VIOLENCE AND DAILY LIFE

VIOLENCE
AND
DAILY LIFE

Reading, Art, and Polemics in the Cîteaux *Moralia in Job*

CONRAD RUDOLPH

PRINCETON UNIVERSITY PRESS
PRINCETON, NEW JERSEY

Library of Congress Cataloging-in-Publication Data

Rudolph, Conrad.

Violence and daily life : reading, art, and polemics in the

Citeaux Moralia in Job / Conrad Rudolph.

p.   cm.

Includes bibliographical references and index.

ISBN 0-691-02673-4 (cloth : alk. paper)

1. Gregory I, Pope, ca. 540–604. Moralia in Job—Illustrations.   2. Bible. O.T. Job—

Commentaries.   3. Illumination of books and manuscripts, Cistercian.   I. Title.

ND3385.G74R84   1997

745.6′7′094—dc20   96-22197

CIP

This book has been composed in Adobe Caslon by The Composing Room of Michigan, Inc.

Princeton University Press books are printed on acid-free paper and meet the guidelines for

permanence and durability of the Committee on Production Guidelines for Book Longevity

of the Council on Library Resources

Printed in the United States of America by Princeton Academic Press,

Lawrenceville, New Jersey

10   9   8   7   6   5   4   3   2   1

TO MY PARENTS

Richard C. Rudolph
and
Mary Alice Rudolph

CONTENTS

PREFACE

There is something extraordinary about the early Cistercians, the twelfth-century monastic reform movement centered at Cîteaux in Burgundy that successfully challenged the entrenched and highly respected traditional Benedictine monasticism. Although unimaginable without Bernard of Clairvaux, the movement itself seethed with energy and creativity—the critical mass that Bernard touched off, neither one likely to have been as successful as it was without the other. Like a prism emitting multicolored rays, Cîteaux seems to refract the white light of early twelfth-century monasticism and spiritual expression, both revealing their fundamental natures and presenting them in new forms.

The strikingly illuminated copy of Gregory the Great's *Moralia in Job* made at Cîteaux around 1111 by an anonymous artist, probably a Cistercian monk—according to some, possibly even Stephen Harding, the abbot of Cîteaux himself—is like the movement that produced it.[1] A copy of one of the most widespread and influential texts of medieval monastic culture, it also reveals a great deal about a number of art historical questions common to many other medieval artworks, shedding its light on such issues as the question of meaning in some monstrous and violent imagery of a seemingly ornamental character, the supposed direct observation of nature for its own sake, the apparent intrusion of the secular upon the sacred, and, inevitably, the role of the artist in all this. It does this despite, or perhaps because of, the fact that iconographically it is largely a unique work. And this leads to the issue of how a unique illuminated manuscript like this might have come about in the first place: in this case the result of an unusually intimate relation between text and image, or more precisely, between text, artist, and image, a relation fundamentally conditioned by contemporary monastic politics and polemics since Cistercian spiritual expression at this time very often acted on a political level. These issues, together with the questions of what, individually, the illuminations of the Cîteaux *Moralia* mean, how, within the limits of their primary audience of the monastic community of Cîteaux, they operated, and why, as a whole, they appear in the text of this particular patristic work at this particular time of monastic reform are the subject of this study.

This has not been an easy task. In fact, the Cîteaux *Moralia* has proven to be more like a mystery than any problem I have worked on. Like many mysteries, however, once solved its former secrets appear glaringly obvious—as I believe they appeared to most monks of early-twelfth-century Cîteaux as they actually sat and read the Cîteaux *Moralia*. Still, for very definite reasons these illuminations are idiosyncratic and the meanings invested in them are the result of both a gradual change in attitude on the part of the artist and a very specific medieval mentality that is not particularly accessible to modern sensibilities. If the meanings of these illuminations are at times based more on a personal response by the artist to the general sense of the text—rather than to its literality—than the modern viewer might expect, it should be remembered that the disciplined method that would result in a consistent dependence was not at all necessarily part of the goal of the medieval monk-artist; his primary relation to theology was an experiential one, an experiential relation by definition being a personal one, though conveyed here through a visual vocabulary that was common to Cistercian spiritual expression.

In this regard, the textual bases of certain of the illuminations defy succinct quotation as often as not, though they are certain. Typically, when the illumination has been conceived in response to the general sense of the text rather than its literality, that sense is dispersed through many chapters of diffuse and at times erratic commentary—something that might be expected from an 1800-page commentary (the *Moralia in Job*) on a thirty-five page book (the Book of Job). Although I give all significant passages in this study, readers are encouraged to turn to the *Moralia in Job* itself in cases like these, as its monk-artist did. James Bliss, *Morals on the Book of Job*, provides a reliable rendering into English of Gregory's often convoluted Latin, although I have preferred to give my own translations here.

This is not an exhaustive study of the Cîteaux *Moralia*. Much work on the formal aspects, codicology, and possible sources of the illuminations has been done by others. Likewise, it is not the purpose of this study to address the full issue of first and second generation Cistercian spiritual expression itself. It is concerned strictly with the meanings of the individual initials and with their significance and impetus as a whole as one aspect of the dialectic of first and second generation spiritual expression.

In this study, "*Moralia in Job*" refers to the writing per se by Gregory the Great (as does the bibliographic abbreviation "*Moralia*" in the notes) and "Cîteaux *Moralia*" refers to the illuminated copy made at Cîteaux around 1111 (Dijon, Bibliothèque Municipale MSS 168, 169, 170, and 173). When dual systems of traditional numeration exist for primary sources, reference is made to the more precise of the two. All biblical references are to the Vulgate. While the discussion of the illuminations is essentially thematic (only the initial to the last book, Book Thirty-five, is affected by its sequential position in Gregory's text), the illustrations have been arranged in the same order as found in the Cîteaux *Moralia*.

I would like to thank M. Nicolas Ruppli, Conservator of the Bibliothèque Municipale of Dijon, for the consideration shown to me during my study of the Cîteaux *Moralia*; and Curator Dr. Charlotte Ziegler, Abbot Bertrand Baumann, and the brothers of the Cistercian monastery of Zwettl, without whose kind invitation to speak there this work might never have been written. I have benefited from support of many different kinds during the writing of this book and am at a loss when I think of how much I have received from the late Robert Benson, Rozanne Elder, Kurt Forster, Françoise Forster-Hahn, Herb Kessler, Steven F. Ostrow, Karl Werckmeister, and John Williams. I am especially indebted to Chuck Rosenberg and John Williams for their perceptive and greatly appreciated readings of this study, which owes much to them; to Jonathan Alexander, whose persistence and unfailing care through the successive drafts of this book can only be compared to a new tale of some homeric hell—his, not mine; and to Chrysogonus Waddell, Cistercian monk and scholar, for his kind help on liturgical questions. An author may write a book, but it takes more than an author to make it happen; and so special thanks must go to the exceptional press readers, Giles Constable and Anne D. Hedeman, for their fine and generous readings of the manuscript, and to Timothy Wardell, my editor at Princeton, for whose interest and constant efforts, no less than the others, I am grateful.

This book is dedicated to my father, Richard C. Rudolph, archaeologist and professor of Classical Chinese, and to my mother, Mary Alice Rudolph, dedicated schoolteacher and doting grandmother.

VIOLENCE AND DAILY LIFE

❧ INTRODUCTION ❧

In the historiated initial to Book Twenty-three of the Cîteaux *Moralia*, an unknown artist painted an astonishing image of seemingly gratuitous violence (Fig. 25). In this vision of almost total anarchy, a small dragon at the bottom of the upright of the initial *P* wrenches its neck around in order to swallow the hind leg of a shod centaur above, its sharp claws tearing furiously at the air in a violent frenzy. The centaur, whose equine half is green, grips the neck of a brilliantly red dragon that forms the circular part of the initial and whose jaws clamp his torso with all their might. The centaur raises his sword aloft to give the death-blow to the dragon, yet—inexplicably enough—looks beyond him, not seeing him, almost as if he were not there. Stranger still is the creature springing off the underside of the dragon, a centaurlike hybrid whose bottom half is canine with a horse's tail and whose top half is a faun with strongly elongated ears. He wildly swings an ax, whether at the dragon's soft underbelly or at the eared snake that strikes at the ax handle is unclear—and perhaps beside the point. The snake's green and frightfully coiling body stretches across the initial, leading the eye to a similarly colored hybrid. This figure, which leaps through the middle of this scene of seemingly incoherent violence, is composed of a small horse below with the upper part consisting of a human head that springs directly from the equine body without the benefit of a human torso. Its face is ocher but it has green fur and locks and large green rabbit ears. In front of it is a horrible little monstrosity whose neckless faun head is attached to an armless anthropomorphic torso that has anthropomorphic legs but canine feet and tail. It dances a hideous dance in midair in front of the human-rabbit-horse hybrid for no apparent reason other than to contribute to the nightmarishness of this almost nocturnal vision. The whole gives the effect of startling exuberance, stunningly addressing itself directly to the viewer in a way that was all but impossible with the more pervasive, conventional artistic devices of eleventh- and twelfth-century manuscript illumination.[1] Even so, the vast majority of the books of the Cîteaux *Moralia* have initials of equal and occasionally greater violence, charm, and/or imagination.

There is, however, a contradiction inherent in this initial. In his *De Consideratione*, written for the first Cistercian pope between 1149 and 1153, Bernard of Clairvaux, the great Cistercian leader and perhaps the foremost ecclesiastical politician of Europe, said about the different levels of monastic contemplatives:

> He is greatest of all who, having dissociated himself from the use of things and from the use of the senses, . . . has formed the habit of flying off on occasion in contemplation to the sublime—not by gradually ascending stages, but by unexpected departures.[2]

In this authoritative and unequivocal statement, the focus of Bernard's attack is on the role of the material, and so on the role of art and architecture, in one of the most fundamental justifications of the existence of monasticism: advanced and exclusive spiritual knowledge and experience.

Certain questions thus force themselves on the historically informed viewer of the Cîteaux *Moralia*. How, conceptually, do these illuminations relate to classic Cistercian spirituality as expressed by Bernard and the other great early Cistercian writers? And if such images can be shown to be related to the text, a spiritual writing, and therefore are spiritually based, what sort of spiritual expression is it?

The *Moralia in Job* was one of the great works of literary expression of the Middle Ages. It was begun by Gregory, a monk, while on a diplomatic mission in Constantinople (579–585) at the request of his fellow monks who had accompanied him, being finished only later (595) during his papacy. It was dedicated to Leander, monk and bishop of Seville, who had met Gregory in Constantinople. Ostensibly an exegetical commentary on the Book of Job, it is perhaps better described as a doctrinal stream of consciousness in which the Book of Job serves as the vehicle for a theological presentation so extensive that it became one of the leading theological source books of the entire Middle Ages and perhaps the leading single comprehensive theological authority before the systematization of doctrine in the twelfth century.[3] In fact, it had such authority that a legend exists actually imputing a sacred quality to the original copy of the *Moralia in Job* that had been sent to Leander by Gregory.

According to this legend, after the deaths of Leander and his brother, Archbishop Isidore of Seville, also a monk, Bishop Tayo of Saragossa was sent to Rome to inquire about it. Here, in conjunction with an elaborate vision, the bishop found the original manuscript of the *Moralia in Job* as if it were the *inventio* (discovery) of an important relic.[4]

For the purposes of understanding the illuminations of the Cîteaux *Moralia*, there are two main characteristics of Gregory's *Moralia in Job* that are of particular importance. The first is that it was written specifically for monks, so much so that Gregory in fact objected to its being publicly read, insisting that its nature was not appropriate to the general lay public.[5] The second is that in trying to come to terms with the main theme of the Book of Job—the apparent contradiction in this world of the material success of the bad and the suffering of the good—Gregory emphasizes the necessity of material and spiritual trials for the good as a spiritual aid in advancing toward perfection.

The Cîteaux *Moralia* itself was the product of a young and—so the sources would like to have us believe—impoverished community.[6] Founded only thirteen years before, the community of Cîteaux was predicated on a strict return to a literal interpretation of the Benedictine Rule. Rejecting the liturgical accretions and social entanglements of traditional Benedictine, especially Cluniac, monasticism, its claim to an authentic return was particularly expressed through its widely discussed embrace of strict asceticism and manual labor.[7] While the earliest written accounts of the monastic ideals of the first generation Cistercians (those monks who came to Cîteaux from the reformed but traditional Benedictine monastery of Molesme) date only from the second generation (those monks who arrived with Bernard at Cîteaux two years after the completion of the *Moralia*), their general dependability in this area is certain. First generation legal documents embedded in the second generation sources confirm the general claims made on behalf of the first generation by the second as a statement of the latter's own lineage and self-image. Thus, while always making a distinction between claim and reality, the second generation descriptions of the way of life of the first give every indication of being historically trustworthy in their general ideals—ideals whose claims by the first generation itself are documented in the evocative illuminations of the Cîteaux *Moralia*.[8]

As I have shown in an earlier study, however, the strict asceticism of the first generation did not extend to artistic asceticism. For while rejecting much of the liturgical, social, and economic bases of traditional monasticism, the first generation was apparently quite accepting of at least part of traditional monasticism's artistic basis. Also, it is not often realized that the architecture of early Cîteaux is not necessarily an expression of architectural asceticism, as it has been portrayed by scholars. Even though Cîteaux was expanding at this time, it was in no position to expend the vast amount of resources on frontline monumental architecture that some older communities could afford. It was only with the second generation that artistic asceticism became the standard among the monks of Cîteaux through written legislation.[9]

But the difference between the first and second generations seems to have involved more than their attitude toward monastic art. While monastic art was in many ways an important matter in itself, at least on one level its permissiblity or impermissiblity—and its form, if it was in fact permissible—was an expression, however much a part of actual practice, of something more profound to the medieval monk: monastic spirituality. It was in the sense of monastic spiritual expression that the first and second generation Cistercians differed most fundamentally. It seems that while the consuetudinary reform of the first generation was very strict indeed, their spiritual expression, their manner of conceiving of and expressing the spiritual state, was rather traditional. This is quite understandable. For the new manner of expressing the spiritual state that arose in the twelfth century, of which Bernard was himself the leading figure, amounted to no less than one of the great developments of the spirituality of the entire Middle Ages. It can even be said that while the effort of the second generation in the area of spiritual expression was something new, the effort of the first generation in the area of an authentic return to the Benedictine Rule was rather an intensification of Benedictine standards—the first generation's sense of spiritual expression also being such an intensification.[10]

In connection with the Cîteaux *Moralia*, one of the most characteristic means of the spiritual expression of traditional monasticism was through the vocabulary—whether literary or artistic—of violent spiritual struggle. This way of approaching the spiritual was something that was by no means rejected by the second generation, which gave it perhaps a secondary status. But with traditional monasticism and with the first generation, it had, I believe, a primary status, although not exclusively so. This is preeminently clear in figural art where it dominates the art of the first generation and is for all practical purposes absent from that of the second. It manifests itself a little differently in the written sources but nevertheless does so in a pattern so strong as to be unmistakable. The question here is not simply one of whether or not the vocabulary of violent spiritual struggle is present. Rather, the distinction must be made as to whom it is addressed, to what level of spiritual adept such imagery is considered to be appropriate. Using Bernard as the quintessential example of second generation spiritual expression, such language is rather common. It is almost consistently found, however, in writings directed to individuals or groups that were seen by the second generation as belonging to a less committed spiritual state than their own, not in those intended for strictly internal consumption.

For example, this pattern is found throughout the writings of Bernard but nowhere more strongly than in his public letters to Suger of Saint-Denis, whose traditional but lax Benedictine monastery had such a high profile in the world of contemporary French monasticism; and to Robert of Châtillon, Bernard's own cousin, who had fled the harshness of Clairvaux for no less than Cluny itself, Cluny being both the ideal of mainstream monasticism and the competitor-to-beat for Cîteaux. In both of these widely circulated letters the imagery of violent spiritual struggle is given place of prominence: at the opening of the letter to Suger and at the closing of the letter to Robert. It plays an important part in the *Apologia*, the ultimate second generation expression of institutional superiority and a treatise that also specifically criticizes the use of violent art as a spiritual distraction. It is found in Bernard's writing for the Templars; in a letter to a renegade canon regular; and in a host of other letters and writings directed outside the Cistercian Order. But it never—or only very rarely, and then typically quite mildly—is found in those writings that were unequivocally addressed to within the Cistercian Order alone.[11] In constrast, the only writing known to be by Stephen Harding himself (aside from the colophon of the Bible of Stephen Harding), a short sermon given to the monks of Cîteaux on the occasion of the death of his predecessor, Alberic, is filled with military imagery of violent spiritual struggle, although not of the literary accomplishment of Bernard's.[12]

Just as the reform of the first generation was in one sense an intensification of Benedictine life and just as the spiritual expression of the first generation was an intensification of traditional spiritual expression, so were the illuminations of the Cîteaux *Moralia* an artistic intensification of the traditional expression of spiritual struggle—although done in a way that was itself of great artistic originality. This use of the imagery of violence to express spiritual struggle is something that in the Christian tradition began as early as Paul, increased in violence with Athanasius and Prudentius, and is found in similar although not necessarily so effective terms in countless medieval manuscripts, sculptures, wall paintings, and liturgical artworks.[13] Indeed, as has been shown elsewhere, Bernard's famous criticisms of monastic art in which he uses violent and monstrous capital sculpture as a rhetorical medium are in fact more directly applicable to the illuminations of the Cîteaux *Moralia*—which he undoubtedly held in his own hands first as a novice and then as a young monk at Cîteaux—than they are, for example, to the capital sculptures of Moissac.[14] While the depiction of seemingly gratuitous violence was not new, then, what was new in this illumination of an authoritative patristic text is the manner in which it is portrayed and the accompanying emphasis on images of daily life, especially manual labor.

The basic art historical problem of the Cîteaux *Moralia* presents itself in the following manner. It is one of the most fundamental methodological tenets of contextual medieval art history that when there is a conscious, significant change in conventional iconography, one may expect a correspondingly significant change in meaning. In the Cîteaux *Moralia* the artist painted a series of illuminations of largely original iconographical conception, and this in a period of art so amenable to the conventionalized representation of images that it actually suggested the concept of iconography as such to the discipline of art history. However, copies of the *Moralia in Job* traditionally did not receive illumination either so lavish or of such subject matter. If a change in iconography indicates a change in meaning, what must the full-scale and largely original illumination of a patristic text that had no tradition of significant illumination at all indicate?

The illuminations of the Cîteaux *Moralia* are more than just lavish or of a slightly unusual subject matter.[15] In the opinion of Arthur Kingsley Porter, the early Cistercian manuscripts, of which the Cîteaux *Moralia* is the most impressive, constitute "one of the principal artistic treasures of Europe." According to C. R. Dodwell, the manuscripts produced under Harding possess an artistic creativity that has few parallels. In Otto Pächt's view, they are works of "rare originality" by a "great illuminator," marking one of the significant points of artistic change in the development of the figure initial—one of the most characteristic of all medieval art forms.[16] The Cîteaux *Moralia* has at times also been a key element in the recurring debate over whether or not the monstrous imagery of the Middle Ages had any specific meaning. More recently, it has been used to support the argument that when medieval initials are related to the text of the books that they head, they are "invariably" related only to the text of the folio on which they appear.[17] And, in its remarkably appealing scenes of daily life, it is believed to represent the first known use of the direct observation of nature in medieval art.[18]

Despite all this, the meanings of the illuminations of the Cîteaux *Moralia* have been almost entirely ignored, being seen from Charles Oursel to Meyer Schapiro—with only minor exceptions—as "entirely independent" of any specific relation to the text of the *Moralia in Job* and with the images of violence being viewed simply as the expression of an "unbridled, often irrational fantasy."[19]

Unbridled and irrational they may be. But they are for the most part not independent of the text. Nor is their meaning "invariably" related to the text of the folio on which they appear. While the latter may be true for most manuscripts, the Cîteaux *Moralia* is not like most manuscripts. The distinguishing feature of the early Cistercians was not what they had in common with the rest of monasticism but rather what was distinctive to them. The same holds true for the Cîteaux *Moralia*. The brilliance of its illuminations and an undercurrent of thematic consistency that may be detected in them cry out from hiding, as it were, that, like an obscure event from Scripture, there is potentially another level of meaning beyond what has so far met the eyes of modern viewers. Subject to the nature of the transformation of the conception of the initial that is one of the main themes of this study, it can be shown that virtually all the initials of the Cîteaux *Moralia* are related either to specific passages of the books that they head or to the general sense of one of the issues raised in those books, although sometimes in an idiosyncratic or seemingly arbitrary way.

In the past, part of the difficulty in detecting the general relation between text and image in the Cîteaux *Moralia* had to do with the question of whether monstrous imagery of the unconventional kind not discussed in bestiaries and other widely known sources—but found with infinite variety and depicted with consummate skill in this manuscript—had any specific meaning. It is impossible to give a complete summary of this issue here, but briefly put, there has never been agreement that it has specific meaning or even that it has general meaning. The disagreement typically revolves around the use of sources, debate on this being particularly fierce in the nineteenth century.

Some scholars, Eugène Viollet-le-Duc, for example, saw this type of monstrous imagery as devoid of specific meaning. The basis of his assertion was Bernard's famous criticism of monstrous capital sculpture in the *Apologia*. In this passage, Bernard asks: "But apart from this, in the cloisters, before the eyes of the brothers while they read—what is that ridiculous monstrosity doing, an amazing kind of deformed beauty and yet a beautiful deformity?" Viollet-le-Duc, and many scholars after him, misinterpreted this passage as proof that, in Bernard's opinion, such monstrous imagery had no meaning. In fact, it can be shown that what Bernard is asking in this rhetorically quite powerful extended passage is not what it means, but why it is there, in the cloister, a place of prayer, of reading, and of teaching. The subject of meaning is never taken up by Bernard. What concerns him in this deceptively descriptive passage over which many have faltered is the great potential such imagery has for distraction from spiritual pursuits—regardless of its meaning or nonmeaning.[20]

The polar extreme to Viollet-le-Duc's broad rejection of meaning was expressed by Charles Auber, who stated in a discussion of meaning in the sculpture of the Gothic cathedral that "in these majestic basilicas, there is not a detail, not a carved head, not a leaf of a capital, that does not represent a thought and speak a language understood by all." Auber attempted to back up this claim with a rickety assemblage of texts which, were it ever applied systematically to a complex art program, would typically be wildly disconnected, textually unconvincing, and have no demonstrated association with the artwork or institution under study.[21]

Emile Mâle reacted strongly to this approach. He distinguished between those monstrous forms which can be reasonably explained by widely circulated texts and those into which meaning was read by scholars who, although having a kind of generalized textual foundation to their claims, did not base those claims on sound historical analysis. According to Mâle, "Didron and Caumont made an exact science of [art history]; these people made it a work of fiction."[22] Unaware of any other basis on which to judge unconventional monstrous imagery, his own view was that it constituted "purely artistic" efforts, completely "free of thought."

But others of Mâle's time did see in this type of imagery a certain content, if only general, like Elphège Vacandard who, quoting A. Joly, thought that there was a psychological basis to it and that it portrayed "a startling image of the deepest side of our nature, of our brutality, violence."[23]

While interest in the interpretation of unconventional monstrous imagery has not lessened since Mâle and his contemporaries, the historiographically most significant scholar since then for the purposes of this study has been Schapiro. In his paper on the aesthetic attitude in Romanesque art, he articulated the theme of "pure" aestheticism touched upon by Mâle in such a way as to logically encompass within it the idea of psychological fantasy expressed by Joly and others, using the Cîteaux *Moralia* as the first specific example of a medieval artwork in his argument.[24] Today, I think that it is fair to say that most art historians would agree with Mâle's distinction between monstrous imagery for which there was a sound textual basis and that for which there was not. But rather than characterize all of the latter as "purely artistic," I believe they would see some of it, depending on the particular instances, also in the psychological terms proposed by Joly, Schapiro, Ernst Gombrich, and others.[25]

Nevertheless, the type of art history that Mâle struggled against has had its successors, though now without the all-encompassing claims. Studies continue to emerge that on the surface offer a seemingly logical explanation but whose logic is in fact based on sources that are unlikely, were often unavailable, or were even unknown in the Latin West at the

time, as Mâle complained. Others still are too ready to offer facile interpretations or weak parallels with external events and general phenom-
ena that cannot be documented to the particular artwork or institution
under discussion, going outside them for a type of "documentation" so
generalized that it lacks any specificity and so credibility. Given that
meaning is established through texts and contexts, the first type of study
exaggerates the role of the text while underestimating that of the context. The second does just the opposite, although the context now is no
longer a specific, historically based context, but rather something more
like the evocation of a generic atmosphere. While I readily affirm that
all—or even the most important—meaning may not be found in texts,
all meaning certainly must be appropriate to the context. Ultimately,
both approaches fail in historical analysis by not relating text to context
convincingly.

The Cîteaux *Moralia* is a preeminent example of monstrous imagery
that was previously thought to have no, or at best only occasional and
then typically generic, meaning but for which specific meaning can be
shown (although I recognize the aesthetic and psychological dimensions
as well). In unraveling how that meaning is embedded and how it operates, I have tried very hard to avoid the extremes of text without context
and context without text. I have tried to keep the direct evidence of my
explanations of the illuminations within the limits of the prefatory matter or book that each one heads, only occasionally going to other parts
of the *Moralia in Job* for support and very rarely beyond it. When I have
gone beyond it, I have done so only for compelling reasons and have
stayed firmly within the widely recognized canon of monastic culture.
The only consistent exception to this has been, naturally, the historical
context, in this case the element of early-twelfth-century monastic reform politics. It may be that other, commonly accepted symbolic interpretations drawn from more distant sources were meant to apply as well,
but I have excluded this type of information for the most part as secondary to the immediate experience of the initials and thus as too indirect for the requirements of this particular study.

Traditionally interpreted as ornamental or generic because they were
typically not seen as illustrating the text of the *Moralia in Job*, the illuminations of the Cîteaux *Moralia* are better characterized as contemporary expressions of concerns discussed in the text and made in response

to—rather than in illustration of—its literality or sense, or some combination of both. These two categories of analysis are fundamental in
understanding the basic impulse of these particular images as manifestations of spiritual expression. They are not the construct of a later age
imposed on the art of an earlier one, nor are they even external to the
Cîteaux *Moralia*. They are taken from Gregory's own classification of literary meaning into "literality" (*textum, litterae verba*) and "sense" (*sensus*), and are found in discussions of exegetical theory contemporary with
the Cîteaux *Moralia*.[26] They are integral to his exegetical method and,
as such, have a special relevance to the Cîteaux *Moralia* because that
method was assimilated by the artist into the artistic process, manifest-
ing itself in the abandonment of an originally conventional and textually unrelated imagery in favor of one that is typically unique and
strongly related to the text in one way or another.

But this assimilation was only gradual, by no means part of the original conception. The Cîteaux *Moralia* was at first conceived of as a luxury manuscript with illuminations of a very traditional character and
with little or no content, as exemplified in those of the prefatory matter
(except the frontispiece) and Books One through Three. Not long after
production had commenced, however, the artist assimilated Gregory's
exegetical method into his work, radically altering his conception of the
initial. In the beginning, this was expressed through the simple symbolism and conventional forms of the initials to Books Four through Seven.
But gradually he turned to the greater visual complexity and vocabulary
of violence and daily life that form the basis of the initials to Books Eight
through Thirty-five, plus the frontispiece—those initials for which the
Cîteaux *Moralia* is so famous.

Indeed, in the process of analyzing the illuminations of this manuscript, it soon became clear that the content of the overwhelming majority was expressed through precisely these two general types of imagery, violence and daily life. By images of "violence" I mean the
depiction of either actual or potential violence, something that com-
prises more than half of the initials made after the artist had fully assimilated Gregory's method and conceived an effective visual vocabulary—Books Eight through Thirty-five, plus the frontispiece. Violent
initials make up approximately the same proportion of the figural illuminations of the entire manuscript. By images of "daily life," I do not

mean images that portray daily life as it actually was but as it was claimed to be, this distinction being basic to an understanding of the initials of the Cîteaux *Moralia* as a manifestation of the ideological use of art. This type makes up more than a third of the figural illuminations of Books Eight through Thirty-five, plus the frontispiece, and more than a quarter of the total manuscript. Together the two types make up around ninety percent of Books Eight through Thirty-five and almost eighty percent of the entire Cîteaux *Moralia*, a clear indication of conscious intent on the part of the artist.

The result was a series of initials of a creativity and exuberance not often found in manuscript illumination before or since. Perhaps the most violent illuminated manuscript of Romanesque monastic culture, the Cîteaux *Moralia* presents a spiritual expression that is intimately bound up with Cistercian reform politics and polemics, and that provides an intriguing view into Cistercian self-conception at a decisive moment in the history of the Order.

⁂ 1 ⁂

TECHNICAL ASPECTS

THE HANDS, LAYOUT, AND FORMAT OF THE CÎTEAUX *MORALIA*

D espite a number of useful studies on the Cîteaux *Moralia*, scholars have never noticed the pattern in the succession of illuminations—not a pattern that constitutes an actual program for the illuminations but one that indicates a certain change of attitude on the part of the artist as work continued on the manuscript.[1] The reason for this may be in part that while the illuminations originally followed a logical succession from the beginning of the book to the end—just as one might expect the book to be illuminated under normal circumstances in a small, early-twelfth-century monastic scriptorium— the arrangement of the illuminations at the beginning of the book was significantly altered sometime during its creation, something that both was an expression of that transformation and, to a certain extent, unintentionally disguised it.[2]

Recognition of this pattern of change has not been helped by the belief of some scholars that more than one artist may have worked on the Cîteaux *Moralia*, an important point in trying to come to terms with the nature of the thought process behind the meaning of the illuminations and their changing conception. Some have argued that the illuminations were by different artists who were more or less responsible for large sections of the manuscript, and some that they were the work of one principal artist with a few pieces done by secondary artists.[3] Both positions are the result of different interpretations of problems that arise in analyzing the application of color to the illuminations, which varies throughout the manuscript. These theories apply, however, only to the application of color. The drawing itself of the illuminations leaves no doubt that they were all drawn by the same hand: the consistency in eyes, nose, hair, the anatomy of unclothed torsos, the arrangement of hands, treatment of drapery folds, clothing types, fibulae, shoe types and treatment, military and equestrian equipment, animal types and details, monster types and details, and vegetal ornament—all of this clearly indicates a single hand despite an obvious attempt at variety. But since there is at least the occasional use of color symbolism in the Cîteaux *Moralia*, and since color plays such an integral part in the often visually striking effect of many of these illuminations, a brief look at the application of color to the drawings is necessary in order to see to what degree it was part of the original conception.

There are two basic coloring techniques in the Cîteaux *Moralia*: the modeled coloring of humans, drapery, animals, and vegetation through the use of a gradation of color tones; and the solid coloring of figures without reference to color gradation and with interior articulation indicated through the simple use of black lines. Within these limits, there was a clear striving for variety.

For example, the technique of modeled coloring is perhaps most characteristically found in the main figure of the frontispiece, the three-dimensionality of whose thigh is modeled through a series of longitudinal brushstrokes of color that are increasingly darker from the center out, ranging from a light wash to an undiluted application of paint (Fig. 2). They run the length of the thigh, curving in a sharp hook at the bottom in order to define the knee. The remaining part of the thigh is "highlighted," highlighting sometimes being done in white paint but in this particular case being indicated through the deft use of unpainted parchment. This technique is also found in variations which have led some to wrongly suppose a different hand, such as the light wash of Behemoth in Book Ten (Fig. 14), the very fine wash of the dogs in Book Nine (Fig. 13)—of a subtlety so fine it cannot be fully captured through modern photographic reproductions—and its more selective use in Book Thirteen (Fig. 17), all of which are found in conjunction with variations of the more characteristic modeling. Without going into a full description of the different artistic devices used in this technique, let me point out the use of small hooks or semicircles to indicate the shoulder and forearm, used in various but strongly related ways in most of the initials just mentioned. Also, the artist at times applies the same techinque of modeling to drapery folds in a radiating manner, resulting in a fanlike pattern, which is also found together with the more characteristic treatment (e.g., Figs. 2 and 15). Thus what identifies the modeling hand is not a brushstroke but an attitude toward artistic representation—an attitude backed by a particular but flexible approach, not a narrowly preclusive technique per se.

The technique of solid coloring has been said by some to be by a different hand and to begin with Book Eighteen (Fig. 20). Here, the clothing of the faunlike figure and the boy he defends is solidly colored, with all interior articulation depicted through the use of black lines, a method that is found with a great amount of consistency from this book on (e.g., Figs. 22, 25, and 36).

But just as the different manifestations of the modeled coloring technique showed a tendency on the part of a single artist toward variety and experimentation (something that is characteristic of the Cîteaux *Moralia* on other levels as well), so is the adoption of the solid coloring technique simply another expression of this same tendency. While the artist is clearly taken with the remarkable visual effect of the new technique, the evidence that it is by the same hand that was responsible for the modeled coloring leaves little room for doubt. For example, the very subtle use of a light wash in the dragon of Book Eighteen and its darker occurence in the cervine creature (Fig. 20) are identical to those in any number of illuminations scholars have characterized as employing the modeled coloring technique, such as the dragon in Book Four (Fig. 8), the monsters and animals in Book Five (Fig. 9), and the dogs in Book Nine (Fig. 13). In fact, the use of the black wash on the lion of Book Eighteen is nothing other than a variation on this same method, using a different color so that it will stand out against its colored ground. In the initial to Book Twenty-nine (Fig. 30)—whose lion is virtually identical to that of Book Eighteen, including the use of an articulating black wash—the drapery of the human figure is solidly colored with a light wash but with a slightly darker application of color delineating the thigh in a way quite similar to that of the frontispiece (Fig. 2). In the initial to Book Twenty-one (Fig. 23), the clothing of the layman in the tree is solidly colored while that of the monk employs the same modeling technique below the waist as seen in the monks of Book Fifteen (Fig. 18). The mixing of coloring techniques is equally pronounced in Book Thirty-one with its general use of solid coloring but modeled clothing of the central figure (Fig. 32), Book Twenty-seven with general solid coloring in conjunction with the fanlike treatment of the cloak of the sitting figure (Fig. 28), and Book Thirty-five where the rider is solidly colored but the breast of the horse is modeled (Fig. 36). The painted blood-flow patterns are identical in the modeled frontispiece and the solidly colored initial to Book Twenty-eight (Fig. 29). And there is even a fair amount of solid colored drapery with interior articulation in black lines in the illuminations that generally employ the modeled technique, such as the initial to the Book of Job, the frontispiece, and the initials to Books Ten and Thirteen (Figs. 1, 2, 14, and 17).

The related idea that all of the monks' robes (Figs. 16, 18, 19, 23, and 35) except that of Book Eleven (Fig. 15) were overpainted sometime after their original creation does not seem to be the case.[4] A variation of the same use of light and shadow that is basic to the modeled coloring technique is seen in the monks of Books Fifteen and Twenty-one, and the small hooks or semicircles meant to suggest the body beneath the drapery in the modeled technique are found in brushstrokes (rather than pen lines) in the initials to Books Twelve (the forearm of the monk on the left) and Fifteen (the right forearm and left upper arm of the monk on the left). In fact, the necessity of such painted devices in the overall figural logic of these initials indicates that painting was unquestionably seen as an integral part of their original conception.

These examples could be multiplied and refined endlessly.

Still, there are problems. Aside from the portrait of Job (Fig. 4), whose drawing is original but which may possibly—although not definitely—have been touched up by a hand other than that of the dominant artist, there is a small amount of sloppiness in the application of some of the solid colors that raises questions. While this is surprising enough in illuminations of such otherwise fine execution, it is even more surprising in that it is largely limited to the colors green and red (e.g., green: Figs. 22, 23, 25, and 28; red: Figs. 22, 28, and 31), colors which at other times are handled with complete skill. Furthermore, some of the initials in which this sloppiness appears also employ well-executed and fairly subtle modeling devices in figures that might otherwise be thought of as solidly colored, such as the legs of the man in Book Thirty-two (Fig. 33) and the toes of the dragon in Book Thirty (Fig. 31)—the latter appearing in a number of works that are solidly colored and well enough executed (e.g., Figs. 20 and 25)—suggesting that the sloppy initials were painted by two hands, the dominant artist and another person. Also, there seems to have been a real struggle to avoid splotching in these colors and in blue, the artist sometimes being successful and sometimes not. At the same time, it is clear that the sometimes splotchy blue and green that are frequently used in backgrounds are often unequivocally part of the original conception of the initial: for example, the initial to Book Thirty-five, the circular part of whose letter form is defined solely through color, lacking a drawn border (Fig. 36). Were these particular instances of substandard craftsmanship the work of someone other than the dominant artist, an apprentice, perhaps, who was allowed a very limited degree of participation in this artwork that was, in the broadest sense, communal? It seems certain. However, this participation was strictly circumscribed. It in no way affected the original conception of the illuminations, and sloppy work is found in only one initial in which color symbolism seems to be involved in the meaning (Fig. 28).

As to the scriptorium, no relation between the succession of scribal hands and the illuminations is detectable that might have played a part in the pattern of change. In a detailed analysis of the scriptorium at Cîteaux, Yolanta Załuska has identified five different scribes in the Cîteaux *Moralia*, such a number not being unusual here. She notes that it is rather rare for a single scribe to copy an entire manuscript at Cîteaux, and that the changes in scribal hands typically bear no relation to the literary structure (e.g., the book divisions) of the text copied and relatively little to the physical arrangement of the manuscript (e.g., the division of gatherings).[5] This is in strong contrast to the clear existence of a dominant artist in the Cîteaux *Moralia* and to the content of the book being the crucial factor in the change in conception of its illuminations. At the same time, it is clear that control over physical changes in the initials, such as their size, did not come from the scribes—unless the dominant artist was a scribe, something that is impossible to tell—since the divisions of work between the five different scribes do not correspond in any way to the pattern of change in the illuminations. Scenarios in which one scribe or another is put forth as the dominant artist can easily be imagined but in the end are unprovable, and the slight paleographical evidence of the word "Iob" embedded in the illuminations to the Preface and Book Ten (Figs. 4 and 14), which could connect artistic and scribal hands, is not enough on which to base any conclusions, given the probable retouching of the Preface illumination and the cramped space of the initial to Book Ten. Likewise, careful study of these five scribal hands in other illuminated manuscripts from Cîteaux—for example, the Bible of Stephen Harding, the one most closely associated to the Cîteaux *Moralia*—reveals no suggestive relation to their illumination.

In the end, close analysis shows an interlocking web of relationships between the illuminations which suggests that all of them were drawn by the same hand and that virtually all were painted by the same hand, with only the occasional and typically partial exception. There clearly was one principal artist whose work dominates the Cîteaux *Moralia* and whose thought, we may assume, underlies its transformation of imagery. The employment of variety was conscious, the recognition of *varietas* being perhaps the standard characterization in the Middle Ages of a work of art that was considered unusually accomplished.[6]

But there is more than *varietas* at work here. It is fundamental to an understanding of the illuminations of the Cîteaux *Moralia* that the transformation of which *varietas* is the vehicle is more than a simple window onto the gradual development of an individual medieval artist. It is the actual working out of a significant intellectual/artistic response in the area of visual culture to a demand from the area of literary culture, a response that formed the visual basis of claims in political culture in an unusually revealing and authentic way. I say unusually revealing because it is not often in medieval art that we witness the gradual transformation of the conception of an artform—in this case the initial, the textually sited image—under the conditions of a "controlled experiment": here we have a series of both changing and unique pieces essentially by the same hand in the same work. And I say unusually authentic because as unique works of art that were meant to function in an intellectual/ spiritual manner, they are the concept of not just an artist but also a member of the specialized audience that read the texts in which these images were sited and that would activate them in that reading.

Although the layout of the Cîteaux *Moralia* is a little complicated, familiarity with it is necessary for an understanding of the illuminations. Gregory the Great's *Moralia in Job* consists of an explanatory letter to Bishop Leander of Seville, an introductory preface, and the main body of the text in thirty-five books (*volumina*, the equivalent of our contemporary chapters). This was all initially divided into six parts (*codices*) by Gregory himself[7] and was often bound in six corresponding volumes.

There was an alternative format, however, and that was to bind it all in two volumes, with the first three parts in the first volume and the second three parts in the second.[8] The Cîteaux *Moralia* originally followed the two-volume format, being structurally unusual only in that the original first volume (the current Dijon, Bib. Mun. MSS 168, 169, and 170) began with the text of the Book of Job that was covered by the commentary of the first three parts of the *Moralia in Job*. The original second volume (Dijon, Bib. Mun. MS 173) correspondingly began with the text of the Book of Job that was covered by the commentary of the second three parts.[9] The fact that the text of the Book of Job was included is not insignificant for an understanding of the meaning of the illuminations and is a point to which I will return.

Disconcertingly to the modern mind, the original second volume of the Cîteaux *Moralia* was made in a larger format than the original first volume. Such alterations, however, were not unusual in sets of the *Moralia in Job*, and the treatment of text and image in the Cîteaux *Moralia* continues without interruption from the original first volume through the original second volume. Since it is about halfway through the original first volume that the change I describe as exploiting the visual vocabulary of violence and daily life takes place, the reason why the change in size occurred then, may be that the excitement at the recognition of the great potential of these conceptually new initials suggested a more imposing format.[10]

Sometime after the completion of the manuscript, the original first volume was divided into three separate volumes corresponding to the first three parts of Gregory's initial arrangement. This division brought about a certain amount of disorder at the beginning and end of some of the new volumes. It also necessitated a dismemberment of that part of the Book of Job that headed the original first volume, so that each of the three new volumes might begin with the text of Job that pertained to it. While all this has certainly added something to the confusion of the study of the Cîteaux *Moralia*, it did not physically alter the original succession of illuminations throughout the text. What did, however, was the insertion of the great initial page of Gregory's Letter to Leander— the frontispiece and the most impressive of all the early Cistercian initials—sometime after the first gathering of the original first volume had been made (Fig. 2).[11] More precisely, I believe that it was added sometime after the first ten books or so of the Cîteaux *Moralia* had been copied and illuminated, as the discussion of the gradual transformation of the conception of the initial in this manuscript will make clear.

The question is, what brought about this transformation, and what does it tell us about the attitude toward art at a frontline monastery of the early twelfth century?

THE UNIQUENESS OF THE CÎTEAUX *MORALIA*

According to Treat Davidson, a cohesive tradition or traditions for illuminated copies of the *Moralia in Job* cannot be worked out.[12] She does attempt, however, to suggest two partial sources. The first is a hypothetical tradition of illuminated copies of the *Moralia in Job* from which she believes the extant late-eleventh- to early-twelfth-century manuscript from the Norman monastery of Saint-Pierre-de-Préaux derives (Rouen, Bib. Mun. MS A.123). Although Davidson states that this was used only as a starting point for three initials that were wholly transformed in the Cîteaux *Moralia*, this seems to be the case for perhaps just one, the initial to Book Six (cf. Figs. 10 and 37). Her discussion of a second suggested source is the development of an idea of Carl Nordenfalk's that the scenes of daily life were modeled on Anglo-Saxon calendar pictures.[13] Here again, Davidson notes the loose relation, a point with which I fully agree. Of the five models in an early-eleventh-century Anglo-Saxon calendar and hymnal suggested by Davidson (London, Brit. Lib. MS Cotton Julius A.VI), only one is convincing as a possible source, the calendar illustration for October, which has a strong iconographic resemblance to the initial to Book Thirty-five of the Cîteaux *Moralia*.[14] Even so, the two instances of use or possible use of these models were not an operative factor in the specific content of the historiated initials of the Cîteaux *Moralia*.

Violent and monstrous imagery, though, is found on occasion in works related to the more narrowly focused subject of Job. For example, some illuminated copies of Prudentius' *Psychomachia*, such as the one in Bern, show Job participating in the struggle between the Virtues and Vices, translating Job's purely personal, nonviolent experience into the imagery of violent spiritual struggle (Fig. 38).[15] In a copy of Philippus

Presbyter's commentary on the Book of Job, there is an initial of a man spearing a dragon (Fig. 39).[16] However, in the *Psychomachia* illustration, Job, who appears as the companion of Patience, is not depicted as actually fighting or even in a threatening manner. And in the Philippus Presbyter, the initial is of a conventional nature. In both, any direct iconographic relation to the Cîteaux *Moralia* is completely absent. Nor is there any conceptual relation such as an unusual emphasis on the seemingly gratuitous violence and participation in that violence by knights and *semihomines* (creatures that are part human and part beast) that is so characteristic of the Cîteaux *Moralia*.

For the most part, then, the images of the Cîteaux *Moralia* are unrelated to traditional artistic sources. The gradual change discernable in them from the conventional and textually unrelated to the unique and textually based indicates a fundamental response to the text. In fact, the reason for their creation actually arose out of the text of the *Moralia in Job*. Precisely because of this, comparisons of its imagery with artworks from different media with different contexts, functions, and publics—such as capital sculpture—are not to the point. The pattern of difference in the monstrous imagery of the Cîteaux *Moralia* even sets it apart from the vast majority of generic hybrids and monsters found in other manuscripts. While these other figures typically carry only a general meaning of spiritual struggle or are even primarily ornamental, the monstrous and hybrid forms in the Cîteaux *Moralia* are invested with a meaning specific to their text.

The relation of the Cîteaux *Moralia* to the work of its own scriptorium is quite revealing along these lines. The scriptorium's only known work previous to the Cîteaux *Moralia* is the Bible of Stephen Harding, a significant number of whose illuminations are by the dominant artist of the Cîteaux *Moralia*.[17] Of the Bible's fifty-six figural initials, canon tables, and miniatures, all but three are either purely ornamental, primarily narrative, or act as straightforward author portraits or symbols of the Evangelists. Of these three, one operates in a symbolically simple manner little or no different from many other illuminated manuscripts (a depiction of Ecclesia and Synagoga at the Song of Songs), while another is more complex but goes outside the text for a significant part of its basic meaning (the initial to John; Fig. 40). Only one, the initial to Wisdom, might be said to demonstrably convey a content of spiritual struggle approaching that of the Cîteaux *Moralia*; but again, this is without a direct relation to the literality or sense of the text in the manner of the Cîteaux *Moralia* (Fig. 41).[18]

On a purely formal level, the descender of the initial to Acts contains a scene of monstrous and semihominal struggle similar in form to some found in the Cîteaux *Moralia* but is wholly unrelated to the text and even to the rest of the initial, seeming to serve only a decorative function (Fig. 42).[19] Related in general form but without *semihomines* or pronounced violence is the initial to 1 Corinthians, likewise serving a primarily decorative function.[20] Significantly enough, these two initials appear toward the end of the book, the production of the later illuminations of the Bible of Stephen Harding quite possibly having overlapped with those of the Cîteaux *Moralia*. One or two other initials have very fine monstrous or semihominal figures but no content, such as the initial to the Prologue to John, and so also do not operate on the level of the Cîteaux *Moralia* initials.[21]

Thus the initials of the Bible of Stephen Harding display at times a use of monstrous and semihominal forms similar to that found in the Cîteaux *Moralia*, but the use of violence to express spiritual struggle is lacking in all but one initial, any direct relation to the text is missing in this type of initial, the theme of daily life is completely absent, and there is no tendency toward a consistent conceptual method. While a number of the elements that contribute to the uniqueness of the Cîteaux *Moralia* are present, they are present only in an incipient way and were not to be exploited to any degree until the Cîteaux *Moralia*.

After the Cîteaux *Moralia*, the use of monstrous and violent imagery in the scriptorium of Cîteaux reverted to the same generic context that had been the case before, regardless of its often very accomplished presentation, as in the lavishly illuminated *Letters* of Jerome where such imagery is generally not related to the text. The anomalous character of the contextual exploitation of potentially generic imagery in the Cîteaux *Moralia* is neatly illustrated by the chronological sequence of three seemingly similar initials from the Bible of Stephen Harding (*c.*1109; Fig. 43), the Cîteaux *Moralia* (*c.*1111; Fig. 13), and the *Letters* of Jerome (*c.*1120; Fig. 44).[22] Of these, the one from the Cîteaux *Moralia* has a direct connection with the text it illuminates, but those coming before and after have none. Thus the conceptual method at operation in the Cîteaux

Moralia that took available generic forms and invested them with specific meanings as the result of a special relation with the text of the *Moralia in Job* did not necessarily lend itself to the illumination of other texts, even within its own scriptorium.

TRADITIONAL LUXURY

The Illuminations of the Prefatory Matter
and Books One through Three

We see, then, that when the artist of the Cîteaux *Moralia* undertook to illuminate his particular copy of Gregory's work, there was no strong artistic precedent to influence him in any direction other than that of traditional luxury—by which I mean that which goes beyond the common, minimal expectations in material and craftsmanship for a monastic copy of the *Moralia in Job* at this specific time. And this is precisely what characterizes those illuminations that extend from the initial to the Book of Job with which the Cîteaux *Moralia* begins through the initial to Book Three, excepting only the great frontispiece. They are very conventional, in some cases even quite modest.

For example, the initial to the Book of Job is an accomplished but unexceptional variation on the conventional image of the inhabited scroll (Fig. 1).[1] (This and many of the illuminations of the Cîteaux *Moralia* are much more subtly executed than current photographic reproduction suggests.) According to Pächt, such imagery carries an implication of mutual antagonism between the figure and the foliage.[2] Even so, the indiscriminate use of this motif from small-scale liturgical artworks to large-scale architectural sculpture is one that tends to reduce its meaning to the level of either the conventional or the ornamental in most, if not all, cases—this example being one of the former. Likewise, the illumination that heads the body of Gregory's Letter to Leander shows nothing more imaginative than a conventional presentation of the *Moralia in Job* to Leander by Gregory, standard fare if ever there was such a thing (Fig. 3).[3] And the Preface is illuminated with an image of Job that is distinctive only in that, rather than showing Job as an Old Testament prophet or sitting on his dung heap, as is traditional, he is specifically portrayed as the author of the Book of Job, holding his volume in his hand (Fig. 4).[4] This small change in traditional iconography, however, offers a hint, no matter how muted, of the potentially unconventional artistic mind of the illuminator in that this depiction actually serves more than the conventional function of an author portrait. For in specifying Job as an author rather than simply depicting him as belonging to the general class of prophets or portraying him as the narrative figure of the dung heap, the illumination presents Gregory's view as expressed in the Preface of the *Moralia in Job* that the Book of Job was written by Job himself and not by another.[5] It is textually grounded, in contrast to the illuminations that precede or immediately follow it.

Following this, however, the initial to Book One is quite mundane, being nothing more than a monochrome rubric, enlarged only enough to fill the interlinear space and not interfering in any way with the lines above or below (Fig. 5).[6] The initial to Book Two is not radically different: it is a large-scale, solid red *S* with very simplified blue, ocher, and green vegetation sprouting from the two extremities (Fig. 6).[7] Still, while remaining a glorified rubric in essence, a greater interest in the initial is now manifested with the introduction of polychromy and an increase in size from one to seven standard text lines, practically speaking. The initial to Book Three, an accomplished but simple vegetal design of eleven lines, but without any figures whatsoever continues this trend. (Fig. 7).[8] While there is no reason to look beyond the scribe for the author of the initial to Book One, the initial to Book Two is clearly by the dominant artist of the Cîteaux *Moralia*, because some of its vegetal forms appear in some of the hybrid monsters of later initials: for example, the downward pointing spray of the lower extremity of the *S* is identical to the upward pointing spray sprouting from the tail of the monster in the initial to Book Eighteen (Fig. 20) Similar comparisons can be made between any number of vegetal forms in the initial to Book Three and the same monster's tail of Book Eighteen.

All of this is more or less what might be expected from a conventionally illuminated, luxury edition of the *Moralia*, the only difference being the hint of contextual potential in the portrait of Job. However, the graduated treatment of the initials to the various books—with the initial to Book One having no decoration, that to Book Two having very little decoration, and that to Book Three having traditionally luxurious

vegetal decoration—indicates a steadily increasing concern for the or-
namentation of the text, although at this time in a way that is without
visual complexity and without any attempt to establish a relation between the text and the content of the initial.

❧ 3 ❧

SIMPLE SYMBOLISM

The Illuminations of Books
Four through Seven

Beginning with Book Four a conceptual change gradually takes place, the incipient signs of which manifest themselves in the initials to Books Four through Seven. While simple enough, these initials are characterized by luxurious but conventional imagery that shares the same trait of relating to the text, even if at times in a general or vague way. Also, three of the four initials are now fundamentally conceived in terms of violent and monstrous imagery, a point of some importance in the relation between text, artist, and image.

For example, in Book Four there is constant talk of spiritual struggle, repeated reference to the devil as "Leviathan," as a "serpent," and as a "dragon," and the repeated discussion of the necessity of the good being tried by the devil.[1] At one point, Gregory explains the passage from the Book of Job, "They who are prepared to rouse Leviathan" (Job 3:8), by saying that those who reject the things of this world and desire the things of God rouse Leviathan against themselves by the example of their lives, and continues:

> For whoever hastens to be ready for action in the service of the divine, what else does he prepare himself for than battle against the old enemy—so that as a free man he may receive blows in combat, he who as a slave in tyrannizing captivity refrained from action?

It is only now that "the mind is ready for action against the enemy."[2] In the initial, this has been straightforwardly expressed by the conventional image of a man fighting a dragon with an ax, an image which, were it not for the textual basis, could easily be misunderstood as generic (Fig. 8).[3]

Book Seven describes the compounding of one sin with another as an "entangling" of the recalcitrant, further characterizing this state as "a habitation of dragons," these dragons denoting nothing other than "malice." The initial to Book Seven takes up this theme, having for its initial *Q* a tangle of dragons that maliciously attack one another (Fig. 11).[4] Like the previous initial, it is related to the text; but it is visually expressed in such a way as to have this relation go by almost unnoticed.

Thus both of these illuminations share an attitude toward the initial that is characterized by a rather strong dependence on the literality of the text that is expressed in a conceptually restrictive and unimaginative way. And while both do respond to a certain degree to the sense of the text with its constant reference to violence and monsters, especially dragons, as images of spiritual struggle, they convey that sense wholly through the use of conventional imagery, imagery that in other illuminated manuscripts might be found in generic initials that have no direct connection with the text and that are not meant to evoke any specific spiritual state, however accomplished they may be artistically.

The initial to Book Five, the most complex of the initials to this point, is very much like the one to Book Four in its simple symbolism and specific relation to the text (Fig. 9).[5] Nevertheless, the first indication of a breaking away from a strict observance of the literality of the text has been introduced here, though it is quite slight, in the two dragon heads that terminate the ends of the interlaced initial *C* and that each grip an animal in its mouth in precisely the same manner.

In this book, Gregory discusses the apparent equality of treatment of the good and the bad on earth. It is no coincidence that the dragon on top, the top being the position of superiority, holds a fish in its mouth while the dragon on the bottom, the position of inferiority, holds a rabbit. The fish is a traditional symbol of the believing Christian, and the rabbit of Lust. Indeed, in the same book Gregory describes the contemplative—the sole intended audience for the *Moralia*—as a fish, since fish "on occasion are able to rise to the heavens by leaps of the mind, lest they always be hidden in the deep sea of cares."[6] This use of the fish as a symbol of the contemplative (practically speaking, only the monk was a contemplative) may very well have been conditioned by its use in one of the most widely read books of monastic culture, Athanasius' *Vita Antonii*, where Anthony, the father of monasticism, describes the monk as a fish—a metaphor that also appears in the equally widely read *Verba Se-niorum*, by an anonymous author, where Anthony again makes a similar comparison.[7] The rabbit apparently was suggested by Gregory's reference in the same passage to the hunting of Esau as "the life of those . . . who follow the flesh," a passage that was considered authoritative enough to be cited as the standard gloss on Genesis 25:27–28, which describes Esau as a hunter.[8]

Nevertheless, the use of the conventional format—in this case of monstrous finial heads attacking nearby creatures—weakens the force of the textual connection, being so common that the initial could easily be misunderstood as a generic design. Indeed, the device of the dragon holding a rabbit in its mouth was repeated in a slightly later work of the scriptorium of Cîteaux except now, significantly, the conceptual antithesis with a fish was not transmitted with the adaptation of the general design to the new letter *G*, although this could have been easily done if the artist had so desired (Fig. 45).[9]

Somewhat different but equally indicative of the tentative nature of the illuminations at this point is the initial to Book Six (Fig. 10).[10] According to Davidson, the artist of the Cîteaux *Moralia* took a historiated *S* from an illuminated copy of the *Moralia in Job* whose existence she hypothesizes as his point of departure for this initial,[11] such a use of models being extremely rare in the Cîteaux *Moralia* and even then employed only in a highly restrictive way. She believes that the initial to Book Thirty-two from an illuminated *Moralia* from Préaux also stemmed from this rarely used, hypothetical model. In this initial, two musicians and a man resting his head on his hand occupy the letter form of a lightly ornamented *S* (Fig. 37).[12] It seems that the artist of the Cîteaux *Moralia* took the hypothetical model that this generic initial was also based on and reconceived it in a more imaginative way. Eliminating the figure with his head on his hand, he composed the *S* of two oliphantlike forms, each with musicians and knife or sword jugglers emerging from the ends, and with the profile faces of the two adjoining figures creating the illusion of a single, frontal face.

If the hypothetical initial used by the Cîteaux artist headed the same book that its counterpart does in the Préaux manuscript, the Cîteaux artist moved it from Book Thirty-two to Book Six, apparently because

of its suitability in referring to that passage in Book Six where Gregory
discusses how

> When the wounded soul begins to pant after God—when, despising all
> the charms of this world, it directs itself through desire to the celestial
> homeland—whatever before was thought to be pleasing and charming in
> this world is immediately turned into a temptation to it. . . . [And] former
> pleasures recur to the memory.[13]

The image, then, is fundamentally a borrowed one. It is perhaps for this
reason that despite its great imagination, the image is rather vague in
meaning, presenting "the charms of this world" but neither condemn-
ing them nor showing the spiritually advancing soul struggling against
them. It is, so to speak, a visual observation from which no conclusion
has been drawn and so functions only imperfectly as an illustration of
the literality of the text and not at all of its sense.[14]

Thus the initials to Books Four through Seven mark a significant
break with the original design intentions as expressed in the earlier initials to Books One through Three, which were nonfigural. They also
mark a significant break with the original content intentions as expressed
in most of the illuminations of the prefatory matter; far from simply
using textually unrelated generic imagery or even letting his fantasy run
free—although run it did—the artist of the Cîteaux *Moralia* had begun,
in this incipient and erratic way, to base his illuminations on the text,
typically through the use of violent and monstrous imagery.

Still, at this point of incipient change the relation between image and
text is rather restricted in regard to both the literality and the sense of
the text. On the one hand, when the image relates to the literality or
exact wording of the text, it generally tends to do so in a way that directly illustrates that wording, rather than in a way that translates it into
a more articulate, original expression. On the other hand, to the degree
that the image relates to the sense or general feeling, it tends to be dependent on conventional format and imagery rather than to convey the
feeling of the text through evocative imagery that is unique to that initial. This is because of the conventional nature of these initials, which in
a way are like a combination of the traditional format of the initial to the
Book of Job (Fig. 1) and the relation to the text of the author portrait of
Job at the Preface (Fig. 4): the initial to Book Four (Fig. 8), for example,

is very much like the initial to the Book of Job in format even though it is distinguished from the latter in its textual basis. Indeed, to the degree that the initials of Books Four through Seven employ conventional imagery, the relation of the initials to the text remains rather weak precisely because of their generic nature. At the same time, to the degree that they do relate to the text, they have been forced to rise above the generic and ornamental, in however incipient a way.

THE VISUAL VOCABULARY
OF VIOLENCE AND DAILY LIFE

The Illuminations of Books Eight through
Thirty-five and the Frontispiece

Beginning with Book Eight and continuing throughout the rest of the manuscript, with the addition of the frontispiece that was inserted only sometime after the original first gathering had been made, a significant intensification of the incipient change that surfaced in Books Four through Seven manifests itself. Here, the simple symbolism and conventional format of the earlier initials have given way to a new visual complexity that combines with a generally more effective visual vocabulary of violence and daily life to produce the great illuminations that are almost without parallel in medieval art. It is these for which the Cîteaux *Moralia* is so famous.

For the most part, the depictions of seemingly gratuitous violence have been seen either as simple images of the struggle between good and evil or as virtually meaningless, the latter being by far the more common interpretation. Scenes of daily life have been regarded either as referring to monastic ideals in the most general possible way or as proto-realistic depictions with little or no content. Here again, it is the latter view that is more prevalent.

This conceptual change is accompanied and to a certain extent aided by a physical change. Beginning here, the amount of space devoted to the visual message conveyed by the initials is at times twice or even more than that of the initials of Books Four through Seven while the size of the figure typically remains about the same or is even less. For example, the initial to Book Four is approximately sixteen standard text lines in height; Book Five, thirteen lines; Book Six, twelve lines; and Book Seven, twelve lines. But with Book Eight, the amount jumps dramatically to approximately twenty-six lines and with Book Nine to thirty-two. At the same time, the human figure in Book Four is approximately ten lines, while those in Book Eight range from seven to eight. Although I do not want to overemphasize the point, this increased amount of space offers greater potential for the development of complexity of content, and so for complexity of thought, and so for complexity of the relation between text and image.

Also, it is in Books Eight through Thirty-five, at Book Eighteen to be precise, that the dominant artist generally switched from his earlier technique of modeled coloring to what he clearly thought was the visually more effective technique of solid coloring, a decision that underlies a great part of the remarkable visual power of these images.

This change in attitude, however, by no means adheres consistently to some artificially conceived "program." While the combination of the artistic devices just referred to were newly at the artist's disposal, he in no way always felt obliged to employ them; some initials are as conventional in their presentation as those found in Books Four through Seven, for example, those to Books Thirteen, Twenty-two, and Twenty-six (Figs. 17, 24, and 27).[1]

Because of the potential confusion in trying to come to terms with the at-first-glance undisciplined presentation of these twenty-six initials of sometimes ambiguous and even enigmatic character, I will first discuss the initials to Books Eight and Nine, which to me represent a breaking away from the earlier use of conventional imagery. After this I will take up the categories of images of violence or implied violence involving humans, violence involving *semihomines*, daily life, and finally two initials of conventional format and one of an unusually complex and overtly symbolic nature. The only initial whose sequential position in the *Moralia in Job* is an active factor in its content is the initial to Book Thirty-five, the concluding initial of the Cîteaux *Moralia*. To the degree that the initials of each of these categories permit, I will first take up those with a specific relation to the text, then those with a general or ambiguous relation.

THE BREAKING AWAY FROM THE CONVENTIONAL

The change that manifests itself in Books Eight through Thirty-five is gradual, the initials to Books Eight and Nine having something of an experimental cast to them: they lack a clear visual vocabulary to express either the literality or the sense of the text in a truly effective manner despite the new visual complexity.

For example, in the initial to Book Eight, it seems that the terror of the two men who desperately climb the stem of the initial *P* in order to escape the two lions below is explained by the passage in the same book that describes how when holy men experience either too great success or too great adversity in the world, they seek rest in the recesses of their hearts (Fig. 12).[2] There the Judge torments them with dreams and visions that have the same beneficial effect as temptations, with Gregory quoting Job 7:13–14, "You will frighten me with dreams and terrify me with visions," and going on to explain these verses as meaning: "Fleeing from external things I turn back to the interior . . . [and there] you terrify me violently through those very mental images of my thought."[3]

The initial is thus directly based on a passage of the book that it heads, but the expression of that text is weak. There is no clear indication of the sanctity of the two men climbing the stem. This can only be inferred, and then indirectly, by a passage elsewhere in Book Eight that describes the color green as symbolic of sanctity, green being the color of the stem of the initial.[4] It is uncertain whether the man with the sword who forms the loop of the *P* is meant to represent the Judge holding the Sword of Justice, a common symbol of judicial authority, or if he is part of the dream, wielding his sword as an instrument of terror. And the reference to dreams and visions is not especially clear, the initial having the potential to be easily misinterpreted as an ornamental display of gratuitous violence.

Only the general relation of the men to the lions—the soul and that which would destroy it—is distinctly apparent, but even then not on the basis of the *Moralia in Job*. Rather, the scriptural affinity of this visual metaphor would have been obvious to an early twelfth-century monk because of such biblical passages as the important and often chanted verses of Psalm 7:2–3:

O Lord my God, I have put my hope in you. Save me from those who pursue me and deliver me so that they might not seize my soul like a lion at a time when there is no one to rescue or save me.

This is evident from the illustration of these verses in the Utrecht Psalter by a very similar scene of a man being mauled by a lion next to a tree

(Fig. 46);[5] here, though, the depiction is one of defeat, rather than the ultimate salvation in the face of adversity that is the underlying message of Gregory's text and that is implied in the Cîteaux initial. (In this and most of the positive iconographical comparisons made in this study, the operative factor is one of a similarity of expression in response to a shared concept, not a shared artistic model.) These specific verses were chanted with great regularity as part of the use of Psalm 7 in the *opus Dei* (Divine Office) in general, as part of Psalm 7 in the Office of the Dead (*Officium Defunctorum*) in particular, as an antiphon in the Office of the Dead, and in the liturgical recitations of the entire Psalter that were said in some monasteries on the death of a brother and on Good Friday—these are aside from the use of the psalm in general Psalter reading or the use of the Psalter in teaching reading. And while there is no need to look for a dependency for the initial on this particular passage, it was in fact cited by Gregory two books earlier in the *Moralia in Job*.[6]

The vagueness of the relation between text and image is equally pronounced in the initial to Book Nine (Fig. 13).[7] In his discussion in this book of Job 9:7, "He commands the sun and it does not rise, and he shuts up the stars as if under a seal," Gregory describes how the sunlight and starlight of those who preach the word of God are removed when the preachers are driven away by those without faith, leaving only the night of the spiritual darkness of this present life:

> Sometimes in sacred Scripture, by the word "sun," the brightness of preachers is meant. . . . They are also represented as the brightness of stars, since as long as they preach what is right to sinners, they illuminate the darkness of our night. Whence, once the preachers have been removed, it is said through the prophet, "The stars of the rain have been withheld" [Jer. 3:3]. . . . They shine like stars in the night because even when they are involved in the things of this world they direct the foot of our endeavor—always ready to stumble—by the example of their own uprightness. But since the preachers had been driven out, there was no one who might show the Jewish people (persisting in the night of their faithlessness) either the brightness of contemplation or the light of the active life. For the truth [both God's way and God himself], having been rejected, abandoned this people, and, with the light of preaching withdrawn, blinded them as a consequence of their wickedness. Rightly it is said, "He commands the sun and it does not rise, and he shuts up the stars as if under a seal." For he

[God] was unwilling that the sun should rise to that people from whom he had turned away the heart of the preachers, and he shut up the stars as if under a seal—he who, while he made his preachers keep to themselves in silence, hid the celestial light from the blind perception of the wicked.[8]

In particular, he mentions the removal from light of two preachers, Elijah and Enoch, who were believed to have been bodily assumed into heaven before death.[9] It seems that it is the removal of these two prophets that is alluded to by the two male deer hiding in the darkness from the bewildered hunter and his dogs who, their spiritual perception having been blinded, stumble about in total confusion, one grabbing his own foot, another biting its own leg. The dark blue ground refers to the spiritual night brought about by the preachers' absence, such a ground often referring to spiritual darkness in the Cîteaux *Moralia*. Furthermore, it may be that the placement of the deer in the upper part of the initial *P* and the hunter and his dogs in the lower part is meant to refer to the comparison in the same extended passage of the lives of those who preach to the heights of the mountains, contrasting them with the lowly earthly regions.[10]

Recognition of the deer as a metaphor of the faithful soul would have been immediate in monastic culture through its constant presence in the popular verse of Psalm 41:2 (Vulg.), "As the deer longs for spring waters, so my soul longs for you, God." This passage appeared in all of the instances mentioned earlier for the metaphor of the lion and its prey, except as an antiphon in the Office of the Dead, and is also used to describe the monk in the *Verba Seniorum*. It is illustrated in the Utrecht Psalter with a scene strikingly similar to that of the Cîteaux *Moralia* of a deer being chased through a forest by dogs (Fig. 47).[11] More immediate to the experience of the initial, however, Gregory compares preachers and the Fathers to deer elsewhere in the *Moralia in Job*, this being not the only example in the Cîteaux *Moralia* of the use of visual imagery from one part of this commentary to illustrate initials in another.[12] What does appear in Book Nine is the use of a hunting metaphor to describe spiritual struggle, the readiness of the Cistercian artist to employ such imagery in all likelihood being strong because of its common use in the sermons and other religious writings of the time.[13]

It seems that what the artist has done in this initial is to take a conventional image of the soul in struggle—the deer, an image so common that at times it functioned primarily as ornament in the scriptorium of Cîteaux (cf. Figs. 43 and 44)[14]—and adapt it to a contextual use. While the conventional image might on occasion have a generic symbolic meaning, there is typically no specific interplay between text and image as the basis of its appearance. The textually based images of Book Nine, in contrast, have nothing in common with their conventional counterparts except species type; and in their undeniable though vague relation with the text they begin to function in a way similar to the text itself.

Contributing to the sense of experimentation in this initial is the highly unusual stem through which the hunter and his pack run lost. While the outline of the stem is in red, the unfinished parts of initials in the earliest Cistercian manuscripts (the Bible of Stephen Harding and the Cîteaux *Moralia*) typically have a sepia outline. At the same time, there is a very fine use of wash in all the figures, the vegetation, and the loop of the *P* (something that does not show up well in photographic reproductions). All of this indicates that the execution of the initial is complete as it stands. But why is the interior of the stem left completely blank, unquestionably on purpose? And given this, why is it composed of a pair of more or less matching strips? Nowhere else in the numerous letter forms of the earliest Cistercian manuscripts is a stem like this found. All the rest are either decorative, act as colored grounds, or serve as architectural backdrops or some other type of space within which figures operate. This suggests an unusual meaning for this particular element of an initial whose other components indicate that it was planned and executed with great care.

In the same passage to which the initial relates, Gregory discusses how the stars or preachers mentioned above are "shut up as if under a seal." He goes on to note that whatever is shut up under a seal is so done with the expectation of bringing it forth at a later time. This, he explains, is the situation with Elijah and Enoch.[15] Given the stem's unique quality of being left blank, it seems that its surface should be considered as representing what it in fact is, parchment; and that as a whole, the arrangement is meant to depict double parchment pendants, whose use was becoming widespread in France and England at just this time (Fig. cf. 48).[16] It should be remembered that the use of seals so foreign to us today was extremely common in the monastic environment of the early twelfth century and references to them appear again and again in the narratives of the letters of the time. It therefore seems that the unusual stem is meant to convey the idea of these two preachers as "shut up as if under a seal." While this interpretation attributes more imagination to the medieval artist than most art historians are willing to recognize, not only are the textual and artistic bases there, but it is entirely in keeping with the great imagination of the Cîteaux illuminator as demonstrated throughout the manuscript.

Thus, at the same moment that an increase in initial size opens up the possibility of a greater complexity of content, there also appears, more significantly, a breaking away from conventional imagery; the original, unconventional imagery of the Cîteaux *Moralia* being able to potentially address the sense of the text in a way that was not possible with stock representations (although this potential is not fully exploited until the following initials[17]). This is because most of the imagery of the illuminated initials of the period that do not literally illustrate the text tend to be conventional and so are perceived as ornamental.[18]

The initial to the Book of Job that heads the Cîteaux *Moralia* is a case in point (Fig. 1). While it is possible that it did have an intended symbolic meaning, its conventional nature reduces any effectiveness along these lines to such a degree that one is left with ambiguity rather than certainty. The tendency is for such initials to be read in a single glance as a non-narrative unit, as a recognized artistic convention unrelated to the content of the text, like the initial to the Book of Job that was made almost exactly at this time at the monastery of Saint-Martial, in Limoges (Fig. 49).[19] But unconventional illuminated initials, at least as found in the early Cistercian manuscripts, have the potential to be less subordinated to the letter form—paradoxically even when comprising the latter in that the letter form is now dominated by the figure, in contrast to the figure being dominated by the letter form—and so are nonstatic, something which in turn contributes to greater visual complexity and potential for content. Thus, whereas the meaning of the initial to Book Four with its lack of visual complexity may be almost instantaneously taken in by the eye and its simple symbolism understood (Fig. 8), the visually relatively complex initial to Book Eight requires more visual study (Fig. 12); it slows down the reader/viewer and potentially offers an opportunity for greater intellectual/spiritual reflection. Rather than being taken in at a single glance, it demands to be read: a characteristic that engages the thought process, as opposed to the more or less strictly visual process of taking in the initials of Books Four through Seven.

It may be that at least some of the vagueness of the initials to Books Eight and Nine is the result of a certain amount of difficulty on the part of the artist in reconciling the imagery of the compositionally centralized primary visual field (the loop of the initial *P*) with the diffuse secondary visual field (the stem). For, generally speaking, those initials of Books Eight through Thirty-five with the weakest connection to the text are these two—the first expressions of a breaking away from conventional imagery—and those three later scenes of spiritual struggle involving *semihomines*, all of which are initial *P*s, the two groups comprising the totality of the initial *P*s in the Cîteaux *Moralia*.

But more fundamental is the vague relation between the visual vocabulary of the initials and the literality or sense of the text. While basing his initials on specific passages of the text for which he felt some attraction but which provided little or no specific imagery, the artist of the Cîteaux *Moralia* was forced to introduce imagery that was idiosyncratic, that came from elsewhere in the *Moralia in Job*, or that was external to it. Part of the problem lies in the inherently non-narrative character of the *Moralia in Job*: in relating the image to the text, the artist generally had the choice of expressing either the literality or the sense of the text, or some combination of the two. There were no narrative or traditional iconic subjects to illustrate. This is something he at first had trouble dealing with effectively.

In the initials to Books Four through Seven he undertook this task with rather conventional imagery and with corresponding results. In those to Books Eight and Nine, he left the conventional behind but still had a certain amount of difficulty: he had only just begun to perceive the greater force of expression that was possible with the introduction of the element of visual complexity but had not yet conceived a visual vocabulary to effectively complement it. Thus the choice in these two initials of the particular imagery of the hunt in which the protagonists are not the hunters but the hunted. Whatever precedent such imagery may have in Western art, its use here renders the initials essentially passive as twelfth-century monastic spiritual expressions—wholly out of keeping with the fundamentally active nature of spiritual struggle as articulated by Gregory and as widely envisioned at the time, and ultimately not expressive of the current self-image of frontline monasticism. It is more in keeping with imagery of the Book of Psalms, which permeated monastic life, than with this specific type of spiritual expression. It is only with the introduction of two new types of figures, the *semihomo* and the monk proper, that such a visual vocabulary is realized in the normally very unconventional imagery of violence and daily life of the remaining initials.

VIOLENCE

For well over a hundred years, scholars have had a great deal of trouble coming to terms with the often related elements of violent and monstrous imagery in medieval art. The debate has not been very discriminating in its use of evidence, the general practice being to cite whatever examples support the position in question: both that such imagery had meaning and that it did not. One of the greatest contributing factors in this regard has been an inability to distinguish between the different kinds of violent and monstrous imagery. The necessity of doing just this is underscored by the statement of the monk Theophilus in his manual on art, *De Diversis Artibus*, written shortly after the Cîteaux *Moralia* was made, in which this contemporary witness himself speaks of such imagery as conventionalized. In this passage, Theophilus refers to the gratuitous use of "horsemen fighting dragons" on gold and silver cups and dishes, freely grouping this type of image with other standard types—both conventional images of power and those that are purely decorative, including flowers on women's saddles—whose functions according to this passage seem to be understood as indicators of aristocratic power through the display of luxury.[20]

In fact, the meanings of violent and monstrous imagery can exist at every point of the spectrum. Often it functions in an essentially decorative manner, whatever its broader social implications may be, as in the monstrous capital 33 of the cloister of the monastery of Moissac (Fig. 50). This is the sort of imagery that Theophilus speaks about, though on a monumental scale, and it is a type that has generally been suggested for many of the initials of the Cîteaux *Moralia*. At other times it operates as little more than a conventionalized representation of the struggle between good and evil, as the case seems to be with capital 3 from the rotunda of the abbey of Saint-Bénigne at Dijon (Fig. 51) and as has been wrongly suggested for a few of the initials of the Cîteaux manuscript. From time to time it is found in relatively sophisticated representations of spiritual struggle, as in the Cîteaux *Moralia*. And sometimes it remains ambiguous even upon close and informed analysis, as in the initial to Psalms in the Second Bible from the monastery of Saint-Martial, whose exact meaning seems to defy interpretation (Fig. 52).[21]

In the Cîteaux *Moralia*, an understanding of the different kinds of violence begins with bringing into better focus the different kinds of participants in that violence. For example, among the fully human figures of this manuscript a distinction must be drawn between overtly knightly figures (those with weapons of some kind, body armor per se not being a requirement; e.g., as in Fig. 14) and contending figures that are not overtly knightly (unarmed humans that struggle with dragons; e.g., as in Fig. 34). As to the former, while the use of military imagery to describe spiritual struggle in general and monasticism in particular goes back to the beginnings of Christianity and monasticism, the specifically knightly predilection in this type of imagery received special emphasis within monastic culture of the late eleventh and early twelfth centuries, and the early Cistercians were among the most active in this practice.[22] In fact, in one of the most venerable of all documents from the early Cistercian period, the *Exordium Parvum*, an official account of the origins of the Cistercian Order, the Cistercian monks describe themselves as the "new knights of Christ" (*novi milites Christi*) and their order as "a spiritual knighthood" (*militia spiritualis*), terms that are found again and again in the *Moralia in Job*, especially in the form of "knight of God" (*miles Dei*).[23] It is the *miles Dei* that the armed human of the Cîteaux *Moralia* is meant to represent.

Having come to this conclusion, however, one must not be misled by a superficial interpretation of the fact that while those figures that are not specifically knightly are always depicted in tenuous (e.g., Fig. 22) or even negative (e.g., Fig. 31) circumstances, the overtly knightly ones are always portrayed as victorious or soon to be victorious (e.g., Fig. 21). Rather, this distinction must be related to the text of the *Moralia in Job* which consistently sees spiritual threats and even momentary defeats as a positive thing. Thus while the two different types represent different kinds of spiritual struggle, they also both potentially depict spiritual combatants of the same general spiritual level, with one type now up and the other now down—a regular feature of advanced spirituality in Gregory's view.

Along these lines, it is wrong to interpret negatively certain of the more lavishly dressed knightly figures strictly on the basis of the contemporaneity of their clothing and hairstyles, as has been done,[24] a view that misses the point of the use of the added force of contemporaneity in the metaphor of the knightly ideal as an expression of the Cistercian claim to be the *novi milites Christi*. The desire for and power of contemporaneity could be quite pronounced in the early and middle twelfth century, and its use in clothing design in an unquestionably positive way was widespread. For example, externally, the most effective example is close at hand in the Bible of Stephen Harding, which employs pointed shoes, tight-fitting garments, and long sleeves throughout and which reserves some of its most extravagant designs for figures whose spiritual authority is unquestioned (e.g., Fig. 53).[25] Internally, the clothing and hair styles of the indisputably positive figures of the knights of the frontispiece (Fig. 2) and the initial to Book Nineteen (Fig. 21) are either identical to or basically the same as others, such as the initial to Book Thirty-five (Fig. 36), that have been described as images of secular pride on the basis of their contemporary treatment of clothing and hair.[26]

Of the scenes of violence involving fully human figures, the majority are relatively straightforward, with specific connections to the text of the books that they head.

For example, in the initial to Book Nineteen, the mounted knight who charges a hissing dragon with sword drawn relates to a passage in that book—which is steeped in violent imagery—that describes how those who advance through spiritual struggle are "strong warriors of the spiritual fight . . . *holding swords and highly expert in war*" [Song of Sol. 3:8] (Fig. 21).[27] The passage explains that these "spiritual swords" are not merely the knowledge of Scripture but the knowledge of Scripture put into action against the threat of temptation:

> For he has a sword but does not hold it who knows divine Scripture but neglects to live according to it. He is no longer able to be expert in war who never trains with the spiritual sword he has.[28]

The initial to Book Nineteen, then, is not exactly the symbolic portrayal of good overcoming evil—which could very well be its interpretation if it were taken generically, if it were removed from its very specific context of Gregory's conception of spiritual struggle. More precisely, this particular depiction of a knight on horseback slaying a dragon is an evocation of the implementation of the moral models found in Scripture in the daily struggles of the medieval monk, with the artist taking the basic idea from Gregory but ultimately phrasing the statement according to his own inclinations.[29]

Likewise, the initial to Book Twenty, which shows a man cautiously holding open the jaws of a menacing dragon, has as its basis a passage in the same book that states that the elect, while in this world, never become overconfident of their spiritual security; instead they are always on watch against the plots of the enemy (Fig. 22)[30]:

> As long as they are in this life, none of the elect ever let the self-confidence of security grow in themselves. At all times mistrustful about trials, they are apprehensive of the plots of the hidden enemy. . . . For one must always be on the alert. . . . [Holy men] are always apprehensive of temptation. . . . They both trust and fear.[31]

The walking of this narrow line between confidence and fear—ever mistrustful of temptation but ever forced to confront it—is something whose sense is quite evocatively conveyed in the visual vocabulary of spiritual struggle in this initial, which is reminiscent of, but not in reference to, the passage from Terence, "I have a wolf by the ears and can neither let go nor hold on."[32] The man gingerly stretches his arms forward to keep the jaws of the dragon from clamping down while at the same time he pulls his body back, right leg poised in midstep, right foot ever so lightly resting on tiptoes, eyes staring straight into the maw of death—ready to spring instantly away at the slightest movement from the mouth that could snap shut at any second, from the claws that are held limp, waiting to strike, or from the tail that reaches beyond him, flicking like a cat's, ready to entangle him.

The tower manned with armed knights that forms the initial *I* to Book Thirty-one is one of the few initials of the Cîteaux *Moralia* for which previous scholarship has attempted an interpretation of any complexity (Fig. 32).[33] Unfortunately, this interpretation is hamstrung by the premise that the initial to a given book refers only to a passage that is "invariably" close to the initial. According to this view, the initial is explained in that the central figure, who is without armor, is the "weakling" referred to in the opening passage of Book Thirty-one, while the armored figures represent those deceived by worldly pride.[34]

This explanation, however, does not take into account the distinctive and clearly purposeful poses of the armored figures: the one on the left expansive and that on the right reflective. Nor does it properly consider the sword and banner of victory of the central figure—something that in no way conveys an identification as a "weakling"—nor the fact that his central position, strong pose, and higher eye level are clearly not subordinate or "weak" in relation to the flanking figures. Furthermore, the absence of armor on the central figure, unlike the flanking figures who wear chainmail and helmets, is consistent with the other images of souls in spiritual struggle throughout the manuscript, for example, the knight of the great frontispiece (Fig. 2). (There is only one other exception to this, the knight on horseback in the initial to Book Nineteen, who wears a helmet.) As succinctly put by Martin of Tours during one of his many miraculous appearances in which he typically showed himself dressed strictly in a brilliantly white robe, "I am Martin, a knight of Christ" (*Ego sum Martinus, miles Christi*). Indeed, the absence of armor in the spiritual warrior is described by Prudentius as indicative of spiritual zeal. Similarly, Michael the Archangel is often depicted without body armor at this time, although he may carry a shield.[35]

Rather, it seems that the initial to Book Thirty-one—which contains the longest discussion of spiritual struggle in military terms in the entire *Moralia in Job*—received its impetus from a passage in that book that is concerned with recognizing the danger of faults before they are present. In this passage, Gregory compares a manned tower to the discernment of the holy men of the Church which, thanks to the eminence of that tower, is able to detect the threat of distant but approaching vices. In a lengthy and characteristically erratic discussion of Job 39:25, "He smells the distant battle," Gregory writes:

> to smell the distant battle is to seek out lurking vices. . . . Concerning this sense of smell, the Lord rightly says in praise of his Church, "Your nose is like the Tower of Lebanon" [Song of Sol. 7:4]. . . . What is meant by the

nose except the foreseeing discernment of holy men? A watchtower is put in a high place so that the approaching enemy may be seen from afar. Rightly therefore is the nose of the Church said to be like the Tower of Lebanon, because as long as the foreseeing discernment of holy men, stationed in a high place, keeps watch with care in all directions, it detects fault before it arrives.

He then immediately refers to Jeremiah who warned "the soul of each elect, saying, 'Set yourself up a watchtower' [Jer. 31:21] . . . to learn beforehand from elevated observation the approaching battle of the vices;" Gregory concluding, "Every vice is detected in the thought of the spiritual knight (*spiritalis miles*) before it can enter by stealth."[36]

It thus seems that the artist of the Cîteaux *Moralia* chose to integrate what really are two parallel ideas, though presented together by Gregory, the watchful Church and the watchful individual soul. He depicted the watchful Church in its two primary aspects, the active and the contemplative lives. This idea is one that in large part originated with Gregory and that appears both in this passage and at greater length a little later in Book Thirty-one.

Further on in this particular passage, the concept of the *miles Dei* is joined to the notion of contemplation:

> The knight of God (*miles Dei*) . . . smells the distant battle because he considers with anxious thought how the leading evils have the power to persuade the mind. . . .
>
> Since we have understood that any knight of the spiritual battle (*spiritalis certaminis miles*) is described in the account [of the watchtower], now let us see the same person once more in the symbol of a bird, so that . . . we may learn his contemplation. . . . Let us understand how high he flies in contemplation through the figure of the bird.[37]

The actual dichotomy of the Church into active and contemplative lives—which was standard by the twelfth century—is taken up only a few pages later in the same book: "When [Isaiah] was describing the virtues of the active life, . . . he added to what heights of contemplation one may ascend, saying, *He will dwell in high places*" [Isa. 33:16]; with Gregory going on to discuss contemplation at length.[38]

The initial thus gives expression to Gregory's discourse on the watchful Church and the watchful individual soul with the Church depicted in the fundamental dichotomy of the active and contemplative lives, an idea attached to Gregory's name and touched upon in this book. The active life stands on the left, represented by a knight (a *miles Dei*) brandishing a sword against all potential enemies; the contemplative life is on the right, represented by a knight (a *miles Dei*) shown lost in thought with his hand to his chin, a traditional gesture of contemplation. The helmet of the knight on the left is red and that on the right green. Given that their apparel is otherwise identical, this opposition suggests that an inherent distinction is being made between the two. In fact, in the previous book the color red is described as indicative of blood and suffering shown for love of the eternal kingdom, something appropriate to the active life. The same book also refers to green as signifying the eternal things for which the holy man longs, such longing befitting the contemplative life.[39] Between these two stands the other component of Gregory's parallel, the watchful "soul of each elect" (also a *miles Dei*), armed in accordance with the military imagery of the passage and holding the banner of victory. Firmly rooted in the text and yet at the same time expressed with a fundamentally independent imagination, it is one of the most ambitious statements in the entire Cîteaux *Moralia*, an ambition that testifies to the artist's mastery of his artistic vocabulary.[40]

In the initial *A* to Book Thirty-three (Fig. 34)[41], the representation of a man restraining two writhing and open-mouthed dragons by wrapping his arms and legs around their necks expresses the warning found in that book regarding Behemoth, the devil, who elsewhere in same book is specifically described as a "dragon":

> Let no one think that he has completely escaped the jaws of Behemoth by a confession of faith alone. . . . We do indeed avoid his mouth with the aid of faith, but we must still watch with great care lest we fall in in this slippery operation.[42]

This is precisely the sense conveyed by the initial. Starting with the centuries-old generic image of spiritual struggle of the man between two beasts as seen, for example, in the rotunda capital of Saint-Bénigne at Dijon cited earlier (Fig. 51), the artist adapted it, making it specific to the idea expressed by Gregory.[43] He did this not only by subtly altering the iconography and thus the content of the image by wrapping the man's legs around the dragons and so overtly enabling him to "fall in," but also by thoroughly translating the stock form of the man between two beasts from the generic language of violence into his own distinctive dialect. The figure holds the "jaws of Behemoth" at bay with his arms, but he is now quite precariously perched at the dragons' mouths, with his feet resting uncertainly on their unchecked claws—a truly evocative depiction of the "slippery" undertaking of life.

With less certainty, a later passage from the same book may account for a major detail of the initial: the dragons' tongues, an element that appears in only one other place in the entire Cîteaux *Moralia* despite the great number of dragons, and then without the emphasis seen here. It seems that their prominence in this initial was suggested to the artist by this later passage that discusses how Christ will bind the tongue of the devil, something that humankind cannot do.[44]

The initial to Book Ten has previously been interpreted by one scholar as referring to a line from the opening passage of Book Ten which describes Job as a "mighty wrestler" (*fortis athleta*) (Fig. 14).[45] This scholar further states that the depiction of the figure of Job, as if passing through the circle of the letter form of the initial *Q*, is meant to suggest that Job's glory is not total, such glory being reserved "for One only."

The word *athleta*, however, refers in its classical sense to an athlete in the public games of Greece and Rome (thus its metaphoric use in Christian literature), especially a wrestler or boxer, something that is simply not shown here in the sword-bearing figure of Job. It is not likely that this was misunderstood by the artist of the Cîteaux *Moralia*. Both the games and the meaning of the word *athleta* were wellknown in the twelfth century. References to the games appear in the pagan and Christian authors of the Imperial and Late Imperial periods that were commonly read at the time, for example, Suetonius and Augustine; and an understanding of the games is taken for granted in a discussion of the Circus Maximus in the contemporary tour guide of Rome by Benedict the Canon and in Hugh of Saint Victor. The word *athleta* is actually defined as "a wrestler" (*luctator*) in the eleventh-century word list of Papias. And wrestling was both practiced in the Middle Ages and depicted in medieval manuscripts; for example, in the contemporary Second Bible of Saint-Martial, the early-thirtheenth-century sketchbook of Villard de Honnecourt, the early-fourteenth-century Luttrell Psalter, and so on.[46] Furthermore, the same device of showing figures passing through the letter form appears in the initial to Book Thirteen without any apparent meaning (Fig. 17); and similar occurrences are found in the related Bible of Stephen Harding, again without any apparent meaning.[47]

Instead, it seems that in an idiosyncratic way, the initial refers to the passage in Book Ten that discusses how

> the righteous, on account of certain things that were not done righteously by them, consider the voice of chastisement as the ministry of charity. . . . They immediately throw themselves down in obedience. . . . [And] they regard the aid of chastisement as their life's *patrocinium* [the protective power of a lord over his servant or vassal], by means of which . . . the wrath of the judge to come is moderated. [But] when [the unrighteous] see themselves challenged with rebuke, they regard it as a striking sword.[48]

Thus the initial depicts a figure marked *Iob*, one of the most righteous figures of the Old Testament, who has thrown himself down and who grasps the edge of Christ's sleeve with his left hand, the latter suggesting the seeking of aid. Christ in turn holds the scales of judgment in his left hand in order to indicate his role as judge and lays his right hand on the head of Job to show his bestowal of aid—his *patrocinium*, his support for his servant, which he is in fact called throughout the Book of Job. He stands on the head of a bound demonic figure with the inscription "be[he]moth" beneath, the unrighteous.[49] The same sword that the unrighteous sees as a threat, here held by Job over Behemoth, the righteous uses as his defense.

While at first glance the image appears to be fairly dependent upon the literality of the text, the artist has actually begun with a literal basis and then developed the initial in a quite independent way.

Take, for example, the sword, which Gregory describes the unrighteous as fearing when from God but which the artist has depicted as held by Job. Gregory described the relationship between God and the righteous as one of *patrocinium*. In a chapter dealing with *patrocinium* in the *Lex Visigothorum*, the archetypal characterization of this protective relation between lord and vassal is one in which the former provides weapons to the latter.[50] Such a relationship was apparently foremost in the mind of the Cistercian artist as well. Developing the feudal idea of *patrocinium*, he does in fact depict the sword of spiritual rebuke as ultimately coming from God—the only place it can come from. God, however, has bestowed it upon his righteous servant, Job, who in recognition of this vassal relationship holds it at shoulder arms as he kneels before his lord.

But a problem arises in that Job is inherently a symbol of both the individual soul and the Church, the latter meaning having come about primarily because of the *Moralia in Job* itself.[51] The sticking point for the modern viewer is the exact identity of Job. Is he the righteous individual soul or is he meant to represent the community of righteous souls within the community of the Church?

Given the emphasis on the individual soul in both the passage in question and the illuminations of the Cîteaux *Moralia* in general, it is clear that the figure of Job is meant to be understood here in this aspect. This is why, contrary to iconographic and literary tradition, he is depicted as a *miles Dei* in complete consistency with the other images of the individual soul as *miles Dei* found throughout the Cîteaux *Moralia* (e.g., Figs. 2, 30, and 32). In portraying Job with sword in hand—something that never occurs in the Book of Job or in the *Moralia in Job*—the artist meant to convey the Gregorian idea that God provides not only trials for the righteous but also the means with which they are to defend themselves in these trials, a spiritual struggle whose ultimate outcome will be the binding of Behemoth, which is the triumph over temptation.

It is the nature of scriptural exegesis, however—of which the *Moralia in Job* was considered to be one of the greatest examples in the Middle Ages—to see multiple levels of meaning operating in the same subject at the same time. Consequently, while the figure of the *miles Dei* is consistent with the body of illuminations in the Cîteaux *Moralia*, it has also been distinguished in a particular way: the inscription *Iob* on the sword, which the artist clearly felt necessary to include. It seems that he felt this was necessary precisely in order to distinguish this figure from the other *milites Dei* in the manuscript. Thus marked as *Iob*, the figure carries an additional level of meaning, that of the Church. Holding a sword, it is more specifically the Church Militant. Given that the relationship of *patrocinium* is basic to the text and elaborated upon in the image, it seems that this divine relationship of *patrocinium* is meant to convey the idea of the divine legitimization of Church authority over the unrighteous and the Church's ultimate victory. In a very normal and common way, then, the uncommon portrayal of Job as the rather common *miles Dei* of the Cîteaux *Moralia* is meant to be understood on multiple levels, and the relationship of *patrocinium* is central to this. The initial thus takes on exegetical qualities that go beyond the text, typically not illustrating the text in the narrow sense of the term, but rather acting as a visual commentary of sorts on issues that are raised in the text.[52]

Indeed, the initial to Book Thirty, while taking up one of the main issues of that book, can at the same time be said to be almost entirely independent of the literality of the text (Fig. 31).[53] With all of the biting that takes place in the initials of the Cîteaux *Moralia*, this is the only one in which a man bites a dragon, as opposed to the other way around. It should therefore come as no surprise that one of the main themes of this book is the importance of overcoming the temptation of gluttony—or that the dragon, constantly used as a symbol for the devil, here enters the body of the man through his mouth. The struggle with the temptation of gluttony was put by Gregory in the late antique literary imagery of the city under siege:

> One cannot rise to the conflict of spiritual combat if the enemy stationed within ourselves, namely gluttony, is not first overcome. . . . Because war is waged pointlessly in the open field against external enemies if a citizen plotting some treachery is situated within the walls of the city itself.[54]

But what of the second dragon? The one whose neck the man stands on with one foot while with the other he crushes its threatening muzzle, effectively standing triumphant on it? Even though the primary visual concept of the initial was formed independently of the literality of the text, the artist freely turned to it for what might be called secondary elements. Immediately following the passage just cited, Gregory continues:

> Some, being ignorant of the stages of struggle, neglect to master the appetite and already rise to spiritual battles. At times they even perform many acts that are of great courage but, being dominated by the vice of gluttony, they lose all that they have done boldly as a result of enticement to the body.[55]

At first glance easily misinterpretable as simply a generic image of gratuitous violence, the initial has been translated by the Cistercian artist into a more personal expression than that of Gregory's civic metaphor into one of one-to-one combat with the devil over control of the appetite and of the relation of this to the larger course of spiritual struggle. Thus this is not actually a representation of a man biting a dragon, but rather of a man giving in to the temptation of gluttony—after he has successfully withstood other temptations—through which the devil enters not his body but his soul.

Based on a specific passage of the book that it heads but even less dependent on the literality of the text is the initial to Book Twenty-nine, an initial that is more ambiguous than the other initials of violent imagery previously discussed but still representative of the same relatively independent process of illumination (Fig. 30).[56] In this initial, a triumphant figure stands on the heads of a lion and a dragon, the traditional imagery of Psalm 90:13 (Vulg.): "You will trample the lion and dragon underfoot." The problem is, the psalm itself is not cited in this book. Nor is the figure meant to represent Christ since he has none of Christ's traditional features in physiognomy, hair, beard, halo, or drapery; and instead of the processional cross or spear in one hand and book in the other that are common attributes of Christ, the figure is depicted as a knight, a *miles Dei*, brandishing sword and shield (cf. Fig. 54).[57]

As with the previous initial, this is a rather idiosyncratic response to the text of the *Moralia in Job*. There is a relation between text and image, but it is one that pays little attention to the literality of the text. This is because the artist here chose to illuminate a passage that provided very little to go on in the way of specific imagery; but what it did provide he developed fully, presenting it in the visual vocabulary of spiritual struggle. The reason that a *miles Dei* is shown in place of Christ in an iconographical composition traditionally reserved for the latter is that the victory of the *miles Dei* over the lion and dragon refers to the statement in the opening passage of Book Twenty-nine which asserts that Christ took on human nature in order to be imitated:

The Lord said, "Be perfect, just as your heavenly Father is perfect" [Matt. 5:48]. Since he was not able to be recognized in that divine [nature] by humankind, he entered into human nature so that he might be seen. He wished to be seen so that he might be imitated.[58]

This is just what the initial shows: the *miles Dei* imitating Christ in his triumph over the powers of the devil. Or, to be more precise, it shows the spiritually advanced monk imitating Christ in overcoming the powers of the devil, which the lion and dragon of Psalm 90:13 are traditionally interpreted as representing in the standard commentary on this psalm, Augustine's *Enarrationes in Psalmos*. In this connection it must be realized that the *Moralia in Job* is so imbued with the thought of Augustine that one scholar of medieval exegesis has said that medieval culture "follows the principles of St. Augustine and the practice of St. Gregory, or rather of St. Augustine through the *Moralia* of St. Gregory."[59] This is not merely a modern characterization. The medieval awareness of the connection between the *Moralia in Job* and Augustine is made clear in the legend concerning the discovery of the original manuscript mentioned earlier where, despite its short length, the relation between Augustine and Gregory is implied.[60]

But why should the particular imagery of this psalm have been chosen? It seems that the opening line of Book Twenty-nine, which states that "Our Lord God Jesus Christ . . . is the power and wisdom of God" (based on 1 Cor. 1:24), suggested the well-known iconographical form for Psalm 90:13.[61] In *In Psalmos*, Augustine specifically sees the lion and dragon as referring to the two powers of the devil: the open power of force and the concealed power of deception.[62] It is power that overcomes power, and wisdom that overcomes deception. In imitating Christ in the victory that he achieved over the devil by taking on human nature, the monk too participates in "the power and wisdom of God" in the defeat of the open power of force and the concealed power of deception of the devil, these two powers being taken up at some length later in Book Twenty-nine.[63] Unquestionably, this is quintessential monastic art—an art only for those imbued with the literature of monastic culture.

Perhaps the most imposing of all the initials of the Cîteaux *Moralia* is the one to the Letter to Leander, an initial that is by necessity only generally related to the text because of its function as the frontispiece to the entire manuscript (Fig. 2).[64] Nevertheless, it expresses the sensibility of the first generation Cistercian attitude toward the *Moralia in Job* superbly. Composed of a fashionably attired and gracefully posed knight standing on the back of his squire, both of whom face two threatening dragons, the image is the ultimate expression of monastic spirituality in terms of violent and monstrous imagery. Indeed, as the initial here makes eminently clear, the aristocratic and knightly background of early-twelfth-century monasticism was a fundamental factor of such imagery.

It is almost astonishing the degree to which violent and knightly imagery could be used as a metaphor for what might be—to the non-monastic mind—the most mundane things. Nowhere is this more articulately put than in Bernard's chastisement of his cousin for literally fleeing the hard life of Clairvaux for what Bernard, at least, saw as lounging in bed in the morning at Cluny. As he writes in a letter directed to a level of monk decidedly below that of the current generation of monks of Clairvaux:

> Arise, knight of Christ (*miles Christi*), arise! Shake off the dust, return to the battle from which you have fled, ready to fight more courageously after your flight, ready to triumph even more gloriously. Christ has many knights indeed who have begun quite courageously, stood firm, and conquered—but few who, having turned around from their flight, have flung themselves back again into the danger that they had avoided, the enemy whom they had fled now fleeing in turn. . . . Because you have fled from the front line of battle, do you think that you have escaped from the hand of the enemy? The foe pursues you fleeing with even greater joy than when he faces you offering resistance, and he proceeds more boldly from the rear than when he encounters you frontally. Untroubled now with arms cast aside, do you take your morning sleep at that hour when Christ arose from the dead, and are you ignorant that unarmed you are both more fearful of and less to be feared by the enemy? A multitude of armed men have surrounded your house, and you sleep? Already they are scaling the ramparts, already they are breaching the walls, already they are rushing headlong through the rear gate.[65]

Following Gregory's recurrent theme of the necessity of spiritual trials and the resultant strength that the striving soul gains from them, the knight shown here represents the veteran warrior. He is well trained, physically and mentally alert, a master of many campaigns whose readiness and ability to engage the enemy is meant to refer to the spiritually advanced monk who has assimilated the principles to be found within this essentially monastic writing. Załuska has given technical arguments proving that this initial was inserted into the manuscript only after the first gathering had been produced, as mentioned earlier.[66] It is my belief that sometime after the initials to the first ten books of the Cîteaux

Moralia were made (specifically after the new visual vocabulary of violence had been conceived), the artist went back and either made or, as is more likely, remade the frontispiece in keeping with the significant change in attitude that had developed during the course of production. The imagery used here and in Bernard's letter is not superficial symbolism by twelfth-century standards, the sort of facile parallel that might be found in a modern sermon. In the most fundamental, nonbiblical text of monastic culture, the Benedictine Rule, Benedict stipulates that the Heptateuch and Book of Kings should not be read at compline, the last of the monastic hours before bed, because the violent imagery of these books might be too exciting for the average monk.[67] In other words, the imagery of the Cîteaux *Moralia* was not for pleasant daydreaming but for strong spiritual stimulation. It is in this sense that the frontispiece is a crystallization in one image of the entire *Moralia in Job*. It represents the spiritual struggle of the advanced, the adept, those of a higher order, whose spiritual hierarchy is indicated here in social terms through the depiction of the knight standing on the back of his squire.[68]

If most of the fully human figures in the Cîteaux *Moralia* represent those who are spiritually advanced enough to contend successfully with the various evils of earthly existence, and if the fully monstrous creatures represent evil, what do the *semihomines* who so stunningly populate the pages of the Cîteaux *Moralia* and who appear for the first time in Books Eight through Thirty-five represent?

In an earlier study, I attempted to show that the general meaning of the *semihomines* and their scenes of seemingly gratuitous or even incoherent violence is revealed in the initial to Book Twenty-three—which I described in the preface to this study—by the figure of a shod centaur who raises his sword to strike one of the two dragons that endeavor to devour him (Fig. 25).[69] This is based on the fact that although essentially no different from the other *semihomines* of this manuscript in general activity, attitude, attributes, and principles of form, this creature is identified, unlike the others, by his tonsure as a monk. Indeed, elsewhere in the *Moralia* Gregory describes as "beasts" the desires of the flesh that "rise up" against the spiritual person, centaurs as symbols of lust, and other *semihomines* as symbols of the irrationality of sin, something that seems to begin as rational but which ends up as devoid of reason.[70] (It is in this sense of the *semihomo* and of semihominal struggle that irrationality is best spoken of in regard to the initials of the Cîteaux *Moralia*, rather than in the sense intended by Schapiro mentioned earlier.) Furthermore, in connection with these monstrous hybrids, Gregory notes that some people are overcome by the struggles that the creatures represent, now "overcoming the rage" of one only to be "subjected by the violence" of another, and so on and so on in damning succession; yet at the same time he states how such trials benefit the spiritual person, to whom they act as spurs to greater advancement.[71]

More than just the primary element of the *semihomo*, however, goes to make up the three semihominal initials of the Cîteaux *Moralia*. For the world that the *semihomines*, monsters, and other creatures of these initials inhabit is one of consistent darkness, as indicated by the dark blue ground in each, a device that we have previously seen can function in the content of the initial. Significantly, the dark blue ground does not typically appear in the manual labor scenes where, in contrast, a light blue ground suggestive of day sky is the rule.[72] And textually, a close reading shows that the semihominal illuminations all share a common basis in that the passages to which their initials relate combine violent imagery with nocturnal or storm imagery.

In an extended passage of Book Twenty-three itself, Gregory describes the present life as "night" and the desires of this world as "tumultuous," noting: "As long as we are in it, to the degree that we perceive interior things, we are shrouded in the darkness of uncertain imaginations."[73] He tells how to those who examine their faults, "the laments of compunction are like the wounds of a beating," but wounds that restore the person thus afflicted.[74] He goes on to say that one type of compunction concerns itself with reflection on the evils of this life and that it is through the rejection of "corporeal fantasies" (*imaginationes corporeae*) that one rises above oneself, observing that humankind was created "whole" but has since become corrupted through its own actions.[75] Toward the end of the passage, he characterizes good endeavors that are free of temptation as a potential snare, describing the assaults of temptation as the "tender direction" of God, an idea to which he returns again and again.[76] In fact, according to Gregory, it is often when one becomes strong that one is tried with temptations and afflictions in order to increase one's strength, and it is through this that one comes to know oneself, recognizing the fundamental incompatibility of body and soul that manifests itself as a "war" between the two—an incompatibility that is very effectively conveyed through the initial's scene of semihominal struggle.[77] Thus this depiction of a monk as a tonsured semihominal—that is, partially "irrational"—creature is actually an accurate and positive one, not a satirical or negative one according to the line of thought of the *Moralia in Job* and its twelfth-century monastic illustrator.

Indeed, with the introduction of the *semihomo*, the struggle is no longer one of extremes but rather of degrees. For in a culture in which the physical was readily used to represent the spiritual, the *semihomo* is a creature whose body lies somewhere between human and bestial, and so whose nature lies somewhere between good and evil.[78] Thus when we ask whether another such scene of seemingly gratuitous violence as the initial to Book Twenty-eight is generic or related to the text of the book that it heads, a close reading of that book suggests that it very evocatively represents one of the main ideas expressed in the text, although, as it were, in a generic way (Fig. 29).[79] In Book Twenty-eight, one of the major themes is the constant spiritual struggle of humankind, a struggle described over and over as "a raging sea" that "secretly assails within," as "a storm of temptation," as "a turbulent sea darkened by the confusion of its own restlessness," and as "a storm of the heart."[80] What the artist of the Cîteaux *Moralia* has done is to take the sense of that specific passage and translate its verbal imagery of raging sea, storm, darkness, and chaos into the visual imagery of the storm of battle, in all its confusion, against a sea-blue ground. Even the word used by Gregory for a storm, *procella*, also carries the meanings of "violence," "commotion," "attack," "battle," and so on; while the sense here is quite effectively conveyed, the literalit is rather difficult to convey visually.

Some of the imagery of these scenes of gratuitous violence can be very strange indeed. Even so, at least some of it contributes to the content of the initial in a significant way. For example, at the bottom of the letter, seemingly oblivious to the absolute chaos that reigns above, a nude, bald, and bearded dwarf with severely atrophied legs rides a saddled, nude man who ambles along on all fours, bridled. What could ever account for such a bizarre arrangement?

At the culmination of the extended passage to which this initial relates, and which continues to employ the imagery of a stormy sea as a metaphor of the violence of spiritual struggle, Gregory explains how

> If a mind restrains itself by love of God and neighbor when the turbulence of temptations have suggested to it any wrong things, this very love acts as an obstacle to them and breaks the wave of evil urging. . . . [In this way, God] checks the violence of this rising sea by means of obstructing barriers.

Gregory immediately provides a number of examples of how this might take place, of which this is the first:

> It may be that anger exasperates within. But, lest heavenly peace be destroyed, the action of the tongue may be withheld from the upheavals of the mind so that that which makes a tumultuous sound in the innermost parts of the heart may not come out in words.[81]

Choosing to express this related concept of suppression in a manner congenial with the larger theme of the violence of spiritual struggle, the artist may have had his imagination sparked by earlier verbal imagery of the *Moralia in Job*. For example, in Book Seven, Gregory cites James 1:26 which advises the spiritual person to "bridle" his or her tongue. And only two books before Book Twenty-eight, he cites Psalm 31:9 (Vulg.) which refers to binding the jaws of those who do not come near God with bit and bridle like a horse or mule—a verse that was illustrated with the actual bridling of a mule and riding of a horse in the Utrecht Psalter and the restraining of a mule and horse by their bridles in the Stuttgart Psalter.[82]

Apparently expressing the general sense of the passage from Book Twenty-eight in the more specific imagery of James 1:26 and Psalm 31:9, which he had read previously, even recently, the Cîteaux artist approaches the same idea differently from the Utrecht and Stuttgart Psalters, in a way that was clearly meant to be seen as humorous or satirical by twelfth-century standards. Thus while the general depiction and much of the detail come out of the imagination of the artist, the pair's removal from the chaos above, the quite literal bridling of the "tongue and jaws," and the rider or "neighbor" seem to have specific meaning. Far more than a minor touch of "symbolism," the pair at the bottom of the initial refer to Gregory's concluding reference to the gift of the suppression of inappropriate feelings, with the artist amending it to the larger subject of spiritual struggle in the same way that Gregory did in his extended passage.

Like the other two initials of semihominal struggle, that to Book Eighteen seems to refer to the sense of a specific passage in the book that it heads (Fig. 20).[83] This book, which begins with an admonition to the reader to be aware of the deeper meaning of Scripture, has at its core an extended metaphor of spiritual darkness. Gregory begins by noting that certain passages in Scripture have such a clear absence of literal meaning in them that

> they compel the reader to look for something else in them. . . . [That] when we find a more obscure meaning, it is as if we are stung by some kind of goad so that we might be alert to an understanding of the deeper things.[84]

He then goes on to repeatedly refer to darkness, night, storm imagery, "the darkness of allegories," and earthly life as a stormy sea. He once more discusses how God allows humankind to be tried, describing how seeing the "violent death" (*interitum*) of another often causes one to be more careful about one's own actions, and how the reprobate are dragged off to punishment. He also notes that it is reason that separates humankind from animals.[85] Showing the storm of battle against a dark ground, it seems to be no accident that the *semihomo* in this initial carefully defends himself with a shield as he watches the ruin of another: a small, screaming boy who pathetically curls up in ineffectual defense as a scaleless dragon crushes his neck as it prepares to drag him off. Nor is it that the only pure animal form in the initial, a dog similar to a greyhound beneath the faunlike *semihomo*, savagely turns on itself, irrationally tearing at its own back in apparent response to the even greater chaos above.

On occasion, it appears as if some of the details of the Cîteaux *Moralia* initials come out of the general verbal imagery of the *Moralia in Job*— something that seems to be the case here. The imagery of the crushing of the neck of the boy by the dragon and of the cervine creature by the lion quite likely comes from Gregory's repeated reference outside of this book to the neck as denoting pride, a usage so common as to imply no specific reference to a particular passage.[86] The point here then seems to be that through pride the devil may crush the unwary soul, the depictions of the boy and the cervine creature in all likelihood being positive. This type of imagery, however, seems to be a minor component of the Cîteaux *Moralia* initials. It is an expression of the artist's imagination in that the details of the chaos do not refer to the specific passage of his attention, and so serve primarily to contribute to the element of fantasy in the initial.[87]

Those hybrids apart from *semihomines* proper that also appear for the first time only in Books Eight through Thirty-five must be viewed differently. It would be a mistake to look for too subtle a distinction among them in an attempt to come to any finer shades of meaning for the initials under discussion on the basis of such monastic staples as Cassian and Athanasius. I say this despite the fact that these authors and others offer many examples of how such a mentality might express itself and thus be recognized by reader/viewers of the Cîteaux *Moralia*. For example, Cassian relates in his *Conlationes* how *plani*—a type of spirit rendered as *fauni* (fauns) in some manuscripts, a fauntype appearing in the initial to Book Eighteen—delight in tormenting and destroying humans. In the same passage, he gives a long list of similarly monstrous spirits that are mentioned in the Bible, including centaurs, satyrs, and dragons, all of which are found in the Cîteaux *Moralia*.[88] Likewise Athanasius, in his highly influential *Vita Antonii*, notes with repeated reference to Job that demons like to attack monks, to deceive them by reading along with them, to imitate animals, to appear in monstrous form, to model their apparitions after the monk's thoughts, and that when frustrated, they even savagely attack each other—all of which could be read into these initials.[89] Certainly, the use of monstrous, semihominal, and animal imagery was something with which the twelfth-century monk was quite at home. One even wonders if the concept of the *semihomo* was interpreted at the time in the sense of Paul's "animal man" (*animalis homo*).[90] But in the end, such material diverges from the direct evidence of the *Moralia in Job*, which unquestionably provided the primary conceptual basis in the creation of the Cîteaux *Moralia*—and so the immediate experiences of the artist and the reader/viewers. Instead, the hybrids apart from *semihomines* proper are best seen broadly. They are part of a type of imagery that may have been loosely formed by other sources, but they are not specific to those sources. It may also be that their general presence is not unrelated to a phenomenon noted by one scholar who points out that interpretive rather than literal images tend to be found in poetical and philosophical parts of the Bible, where divine revelation is most dense.[91] These images represent the extreme of interpretive images related to the philosophical or semi-philosophical text of the *Moralia in Job*, primarily addressing the sense rather than the literality of the text.

Finally, if these three initials of semihominal struggle do take on a generic quality, it is equally true that the ideas they represent are of a generic and repetitive character as well. In fact, to the modern mind, the elements of variety and originality are found more strongly in the artist's images than they are in Gregory's text. And, if the visual vocabulary of choice for the expression of spiritual struggle is that of violent and monstrous imagery—whose great variety and originality can only in part be explained by the text, the rest being provided by the imagination and independence of the artist—how much better than the simple braining of a dragon with an ax of Books Four through Seven do the images of semihominal struggle of Books Eight through Thirty-five express the sense of the complete absence of a dualistic conception of that struggle as found in the passages in question? Indeed, despite the almost constant presence of dragons and other monsters elsewhere in the *Moralia in Job*, these three books, which discuss spiritual struggle at length, make no reference to monsters at all.[92] But at this point in the artist's developing conception of the visual vocabulary of spiritual struggle, they did not need to. All that was needed was the topic of spiritual struggle per se. This was then evocatively expressed according to the first generation Cistercian conception of the spiritual state in terms of extreme physical violence, monstrous creatures, and general military imagery. The result was a series of visual cacophonies of unsurpassed imagination and sensibility to the text.

DAILY LIFE

Of the initials representing daily life—which also appear for the first time in Books Eight through Thirty-five, as do their main protagonists, monks proper—some are directly related to the literality of the text of the books that they head and others more generally to the sense.

Among the former that depict monks is the initial to Book Eleven. Here, a Cistercian monk lies prostrate at the feet of a hierarchically larger angel, a haloed angel who holds a book and blesses the monk as the monk looks beyond him, not seeing him (Fig. 15).[93] This represents the primary activity of the daily life of the monk: prayer, whether communal or private. Now, one of the themes of Book Eleven had particular currency in the early-twelfth-century monastic reform, that of the criticism of those who perform spiritual acts for temporal gain. This was something that the early Cistercians had in part left Molesme to be rid of and something that in the polemics of the time was typically equated with the finanically lucrative and elaborately staged *opus Dei* of traditional monasticism, as opposed to the private prayer shown here.[94] In stark contrast to those who practice the spirituality of avarice, Gregory offers the example of the "Angel of Great Counsel" (*magni consilii angelus*), an appellation that in Scripture is found only in the Septuagint translation of Isaiah 9:6 and that was known in the Middle Ages primarily in the pre-hieronymian Old Latin Version of the Bible and in Jerome's commentary on Isaiah.[95] A little further on, Gregory notes how those with "great discernment of counsel" (*magno consilii iudicio*) on occasion fall through pride at this discernment, but "those who prostrate themselves in their faults hasten to tears of penitence"—something that is clearly shown here.[96]

But who exactly is the Angel of Great Counsel? In his cover letter to the *Moralia in Job*, Gregory states that as his biblical source he intends to use the Vulgate for the most part but that he will also use the Old Latin Version when it is useful to do so, as it was in this case. The first generation Cistercians were highly aware of the differences to be found in the various texts of the Bible, the great artistic undertaking of the Bible of Stephen Harding being a progressive attempt at a critical edition.[97] In his commentary on Isaiah—a work given priority of place in the twelfth-century library catalogue of Clairvaux and undoubtedly possessed by Cîteaux as well—Jerome referred to the Angel of Great Counsel and interpreted it as referring to Christ, an interpretation followed by Gregory in the *Moralia in Job*.[98] This is the basis of the initial to Book Eleven: a Cistercian monk prostrates himself at the feet of an angel—

Christ, bearing what apparently is the Book of Life—the penitent monk looking straight ahead, not seeing what is not present in visible form before him but being blessed by it. On one level, it is a rather sensitive depiction of monastic spirituality in that it presents the intimate relation possible with the divine through private prayer as a Cistercian response to spiritual acts for temporal gain, specifically the highly ceremonialized *opus Dei* of traditional monasticism that could at times be performed as much for the eyes of man as for the eyes of God—to closely paraphrase Suger of Saint-Denis.[99] But on another level, it itself was about to be branded as retrogressive. For although the depiction could be said to be in accordance with the Benedictine Rule which recommended that monks pray "with tears and from the heart," the second generation was actually soon to prohibit precisely the type of prostrate prayer shown in this initial. As such, it is an expression of specifically first generation spirituality.[100]

Manual labor (*opus manuum*), too, was one of the key issues of the early-twelfth-century monastic reform. It was a very important element in the early Cistercian claim to greater fidelity than traditional Benedictine monasticism in imitating the primitive observance of the Benedictine Rule, and therefore in the Cistercian claim to moral superiority. As such, the restoration of manual labor was one of the most prominent points of distinction between the old and the new monasticism,[101] and images of monastic *opus manuum* should be understood as something completely distinct from images of lay labor. The Benedictine Rule is explicit: "They are truly monks if they live by the labor of their hands."[102] It should come as no surprise, then, to see in the famous initials of monks cutting down trees, harvesting, draining swamps, and so on—initials that are traditionally taken at face value—probably the earliest known programmatic depiction of monastic manual labor. In fact, scenes of monks at hard labor comprise almost one-half of all the initials of daily life and two-thirds of those involving monks, a solid indicator of the intent of the artist. This emphasis on hard labor is significant. It would have been seen in the twelfth century as a claim to be in institutional contrast to the highly ritualized weeding of the kitchen garden, accompanied by chanting and prayers, that was seen as fulfilling the Benedictine Rule's requirement of labor at such traditional Benedictine monasteries as Cluny.[103]

And make no mistake, these are in fact monks, not the *conversi* that they are sometimes described as representing. (At Cîteaux, *conversi* typically were illiterate lay brothers who lived a semimonastic life and whose primary duties consisted of manual labor, although they did participate in the *opus Dei* in a secondary way.) These initials portray the issue of monastic labor in a way that is both polemical and based on the Benedictine Rule. To employ *conversi* in this task would be meaningless, since on the one hand the issue of monastic labor in the twelfth century was one that concerned monks, not *conversi*; and on the other, not being monks, the Rule did not refer to them. Furthermore, the initials are based on an intimate relation between text and image. In order to understand them, one had to read the text of the *Moralia in Job*, one had to be literate. To depict in the text of the *Moralia in Job* the exegetical spiritualization of the daily life of a social group other than the one reading it—especially one of a lesser social standing, incapable of advancing in this textually based culture, and recognized as more carnal and less spiritual than the group reading the text—and to depict it as activated through that text, would be so vicarious in this particular case as to be something less than improbable.[104] Just as there has been a lack of discrimination regarding the identity of the figures in the scenes of violence, so has there been in the scenes of monastic labor.

The most striking image of manual labor—and perhaps the most striking letter form of all the initials to the individual books, rivalled only by the stunning initial to the Letter to Leander—is the initial *I* to Book Twenty-one, an initial that startles the viewer when the page is turned, projecting boldly into the margin, nearly a half-column of text high, and almost completely unaffected by its function as a letter (Fig. 23).[105] Traditionally seen as a straightforward image of daily life, the initial depicts a tattered monk with his knife in his belt and his leggings slipping down, chopping away with all his might at the base of a tree that is unusually large for a medieval manuscript and that forms the body of the initial. Meanwhile, above, a layman is also busy cutting, but this time branch by branch.

One of the main themes of Book Twenty-one is the importance of the avoidance of temptation. According to Gregory, the senses of the body are the windows of the soul, and it is by thoughtlessly looking out through these windows that a person may fall into the pleasure of sin—

especially lust—through desire, even though this was against the person's original intention and even though the person never actually acts upon that desire.[106] It is for this reason that such danger should be anticipated and the source of such temptation—in this passage, primarily women—be avoided, even if this only involves the sense of sight and nothing more. As an example of the seriousness of the role of the sense of sight in the process of sin, Gregory points out that "Eve would not have touched the forbidden tree if she had not first thoughtlessly looked at it."[107]

Thus in the initial to this book the ragged monk cuts the tree of temptation in accordance with the biblical injunction, "at the root."[108] That is, he cuts himself off from the sight of all such temptations by fleeing the world and seeking shelter in monastic seclusion. The layman, in conceptual antithesis to the monk, cuts the tree branch by branch while perched precariously in its midst, ignoring his impending doom as implied in the inevitable fall of the tree, the theme of the layperson alone being found in a later tomb relief at Saint-Jean at Joigny (Fig. 55).[109] In other words, the pious layperson is contented with halfmeasures by continuing to live "in the world" and will inevitably pay the price for that decision. Along these lines it may even be that the pulling up of the dress of the layman is not just a touch of "realism" for its own sake, but rather the use of a realistic detail in order to illustrate the message at hand—the near occasion and avoidance of the temptations of the flesh.

Certain elements in this initial such as the ragged robes, the shift, and the knife contribute to what has been described as the direct observation of nature in the Cîteaux *Moralia* and left at that. They are indeed the result of the observation of nature, but this is certainly not their point—a subject to which I will return. For now, it is enough to say that the reason such detail was not commonly found in contemporary images of monks was that there was no perceived need for it. Given its prominent appearance here, it seems no great leap of logic to come to the conclusion that there was, then, a perceived need in this case. And, as with the previous image of daily life, the underlying issue seems to be a polemical one. The Benedictine Rule—a chapter of which was read "in chapter" in every Benedictine monastery every day—states that monks are to be given suitable clothing, stipulating that it be found locally and that it be inexpensive.[110] The contemporary and widespread impression, however, was that most monks not only dressed in robes of the finest material available, often imported, but actually considered such matters important. In reaction, Cistercian disdain for such concerns was claimed as a distinguishing mark of the Order.[111] The implication inherent in this initial—one that must have been extremely obvious to any twelfth-century monk, considering the enormous attention given the issue in the polemical literature—is that ragged tunics are suitable enough for the Cistercians, who follow the Rule in its primitive intent.

The same chapter of the Rule also states that monks are to be given a shift for labor and, among other things, a knife—again, items that are extremely unusual, perhaps even unique, in contemporary images of monks.[112] The purpose of the detail here is similar, permitting the image to function on a general level as a claim to a literal adherence to the Benedictine Rule, something that is at operation in one way or another in all the images of monastic manual labor.

Finally, the naturalistic scale of the tree in relation to the human fig-ures is very rare for an artwork of this time.[113] While not denying the Cistercian artist's apparent natural affinity for the observation of realis-tic details, the reason for it is in part to draw attention to the specific act being depicted. For aside from the allegorical interpretation given above, what is being shown here on the literal level is the act of land clearance—not a normal undertaking for a twelfth-century monk. Unlike main-stream monasticism, the Cistercians made a claim to a strict return to monastic seclusion, the "fleeing" of secular civilization with all that that entailed. While other monastic orders of the time might found new monasteries in settled areas, the extreme removal of the Cistercians in the early days to undeveloped regions typically necessitated extensive land clearance, an issue with which at least two other of the depictions of monastic labor are involved. In this initial, the artist has managed to fully integrate the polemical meaning with the allegorical one. Taking the text of the *Moralia in Job* as his original impetus, he has conceptu-ally elaborated upon it according to his own inclination and artistically expressed it with great imagination and originality, introducing imagery not commonly employed in contemporary art in order to refer to issues not commonly addressed there.[114]

One of the most effective initials in the Cîteaux *Moralia* is that to Book Sixteen, which depicts a monk in tattered robes reaping sheaf after sheaf of grain (Fig. 19).[115] While on one level it is very much a straight-forward depiction of early Cistercian manual labor, on another level it is more. For it is in Book Sixteen that Gregory interprets a certain field as "the extent of Holy Scripture," further on describing how

> there are some who, recognizing the severity of their negligence, are anx-ious to be filled with the bread of righteousness and long to reap the say-ings of Holy Scripture. . . . [And] whenever they reflect upon the thoughts (*sententias*) of the Fathers for the edification of their minds, they take with them, as it were, ears of grain from a good crop, . . . the ears of grain sig-nifying the thoughts of the Fathers in that while they are often expressed through figurative speech, we remove from them the covering of the let-ter like the husks of grain so that we may be restored with the kernel of the spirit.[116]

In this metaphor, Gregory specifically refers to the thoughts of the Fathers as "figurative speech" (*figurata eloquia*), by which is meant typo-logically prefigurative speech, whose explication is a function of exege-sis. Exegesis was the focus of scriptural study in the early twelfth cen-tury, and, aside from the *opus Dei*, it was meditative scriptural study (*lectio divina*) that was the true labor of the monk. In illustrating this particular passage, the artist of the Cîteaux *Moralia* was addressing him-self to something much more immediate than just the illustration of an unusually effective metaphor. He was presenting the spiritual labor of the monk in terms of the polemics of early-twelfth-century voluntary poverty and manual labor—in an initial that itself can be understood only through the exegetical process and that in illustrating this passage from the *Moralia in Job* is perfectly attuned to both the literality and the sense of the text. As this initial itself is proof, the exegetical mentality that was so fundamental to the text of Gregory's writing was becoming no less so to the artist's conception of the initials.

As a point of detail, it may be of some significance that in other scenes of harvesting, such as in the Utrecht (Fig. 56) and Luttrell Psalters, the harvesters are all depicted as bent over but with eyes forward, not actu-ally lowered as is the case here. It seems that, fully imbued with the ex-egetical method of Gregory, the Cistercian artist has incorporated the imagery of Job 22:29, "He who has lowered his eyes shall be saved," one of the topics of the exegetical explication of Book Sixteen.[117]

Among those initials of monastic daily life with a decidedly general connection to the text is that to Book Twelve, which shows two monks holding a cloth sheet (Fig. 16).[118] Although its meaning may originally have been more obvious by virtue of an inscription that was once legible between the monks but which has since been erased, the limiting factor of the cloth points directly to one of the main themes of this book: death. In Book Twelve, Gregory writes:

> It is the practice of the righteous to think the more anxiously about how fleeting the present life is the more diligently they have learned to ponder the eternal blessings of the heavenly country.[119]

Continuing with a discussion of the verses from the Book of Job, "Man born of woman lives but a short time" (Job 14:1) and "The days of humankind are short" (Job 14:5), he takes up the subject of the transitoriness of life and the shortness of time, noting that the time of death is fixed. He remarks how the holy long for the end, observing that "Every holy man put into this life, as long as he contemplates how far he is from departing the present life, laments how far he is from the eternal joys," continuing in a similar vein throughout the first half of the book.[120]

Given the absolute pervasiveness of this theme, it seems that the object the two monks are holding is nothing other than a winding sheet. While Cistercian monks were buried in their habits, they were also wrapped in winding sheets, and winding sheets were commonly used for lowering the dead into the grave.[121] The miniature of the burial of Judas Maccabeus in the Bible of Stephen Harding shows a handling of the winding sheet similar to this initial, except that in the burial of Judas the winding sheet has just been used to lower the body into the grave by the pallbearers—they are pallbearers in the original sense of the term, following one of the many medieval meanings of the word *pallium*, here signifying a winding sheet—some of whom now adjust the body for its final rest (Fig. 57).[122] Furthermore, that two of the lessons from the Book of Job that were read as part of Office of the Dead contain verses glossed in Book Twelve would have made this book's association with burial easily recognizable to any early Cistercian monk because of the great importance of the Office of the Dead.[123]

If there are any minor inconsistencies in the logic of the holding of the cloth, it should be remembered that the point of medieval imagery was the message, not a realistic presentation of daily life, whatever tendencies the Cistercian initials have in this direction. Such incongruities are common in medieval art (in fact, one appears in the holding of the ax in the initial to Book Fifteen), and the subjection of the image to the letter form—which affects the winding sheet greatly—is the rule rather than the exception. At the same time, a subtle shading on the left side of the cloth indicates that a three-dimensionality consistent with the holding of a cloth was intended, though the artist's attempt at a perspectival rendering on the right side was not able to communicate this effectively.

Fundamental to the very idea of monasticism, which is commonly described in contemporary sources as a dying to this world, this image too constitutes a depiction of daily life in its liturgical and spiritual aspect.

What is often described as a precocious realism in the Cîteaux *Moralia* is perhaps better described in some initials as an effective presentation of the spiritual messages of voluntary poverty, manual labor, and adherence to the Benedictine Rule, transmitted with a certain amount of humor, inventiveness, and polemics on the part of the artist. This was the case with the initial to Book Twenty-one that portrayed a ragged monk with knife in belt chopping down a tree, and it is precisely what is at operation in the initials to Books Fifteen and Thirty-four.

The initial to Book Fifteen depicts two monks splitting logs (Fig. 18).[124] While it has only a general relation to the text, it perfectly expresses the subject of voluntary poverty that occupies virtually the entire book. In perhaps the most evocative chapter, voluntary poverty is presented in contrast to the worries of the rich person in this world:

> First, he pants from avarice to gather together the objects of his covetousness, . . . [wearing] himself out in the very exhaustion of his own concupiscence: how to snatch up the things he covets, how to carry off some by flattery, others by threats. But after he attains his desire, having acquired these things, another affliction wearies this man—that he must guard with anxiety and fear what he remembers he acquired with grievous labor. On every side he fears those who lie in wait and is terrified that he will experience what he himself has done to others. He goes in dread of anyone more powerful than himself lest he suffer violence from him. And the poor man, when he sees one, he looks upon as a thief. . . . In all this, therefore, the wretch suffers things as great as those he was afraid to suffer because

fear itself is a punishment. Afterwards, he is led to hell as well, subjected to eternal torments. . . . In contrast, there is a wonderful security of the heart in not seeking what belongs to another, but remaining content each and every day.[125]

The conclusions mentioned earlier about the relation between the Rule and the depiction of monks in tattered clothing are applicable to all other similar occurences in the initials of monastic labor, including this one. But apart from its general polemical aspect, is the choice of a scene of manual labor related in a more specific way to some particular idea of the book? And if so, is there any deeper meaning imbedded in this initial?

The depiction of *opus manuum* seems to have been suggested by a passage from Book Fifteen in which Gregory describes how the avaricious do not so much possess things as they are possessed by them, concluding:

> Therefore, considering these designs of the wicked, let the holy man spurn them. . . . Because he sees it to be imcomparably good, he chooses to groan under the lash here for a short time rather than to suffer the pains of eternal retribution.[126]

Suffering in this world rather than in the next is, in fact, what is being portrayed in the initial. But given this, why the clearly humorous depiction of a slight monk, with neck stuck out like a buzzard, "groaning" under the burden of his relatively easy job of holding the ax while a larger monk—who is doing the real work of swinging the mallet—looks inquiringly at him? How does it relate to the previous idea that it is better to groan under the lash than to suffer in hell, an idea in which I think most would have difficulty finding humor?

While the humor comes solely from the artist himself, its impetus comes from the most authoritative source on manual labor in monastic culture, Chapter Forty-eight of the Benedictine Rule, the Rule being a constant in all of the specifically monastic images of manual labor, just as it was in all of the Cistercian claims to a return to the Rule's ideal of manual labor. In Chapter Forty-eight, it is said in regard to manual labor that all things are to be done in moderation because of "the fainthearted" (*pusillanimes*).[127] It was in large part this clause on the fainthearted that was used by traditional monasticism to obviate the requirement of manual labor for all practical purposes, and it is precisely this issue that is being presented here, with wit, but also with a strident claim to compliance to the original intent of the Rule—with the weaker brother taking the lighter task and the stronger one the heavier, exactly as described in one account of Cistercian *opus manuum* as it took place around only four years later.[128] Again, this is monastic art in its most undiluted expression: an art by monks, for monks, and about monks—the interpretation of "groaning under the lash" in terms of daily life and the polemics of Chapter Forty-eight being nowhere called for on the basis of Gregory's discussion. An early-twelfth-century Cistercian monk, who heard this chapter read exactly five times a year in chapter and who partook by the very fact of his way of life (especially manual labor) in the polemics of monastic reform, would have had little trouble in instantly recognizing this element, one of the most important and widely discussed passages of the Rule, and its relation to Book Fifteen.[129]

A variation on this is seen in the initial to Book Thirty-four (Fig. 35).[130] This depiction of two ragged and stocking-footed monks drying themselves out in front of an open fire represents nothing less than the triumph of the aristocratic monks of Cîteaux over material trials and self-pride.[131] While not dependent on any specific passage, it captures the essence of the opposition between pride and poverty of spirit that is one of the principal themes of this book. This is perhaps most succinctly put by Gregory when he writes:

> . . . because all the elect unceasingly perceive that they have cast themselves into the poverty of the present life through the faculty of inherent strength, it is well said, "I am a man who sees my own poverty" [Lam. 3:1]. For whoever continues to desire visible things does not understand the evil of his pilgrimage and does not know how to see the very thing that causes him to suffer.[132]

Indeed, in its cheerful depiction of swamp draining, this initial seems to have been so extreme in its representation of voluntary poverty that a monk of some later generation tried to deface what seems to have originally been a rather humorous scene, judging by the standards of medieval monastic spirituality.[133]

At the same time, this initial, the one to Book Fifteen (splitting logs, Fig. 18), and the one to Book Twenty-one (cutting the tree, Fig. 23), as has been briefly mentioned, carried another polemical level of great force in the current controversy over monastic reform. For the activities of all three of these are not best described as typical daily labor, but rather they show some stage of physical expansion such as swamp draining and land clearance. These were undertakings for which the early Cistercians were well known. The reason was that at this early date such activities were still the direct result of the Cistercian ideal of separation from society by physical removal to "desert places," traditional Benedictine failure in this regard being seen as one of its greatest faults. Monastic seclusion was such an important part of the Cistercian claim that it was given priority of place in the early statutes, being listed as the first in a distinguished and very focused series of enactments.[134] Nor is it a coincidence that the *Exordium Parvum* recounts how in the days of Stephen Harding's abbacy but before Bernard's arrival (between 1109 and 1113 or just at the time the Cîteaux *Moralia* was being illuminated), the lands, vineyards, meadows, and farms of Cîteaux increased greatly, while there was no decrease in religious fervor—this situation undoubtedly playing a part in the particular types of labor shown (as well as probably accounting for the financing of the Cîteaux *Moralia*).[135] In expressing the senses of their various books—whether the subject is the overcoming of self-pride, the embrace of voluntary poverty, or the avoidance of temptation—these initials of physical expansion in the service of monastic seclusion do so not in terms of daily life per se, but daily life as a polemical and multifaceted statement of the Cistercian claim to moral superiority.

Toward this aim, the use of realistic details in no way necessarily adds up to realism. The historical truth (in the sense of historical evidence) to be found in scenes of everyday life is rarely, if ever, in my experience, that of a historically true account of everyday life.[136] Rather, what should be understood by historical truth is typically the depiction of the ideological claims of the person or persons who bore primary responsibility for the determination of the image's content. It is in this sense that the realistic details of the Cîteaux *Moralia* should be understood. Despite what seems to be a whimsical affinity for detail on the part of the artist, the choice of ragged clothing for the monks at labor, among other things, was not the result of whimsy. Such a thing was extremely foreign to contemporary visual expression and it was precisely this difference that signalled to the twelfth-century reader/viewer that such a "detail" was an active part of the content. The raggedness of the clothing spoke of voluntary poverty. The unusual size (and so more realistic appearance) of the tree drew attention to land clearance and thus to monastic seclusion. The depiction of a monk harvesting—whose difficulty and required skill, alien to the aristocratic upbringing of the monks, is attested to in contemporary Cistercian accounts[137]—acted as a witness to a strident manual labor. And all of them put forth the claim to monastic humility and a literal adherence to the Benedictine Rule. Indeed, the degree to which the polemical goals of the artist could change the conception of the initial is strikingly conveyed through a comparison between the conventionalized human chopping ornamental vegetation in the initial to the Book of Job (Fig. 1) and the Cistercian monk chopping the tree in the initial to Book Twenty-one (Fig. 23)—both unquestionably by the same artist—a characterization of which would amount to a summary of this book.

The Cîteaux *Moralia* also has a number of initials depicting scenes of daily life employing strictly lay imagery. For example, the initial to Book Thirty-two, an *S* composed solely of a thresher wildly swinging a flail, has as its basis one of the main themes of that book and one of the most common verbal images of the entire *Moralia in Job*: the flail or scourge (*flagellum*) of God (Fig. 33).[138] The flail of God is one of the terms used by Gregory to describe the afflictions that God sends to the spiritually advanced in order that through their unquestioning acceptance of such blows, even though they may be unaware of the exact cause of them, they might advance even further:

> Whoever struggles to protect himself against flailings (*flagella*) attempts to annul the judgment [handing down] these flailings (*flagellantis*). . . . The heavenly flailings (*flagella*) did not strike blessed Job so that they might erase the faults in him, but rather that they might enhance his merit. . . . Not seeing his fault amid the flailings (*flagella*) and not realizing that these same flailings (*flagella*) were the cause of an enhancement of his merit, . . . he [nevertheless came to] accept that everything he suffered was just. . . . For whoever submits to blows now, even though unaware of the causes of the blow, if he accepts this judgment against himself believing it to be just, by this very act he has already made up for his wrong—on account of which he is glad that he has been justly striken.[139]

The interesting thing about the Cîteaux initial is that the artist chose to interpret the words *flagellum* and *flagellare* in their specifically agrarian sense of "a flail" and "to flail," rather than in the figurative sense of divine affliction used by Gregory, the exegetical interpretation of a word according to its various meanings being quite common in the Middle Ages and something that occurs frequently in the *Moralia in Job* itself. Taking advantage of the double sense of these words, the artist visualized them in terms of daily life—not without a touch of humor—leaving the interpretation of the image in terms of the Gregorian theme of the beneficence of divine affliction up to the reader/viewer, a theme that would have had a high recognition value at this late point in the *Moralia in Job*. Thus the very illumination has become a visual text meant for exegetical interpretation, something completely attuned to the extreme exegetical mentalities of both Gregory and early-twelfth-century monasticism.[140]

On perhaps a less profound level but one equally tendentious toward daily life is the initial to Book Twenty-seven, which portrays two youths spreading a large sheet of cloth while an older, well-dressed man sits on the ground (Fig. 28).[141] Oursel has suggested that the standing figures represent a monk and a *conversus* pleating cloth, and the man at the bottom a *conversus* carding wool.[142] This is not possible. To begin with, neither of the two standing figures wears a monastic habit, identifiable in all of its other appearances in this manuscript by cowl, cut, and color. Furthermore, the noticeably long hair of the youths identifies them as the long-haired servants and squires so criticized by contemporary writers. Although such figures might be depicted in the Cîteaux *Moralia*, it is as likely that monks or *conversi* of early Cîteaux would dress and groom themselves in such a manner as it would be if they dressed and groomed themselves like the fashionably attired knights—equally criticized for their appearance—of the other initials. Furthermore, while the elegant clothing of the seated man would not be be impossible for a carder to be depicted in in this manuscript, given the underlying spiritual metaphor of the illuminations, the fact is that both his hands are visible and he simply is not holding a carding comb, without which such an act cannot be indicated.[143]

Perhaps the least clear of all the initials of the Cîteaux *Moralia*, it seems that it refers to a discussion in Book Twenty-seven of the passage from the Book of Job, "He will spread out clouds as his tent . . . and cover the ends of the sea." About this Gregory says:

The Lord spreads out clouds when, revealing the path of preaching for his ministers, he spreads them out in every direction throughout the extent of the world. And it is well said, "as his tent," since it is the practice to pitch a tent on a journey. When holy preachers are sent into the world, they journey for God. Whereupon it is written, "Behold, I send my angel before you, and he will prepare your way" [Mal. 3:1]. . . . In this journey, the tent of God is identical with the hearts of the saints, with which he [God] is covered as if resting on the way. By coming through them [the preachers] to the minds of humanity, he brings about the things he has ordained, [but] he is not seen.

Somewhat altering the imagery, as is common with Gregory, he immediately continues:

This is why the entire Synagogue is also called a tent when the Lord complains through Jeremiah that the priests have ceased from preaching, saying, "There is no one any more who will spread out my tent or raise my curtains" [Jer. 10:20].[144]

In the Cîteaux *Moralia*, the artist has conceived the covering of God with the tent (or curtain) of his saints as he rests along the way in terms of daily life, with the long-haired servants pitching the tent (or raising the curtain) of their master who rests nearby. A glance at other medieval representations of covering something with a large cloth confirms this interpretation. For example, the verse from Psalm 84:3 (Vulg.), "You have covered all of their sins," likewise expressing divine activity among humankind, is illustrated in the Utrecht Psalter with a more expansive and energetic but quite similar arrangement of the spreading of a cloth as that in the initial to Book Twenty-seven (Fig. 56).[145] The tent (or curtain) itself, which represents the hearts of the saints, is green, a color that is repeatedly described in the *Moralia in Job* as referring to sanctity.[146]

But why did the artist choose this particular passage as the basis of his initial? Further on in the same passage, Gregory describes how the clouds that God has spread out as his tent have covered the ends of the sea, referring to the conversion of Britain, the only place in the *Moralia in Job* that this event is mentioned. Is it a coincidence that some scholars believe the Cîteaux *Moralia* was illuminated by an Englishman, Stephen Harding?[147] Or did one of his monks base the illumination on this passage in conscious reference to the evangelization of his abbot's homeland? Unfortunately, the evidence does not allow an answer one way or the other.

The artist, then, illustrated his chosen passage using the visual vocabulary of daily life but in a way that, while clearly considered attractive to the first generation, was frowned upon by the second in the person of Bernard, who was prominent among those who condemned long-haired servants and fashionably dressed knights.[148]

The initial *E* to Book Thirteen shows two men harvesting grapes, the one in the upper half being depicted against a dark blue ground and the one in the lower half against a green ground (Fig. 17).[149] The figures refer to a passage in that book which culminates a long discussion of the adversities of the Church by invoking the blood of Christ—of which the fruit of the vine as the source of the wine of the Eucharist is a venerable symbol: "It happened that the blood of our redeemer which his persecutors—raging—had spilled, afterward, believing, they drank, proclaiming him to be the Son of God."[150]

Translated into the visual vocabulary of daily life, the man in the upper half of the initial cuts the vine with a knife—spilling the blood of Christ, the true vine (John 15:1)—while the man in the lower half receives the fruit of the vine, looking upward in enlightenment. Taking this imagery a bit further, it is probably the case that the dark ground of the upper half of the initial is meant to indicate the darkness of spiritual ignorance of those who uncomprehendingly put Christ to death, and the green of the lower half their regeneration in that afterwards they drank his blood and believed.[151]

The traditional subject matter and format of this initial render it one of the most conventional in Books Eight through Thirty-five. It is probably for this very reason that it is the only initial known to have been directly copied from the Cîteaux *Moralia* in the later work of the scriptorium.[152]

Oursel interpreted some of the fashionably dressed figures of the Cîteaux *Moralia* as Cistercian *conversi*, apparently because he was hesitant to see a "secular" intrusion in the highly spiritual text of the *Moralia in Job*. Iconographically, far too strong a distinction has been made on occasion between the sacred and the secular in the art of this period in that what on the surface appears to be secular in sacred art is often in fact sacred. It is really a modern idea to make such a severe distinction between the two. The mere fact of their constant merging in the Old and New Testaments, not to mention the indigenous culture of Western Europe, should make this plain. In a culture dominated by the exegetical mentality, it could often matter little whether the figure was secular or sacred—indeed, the sexually explicit love poetry of the Song of Songs was one of the most popular sources of exegetical study in celibate monastic culture. A close look at the general identity of the lay laborers in the initials of the Cîteaux *Moralia* illustrates this. To the early Cistercians, social separation proper was equally important or even more important than physical separation in the Cistercian moral claim. Their original ideal proscribed the possession of serfs and other means of social entanglements such as parish churches, altars, lay burial rights, tithes, bakeries, mills for other than their own use, and manors.[153] The statutes specifically mention that the social disengagement of the Order was to be effected on the agricultural level through the labors of *conversi* (lay brothers) and hired hands.[154] Nevertheless, it would be misleading to look for too much significance in the identities of the lay figures in this manuscript, to see in them images of either *conversi* or hired hands. I say this because they cannot be *conversi* since *conversi* wore habits. And they cannot be hired hands since their pointed shoes and trimmed (and in one case embroidered) clothing indicates a higher social level. Rather, it seems that they represent generic human beings whose lay status sometimes plays a role in the content of the initials and sometimes does not.

For example, the lay status of the person in the initial of the tree being chopped down most definitely entered into the content of that image (Fig. 23). In contrast, the use of lay figures in the initial depicting the spreading of God's tent is appropriate to the imagery of a feudal lord travelling, something that must have been a very familiar sight, especially during the yearly war season, but it in no way contributes to the content of the idea expressed (Fig. 28). In the scene of the grape harvest, the traditional metaphoric element is so strong as to make any more "realistic" depiction of daily life such as appropriate social status and the "realistic" depiction of details as is found in the grain harvest scene beside the point (Figs. 17 and 19). These are not laymen per se harvesting the fruit of eternal life, but rather generic human beings, souls. Indeed, their relatively elaborate dress indicates that they are not to be seen as actual agricultural laborers. In fact, in at least one case, it seems that the social status of the figure was primarily determined by formal considerations. For example, in the threshing initial, the identity of the laborer as a layman is not just unrelated to the content, it seems that his dress was probably dictated by the demands of a letter form which would have been very difficult to accomplish with a robed monk (Fig. 33). Likewise, his pointed shoes, which are generally associated with aristocratic and urban circles, would have been ill suited to the work of harvest time. However, they terminate the lower part of the letter *S* very effectively and not unlike some of the fine Cistercian ornamented rubrics (e.g., Fig. 6). (The threshers in the Luttrell Psalter are, in contrast to almost all of the other laborers in that manuscript, barefoot.[155]) Thus, most of these figures speak against the idea of the Cîteaux *Moralia* as based on the observation of nature for its own sake in the broader sense of the term, although such a thing may be true on a selective basis, and the artist clearly had a personal tendency toward this. It seems that the "secular" figures were meant to be understood simply as generic human beings— more or less dressed as the social counterparts of the monks they appear with—and not as part of a socially comprehensive construction of a claimed way of life, however interesting such a thing might be.

A comprehensive construction does exist, though, on the spiritual level. The initials are in large part made up of images referring to the *opus Dei*, *opus manuum*, and *lectio divina*: the main elements of Benedictine life, regardless of old or new reform. In depicting these three elements that, along with spiritual struggle, make up the totality of monastic life—and in doing so with a strong polemical slant—the artist of the Cîteaux *Moralia* did present a construction of the claimed Cistercian way of life, one that was expressed to a large degree in terms of central monastic issues.

Within Books Eight through Thirty-five there are also two initials of conventional format, the initials to Books Twenty-two and Twenty-six, but even these are related to the text, if only in a general way. The initial to Book Twenty-two, which is a variation on the traditional iconography of the Fall of Pride—with the horse's lip curling as it neighs, trampling its rider whose hooded cape still flutters through the air after his fall—conventionally illustrates that book's theme of the necessity of humility and the risk of pride, which can bring about one's fall (Fig. 24).[156] Book Twenty-two never refers to the actual Fall of Pride. Nor does it need to. The theme permeates the book, and the artist has simply expressed it in a generic way, a way that would have been recognized by all.[157]

The figure that makes up the letter *I* of the initial to Book Twenty-six has sometimes been described as a priest and the matter left at that (Fig. 27).[158] It is possible, however, to be more precise, a precision that reveals the content of the image. What is depicted is the portrait of a tonsured saint of episcopal rank holding the ghost of a bishop's staff in his left hand and blessing with his right: a figure of ecclesiastical authority.

I identify him as a bishop because of the episcopal configuration of his vestments. These are from the innermost to the outermost the alb, tunic, dalmatic, and chasuble, as opposed to the strictly priestly configuration of alb and chasuble. (The ornament on the chasuble is an orphrey, lacking the requisite crosses that would indicate its status as a pallium.) Also, the stole (between the alb and the tunic) is worn in the episcopal, not priestly or diaconal, mode. The episcopal mode, which is depicted here, is parallel; the priestly is crossed; and the diaconal is over right shoulder and crossed under the left arm. The figure originally held an episcopal staff, not a cross as is sometimes said, traces of which can be seen in close examination of the folio. This is supported by the fact that the edge of the cuff that would have been overlapped by such a staff was never completed.

The specificity of the details suggests that they were meant to indicate to the initiated reader/viewer a particular identity for this figure of authority. Given that Gregory, but not Leander—who was also a saint and who is described as such in the sources—is distinguished with a halo in the illumination that heads the body of Gregory's Letter to Leander (Fig. 3), it seems that in the context of the *Moralia in Job* this identity could only be that of Gregory himself: monk, bishop, and saint. The reason that a portrait of Gregory should appear at the head of Book Twenty-six is that it makes reference to one of the book's themes of the need to recognize the legitimacy of temporal power within the Church, as opposed to a more narrowly defined spiritual power, even when some of its prelates conduct themselves irresponsibly in regard to that power. As put by Gregory:

> [Although] the Lord is the reason that the holy Church has grown to the height of religious authority in all parts of the world, they [those who criticize the exercise of temporal power by the Church] misrepresent this same temporal power—which it in fact employs correctly—disparaging it as the vice of arrogance. . . . The reason for this is that they see certain individuals who, under the pretense of religion, are swollen with the vice of arrogance. [But] the vice that they justly censure in these individuals they unjustly bring as a charge against all, clearly not considering in the least that there are in it [the Church] those who, while disdaining to rule temporal things, are known to do so properly. . . . And if there are perhaps some within it who serve not God but their own glory under the pretext of religion, it strives either to bring them into strict order, if possible, or to endure them with patience, if not possible.[159]

Gregory appears in the initial not only as the author of this particular passage, but also as one who as bishop of Rome was fundamental in the gradual establishment of the temporal power of the Church and who did not abuse that power, but nevertheless demanded respect on the basis of the episcopal office for those prelates that did. Along these lines it should be remembered that one of the factors in the phenomenal success of the early Cistercians was their characteristic recognition of local episcopal authority, a recognition that was required by statute and that was widely held to be one of the distinguishing features between the early Cistercians and mainstream monasticism. Such recognition entered the realm of early Cistercian spirituality and polemics because it was fundamental to the early Cistercian rejection of temporal entanglements, which were left for the bishop on the basis of the authority and precedent of Fathers like Gregory. In this policy, observance by the first generation was significantly more pronounced than that of the second, which systematically decreased the earlier recognition of episcopal authority.[160] Thus, this initial too expresses a distinctively first generation sensibility.

Finally, there is one initial of an unusually complex and overtly symbolic nature, the cryptic initial *H* to Book Twenty-four (Fig. 26).[161] Traditionally seen as a depiction of jugglers, this initial is entirely composed of a man looking at and assuming the pose of a small ape which stands on the head of a sinister-looking dwarf, the dwarf holding out a rabbit at the level of the man's genitals and looking directly at the viewer.

Exceedingly enigmatic, it expresses one of the themes of Book Twenty-four that describes how in yielding to the temptation of lust, rational human beings become like irrational animals, fixing their eyes on the lowest of things and following these as models. In a discussion of how one ought to model one's behavior on those spiritually more advanced than oneself, Gregory writes:

> Sometimes [Scripture] refers to as "men" those whom by their reason it distinguishes from the beasts, that is, those whom it shows to be unimpaired by the bestial stirring of the passions. . . . In turn, those who give way to carnal desire are no longer "men" but are called "animals." . . . They are called "men" who are supported by rationality and righteousness, and they are described as irrational "animals" those who are slaves of carnal pleasure. . . . Therefore, we ought to fix our attention on the way of life of the righteous, so that we might [more] finely understand our own. It is plain to see that their visible form (*species*) is held up as a kind of invisible form (*forma*) for us to imitate. . . .
>
> But the reprobate are unaware of this since they fix the eyes of their mind at all times on the lowest of things. And if they ever come onto the way of the Lord, they direct themselves not to the footprints of those who are better than themselves, but always fix their gaze upon the examples of those who are worse.[162]

Some of the details of the figures are important in this interpretation. For example, the devil is often described in medieval literature as small, including by Gregory himself.[163] Also, differentiation was made in the Middle Ages between the tailless ape and the tailed monkey, the absence of a tail being seen as the crucial distinction between the two and as an indicator of the ape's inherent wickedness—the simian here clearly being meant to be understood as tailless.[164]

Thus, in the initial, as the devil tempts the man with lust—as implied by the small, wicked-looking man holding the rabbit toward the man's genitals—the man looks at the ape, a symbol of irrationality and filth, and emulates it, assuming an almost identical pose. Whereas it is usually the ape (or animal) who imitates the human, here the irrationality of sin causes the reverse process: the human imitates the animal.[165]

Whether conceived in terms of the visual vocabulary of violence and daily life or even of traditional iconography and cryptic symbolism, each of the initials of Books Eight through Thirty-five is related to the text of the particular book that it heads. At times this relation may be specific, being in response to the literality of the text, yet with meanings that can be quite complex. At other times it may be general, being more in response to the sense. Such an initial's meaning may be easily guessed, but to pin down a specific passage as its basis is often impossible—the latter being more a goal of the modern art historian than of the early-twelfth-century Cistercian monk. Sometimes the initials present an image which, when viewed in conjunction with a knowledge of the text, is readily understandable. Sometimes they have a meaning that is less accessible, operating more like a verbal image in a sermon given by a monk in chapter that has to be explained to his fellow monks.

But, with the exception of the initial of the Fall of Pride, one thing that all these initials have in common is a certain personal idiosyncrasy of conception. There is a seeming arbitrariness at play; a commonly recognizable visual vocabulary is used, generally speaking, but the near-total absence of traditional iconography—or the use of traditional iconography bent to nontraditional purposes, as in the initials of Gregory and of the grape harvest—puts the initials of the Cîteaux *Moralia* on a personal level not commonly found in other illuminated manuscripts of the time. What is at operation here, however, is not exactly an undisciplined evocation of various themes in the text, but rather the artistic expression of a very specific attitude: this attitude creates the appearance of a lack of discipline in the illuminations because it was the attitude itself, not the artist, that was fundamentally undisciplined.

❧ CONCLUSION ❧
TO BECOME WHAT ONE READS

The Exegetical Spiritualization of the
First Generation Cistercian Experience

In his monumental study of Gregory the Great, F. Homes Dudden said of the *Moralia in Job* that it "disgusts the modern reader. . . . [It is] the endless allegorizing, the twisting of every word and phrase into a symbol of hidden truth that is so inexpressibly wearisome." According to Dudden, Gregory's exegetical method is so undisciplined that "any passage . . . may mean almost anything . . . and the expositor is inevitably tempted to substitute his own fancies for plain teaching and to involve himself in a labyrinthine confusion of symbolical obscurities."[1] Gregory himself states that the variety of his method was specifically designed to avoid "disgust" in the reader, although apparently not of the type felt by Dudden. Gregory expresses the medieval attitude toward the same method criticized by the latter in a quite different way when he wrote in the *Moralia in Job* that "we ought to transform what we read into our very selves so that when our mind rouses itself through the act of hearing, our life may act in agreement by putting into effect what it has heard," noting further on that in Scripture, "we recognize about ourselves both what is monstrous and what is beautiful."[2] Indeed, according to Gregory, religious reading was itself a spiritual exercise.[3]

In this conception of an interrelation of reading (*lectio divina*) and meditation (*meditatio*), Gregory followed an established tradition that was very important to his monastic audience of the early twelfth century, as it had been to that of the late sixth. To cite two of the more authoritative examples, Cassian, in his highly influential *Conlationes*, instructs his reader to "submit yourself to sacred reading . . . until continual meditation permeates your mind and forms you, as it were, in its own likeness."[4] And Jerome, who was described by Gregory of Tours as second only to Paul, advises in his widely read collection of letters that "reading should follow prayer and prayer should follow reading."[5] This connection between reading and meditation or prayer was so strong in monastic circles that in the words of one of the best-known Cistercian writers, William of Saint-Thierry, who wrote not long after the Cîteaux *Moralia* was made: "Meditation usually follows a form similar to the reading"; that is, it usually follows a form similar to the reading that it accompanies.[6] Thus, according to this tradition, reading and meditation are interrelated, and it is in part through meditation associated with reading that one advances spiritually, that one becomes what one reads.

Exegesis was one of the two major bases of this type of meditational reading, the other being ascetic literature.[7] In fact, the exegetical tendency was so strong around the time of the Cîteaux *Moralia* that on occasion a reader might gloss a letter that he or she had received and return it to the sender; and Hugh of Saint Victor, misunderstanding a question, glossed a prayer on his death bed literally with his dying breath.[8] Even so, the symbolic mentality that was inherent in medieval exegesis increased exponentially with the extreme exegetical attitude of Gregory, an attitude often adopted by his readers. An example of this is the apparent origin in the *Moralia in Job* of the famous story of the Angles in the Roman slave market. At one point in the *Moralia in Job*, Gregory makes the simple statement that now that Britain was in the process of being converted, its formerly barbaric tongue had begun to resound in divine praise with the Hebrew "Alleluia."[9] By the time of the writing of the first Life of Gregory one century later at Whitby, this—the only reference to Britain in all of the 1800 pages of the *Moralia in Job* in the modern critical edition—had been expanded and glossed, so to speak, by a British exegete into the apocryphal tale of Gregory's encounter with a group of young, fair-featured slaves at the slave market in Rome.[10] When told that the slaves were "Angles" (*Anguli*), Gregory—conceived of by the British exegete as unable to carry on a conversation free of exegetical interpretation, apparently with the *Moralia in Job* as his basis—responded, "angels" (*angeli*) of God, a reference to the common term for divine messengers in the Bible, here interpreted as bringing a divine message to him regarding the evangelization of Britain. When told that their king was named "Aelli," he felt that this indicated that the praise of God, "*alleluia*," must be given there. And when told that they were from the "Deire" tribe, he saw this as meaning that they would flee "from the wrath" (*de ira*) of God to the Christian faith. Thus the British exegete adopted precisely the same method employed by Gregory in the *Moralia in Job*, in which every word or phrase could be interpreted in such a way as to suit the author's purpose, and applied it to Gregory and a passage of the *Moralia in Job* themselves.

It is this attitude that was assimilated by the artist of the Cîteaux *Moralia*, although the degree to which it was applied to the different initials varies considerably. Just as Gregory identified with his subject, Job, so the British exegete and the artist of the Cîteaux *Moralia* identified with theirs, Gregory. (Gregory's identification with Job was one of the major aspects of the *Moralia in Job* noticed by the author of British Life of Gregory.[11]) And just as the exegetical sense of the vast majority of the interpretations are "moral" (tropological) in the *Moralia in Job* (whence its title), so are they in the initials of the Cîteaux *Moralia*. This is the authentic hermeneutic experience as described by Karl Morrison, which is actually a reexperience of the author's state of mind, or in this case methodology.[12] It is in this sense, that of Gregory's methodology—his urging the reader (in the Cîteaux *Moralia*, the artist) to go beyond the text to the "truer" sense of what was being read and to become what one reads—that one must view the initials of the Cîteaux *Moralia*.[13] However, since the creative process is not to become but to cause to become, in using the *Moralia in Job* as a spiritual exercise the artist—or rather the monk-artist, a person who was himself one of the potential specialized readers of this text in a way that was typically not the case for secular artists at the time—transformed what he had read into artistic expressions of his own spiritual struggle and daily life, recognizing both "what is monstrous and what is beautiful," what pertains to the animal and what pertains to the human, and what pertains to both as embodied in the figure of the *semihomo*.

At the same time, this was effected in a way that was largely undisciplined, like Gregory's own work: the artistic equivalent of Gregory's doctrinal stream of consciousness. Indeed, in his famous discussion of his exegetical method, Gregory himself encourages the reader (or artist) to choose whatever interpretation he or she prefers, a mind-set wholly consistent with the Cîteaux initials.[14] In fact, far from it being enough to

just read a text, monastic *lectio divina* itself implied the spiritual exposition of the text,[15] a process that is the basis of the well-known initial to
the Gospel of John in the Bible of Stephen Harding (Fig. 40). In this illustration of monastic *lectio divina*, a Cistercian monk sits in profile on
a cushioned seat as if reading in the cloister, while the eagle of John digs
the razor-sharp talons of one claw into the monk's visible eye, ear, and
mouth—the primary sense organs of communication. In the other claw,
it holds a scroll with the opening words of the Gospel, "John: In the beginning was the Word, and the Word was with God," perhaps the most
common biblical source for the belief that Christ is an uncreated, and
therefore equal, member of the Trinity. In direct physical and conceptual antithesis to this, the monk points to his own scroll, which bears the
Arian formula, "Arius: There once was a time when he [Christ] was not,"
attributed to Arius himself, condemned in the Creed of the Council of
Nicaea of 325, and often paired by the Fathers with the passage from
John.[16] One need not look for actual Arians in the twelfth century. It is
universally accepted that this and other Early Christian heretical desig-
nations were commonly used against the full range of spiritual, intellectual, and social dissent in the later Middle Ages. Thus, far from being
the depiction of an Arian Cistercian monk being punished by the eagle
for his heretical views or even Arius himself in Cistercian robes as is
sometimes suggested,[17] the initial is a brilliant evocation of the famous
opening passage of John as the subject of the monk's *lectio divina*. In his
commentary on the Gospel of John, recommended by Cassiodorus in
the *Institutiones Divinarum et Saecularium Litterarum* and described by
M.-D. Chenu as the "supreme and unchallenged" authority on John,
Augustine discusses the passage "In the beginning was the Word, and
the Word was with God" in conjunction with heresy—citing the Arian
heresy in particular—and with the role of the senses in spiritual advancement as a continuous theme, ultimately concluding:

> Note! Your eyes and your bodily senses have been lifted up to us [as the
> exegetical source], yet not to us . . . but to the Gospel itself, to the evan-
> gelist himself. . . .[18]

In reading, hearing, and discussing the Gospel of John as part of *lectio
divina*, the monk in the initial has lifted up his senses to the Gospel itself, to the evangelist himself, employing them in the process of divine

enlightenment. This is why they have been seized by the embodiment of that Gospel, indicating the seizure of the mind or consciousness of the monk, the mind being that which makes the transition from the material world of the senses to the immaterial world of the spirit. The idealized Cistercian monk does not simply read the text of the Gospel: he internalizes it with an aim toward its spiritual exposition, assimilating the revelatory message of the eternity and equality of the second person of the Trinity inherent in this passage, the core of the central mystery of Christianity. He then opposes this knowledge to the "false knowledge" of the time—whether actual heresy, heterodoxy, or simply the new theology of the early-twelfth-century philosophers, like Abelard, who was repeatedly compared to Arius by Bernard[19]—pointing in refutation at the Arian formula as the antithesis of the opening passage of John in precisely the same way that Ildefonsus points in refutation at the opponents to Christianity in the Parma Ildefonsus (e.g., Fig. 58).[20]

The transposition of the practice of spiritual exposition from *lectio divina* to the illuminations of the Cîteaux *Moralia* undoubtedly helped legitimize to the literate monk-artist—and, theoretically, to his superiors and the community in general—his independent approach to the initials of that book. For the artist himself does seem to have been personally responsible for the illuminations, as is indicated by the gradual nature of their change, although he may have had to seek permission from his abbot as a matter of monastic discipline regarding this.[21]

Along these lines what most of these illuminations have in common is a readiness to take one idea almost arbitrarily from among the many in the books that they head and express it in a way that is both artistically original and not particularly dependent on the literality of the text, or if there is a distinct literal connection, then they often elaborate upon the text. In other words, they typically do not actually illustrate the text per se but rather are visual commentaries, so to speak, on issues taken up in the text.

Furthermore, not only could the copying of religious books at times be considered a spiritual exercise, but the exegetical process was seen as potentially under the same divine inspiration as the original biblical text.[22] And while the direct inspiration of the Holy Spirit was attributed to only the greatest exegetes, such as Gregory, the contemporary writings of Theophilus Presbyter and others make it clear that this was only a matter of degree and that specifically artistic inspiration was also currently being attributed to a more indirect kind of divine inspiration in monastic circles in the twelfth century.[23] Since the uniqueness of the Cîteaux *Moralia* initials stems from the high degree of the personal element in them, an element that we have seen is connected with the exegetical process, it seems that their production functioned as a spiritual exercise to a distinctly greater degree than those in other manuscripts precisely because of their unique character. The attitude here, while having a specific basis in the *Moralia in Job*, has its counterpart in the unstructured and at times highly personal attitude commonly found in many monastic florilegia, the sometimes idiosyncratic collections of passages from the Fathers and others whose purpose was often to contribute to a certain argument already inherent in those writings.[24] In this sense, the illuminations of the Cîteaux *Moralia* comprise, if I may use the term, a visual florilegium of the *Moralia in Job*. Thus while some patristic texts of early Cîteaux received moderate artistic attention and others luxurious, it would be misleading to look for an explanation for the unique treatment of Gregory's text in an unusual emphasis put on Gregory by the first generation Cistercians. Gregory was not of any greater importance to the first generation Cistercians than he had been to monks of previous centuries or would continue to be to those of later ones. Rather, the reason that the Cîteaux *Moralia* received the level of integration of text and image that it did had to do simply with the internalization on the part of the individual artist of Gregory's dictum to become what you read—something that may have been spurred on by the tendency in the twelfth century toward self-examination, a practice that was more prevalent and more profound than at any time since the fifth century.[25]

More specifically, what seems to have happened was that after initially illuminating this patristic work in the conventional and unexceptional manner described in the discussion of the illuminations of the prefatory matter and Books One through Three (excluding the frontispiece), the monk-artist began in Books Four through Seven to internalize Gregory's exegetical attitude, although only in a visually and conceptually incipient way. This happened, significantly, only after the important methodological statement of the opening passage of Book Four, the culmination of similar statements in the Letter to Leander and Books One and Two:

He who examines the literality (*textum*) of the holy word and fails to recognize its sense (*sensum*) provides himself not so much with knowledge as he confuses himself with ambiguity.[26]

In Books Eight through Thirty-five (plus the inserted frontispiece), he introduced visual complexity into his expressions of the literality and sense of the text, and combined this with an effective visual vocabulary of violence and daily life. It was primarily through this imagery that he addressed the two main characteristics of the *Moralia in Job* mentioned earlier that are of importance for this study: that it was written specifically for monks and that in it Gregory emphasized the necessity of material and spiritual trials for those who wished spiritual advancement. This gradual transformation from conventional and textually unrelated images to largely unique and textually based ones indicates that the latter were deeply in response to the text, the direct result of the artist's assimilation of Gregory's exegetical method into his work.

Thus the Cîteaux *Moralia* concludes with perhaps its most definitive image of the triumph over material and spiritual trials (Fig. 36).[27] If the triumph of the early monks of Cîteaux over such trials could be portrayed in terms of material poverty, it could also be portrayed in terms of material splendor: the concluding initial presents, in the same knightly imagery found in depictions of spiritual struggle throughout the book, the restored monk, here shown restored as a prosperous contemporary knight, from his hawk to his pointed shoes to the bells on his fine horse, on the level of pure appearances precisely the type of knight that was criticized by the second generation in the person of Bernard of Clairvaux.[28] In the same way that Book Thirty-five is concerned with the "twofold" material restoration of the physically (and spiritually) assaulted Job, so is the initial to it conceived in terms of the material restoration of the spiritually (and physically) assaulted, armed *semihomo* or spiritually struggling monk of the previous initials. In this depiction of material and spiritual restoration, the image of the restored *miles Dei* is the conceptual counterpart to the Job of the illumination to the Preface discussed earlier (Fig. 4), which shows Job materially restored as a prosperous contemporary man of affairs rather than in the traditional iconography that portrays him either haloed and robed as an Old Testament prophet or as a leper sitting on his dung heap.[29] Thus in this concluding initial, the artistic conclusion to the monk-artist's meditation on the *Moralia in Job*, the outcome for the spiritually struggling *miles Dei* is the same as it was for the spiritually struggling Job: eventual restoration after the many trials that both strengthened and proved his spiritual prowess.

But given this special relation between the artist and the initials of the Cîteaux *Moralia* as part of the creative process, how did these initials function in regard to the reader/viewer? This is best thought of in terms of personal and public functions. To begin with, the fact that both of the two original volumes were headed with the text of the Book of Job on which they comment—a very unusual feature[30]—indicates that the original function of the manuscript included personal reading: the full text was provided so that the reader could refer to the context of the individual passages discussed by Gregory during personal scriptural study. The critical nature of this uniting of biblical text and commentary was tacitly acknowledged when the original first volume was divided into three smaller volumes and an effort was made to ensure that this arrangement continued in the new volumes, thus implying a continuing function on the personal level.[31]

Given this basic personal function, the initials of the Cîteaux *Moralia* make a claim in their particular relation with the text to act as spiritual aids to the reader/viewer in that in order to understand them he had to understand the text, and even ponder it in some cases—as he might the initials themselves, the equivalent of the meditation associated with reading mentioned above. In some cases the reader/viewer either had to know the text in advance in order to understand its illuminated initial or, as is more likely the case, he had to keep the image in mind as he made his way through the text, something that must also have been an aid in maintaining attention in the process of reading this long and diffuse work. Furthermore, given that *meditatio* involves the actual implementation of what one has learned from the reading that has been the subject of its focus,[32] the initials of the Cîteaux *Moralia*—especially those of daily life—should be seen as having had a potentially immediate and directing relation with the twelfth-century monastic reader/viewer. The initials were thus active factors in the processes of *lectio divina* and *meditatio*.[33]

However, the original intention also took into account a public function as well, one that has both internal and external aspects. Internally, within the monastery of Cîteaux itself, the pointing or punctuation that fills the pages of the manuscript indicates that it was at least in part intended for public reading, specifically in the refectory, at the *collatio* (in this case, the reading in the cloister just before compline), and perhaps at other times as well (see, for example, the text of Fig. 25). The pointing guided the reader in the public chanting of the text by indicating any minor (*punctus flexus*) or major (*punctus elevatus*) medial pause, full stop (*punctus versus*), and so on.[34] While it is unknown whether the images would have been publicly displayed on such occasions, it is not too much to assume that the comparatively few monks of this new monastery with its small library would have been familiar with this manuscript—one of their two greatest treasures, a work whose unique character had probably created a minor sensation throughout the community—and would have kept its images in mind at various points of the reading and presumably have identified with these new mental images. In light of this, one of the striking things about the initials of the Cîteaux *Moralia* is that they take up almost none of the many doctrinal issues for which the *Moralia in Job* was considered important, such as Gregory's discussions of hell, judgment, the nature of God, and so on. The immediate concern of the initials is not a theological one but an experiential one, a monastically experiential one. The tendency is toward the depiction of the struggle, the triumph, and the restoration of the spiritually advancing monk in terms of violence and daily life, in terms of traditional spiritual struggle and contemporary monastic reform polemics. Indeed, while the use of violence to express spiritual struggle was mainstream, the fact that Cistercian monks themselves appear so often in scenes of daily life is indicative of the polemical aspect of this manuscript. Thus internally, both these types of initials would have acted as expressions and projections of corporate confidence in the first generation's self-identification with the major theme of the *Moralia in Job*, the apparent contradiction in this world of the material success of the bad and the suffering of the good.

Externally, outside the monastery, the initials would have acted as expressions and projections of corporate superiority for the same reasons. They would have done this to the extent that they were shown to outsiders, which, though probably very infrequently, cannot be discounted entirely. Despite the fact that the *Exordium Parvum* records that potential monastic recruits kept their distance at this time, it is believed that it deliberately plays down the early success of Cîteaux in order to dramatize its expansion with the arrival of Bernard and the group he brought with him two years after the Cîteaux *Moralia* had been made.[35] The historical evidence suggests that Cîteaux had been so successful that a new daughter-abbey was being planned around IIII, something that would have been impossible without a certain amount of success within the monastic world. The situation with the secular world seems to have been comparable. It was in large part secular recognition that financed monastic institutional prosperity, and Cîteaux was apparently successful along these lines—significant material success being the basis for the production of the Bible of Stephen Harding and the Cîteaux *Moralia* themselves. In fact, the practice of holding a ducal court at the monastery was discontinued only during or, more probably, after the making of the Cîteaux *Moralia*.[36] Given that monastery treasures were regularly shown to important visitors, one might assume the probability that the illuminations of the Cîteaux *Moralia* received a certain amount of individual display to an external audience, one entirely removed from the primary context of *lectio divina* and *meditatio*.

Nevertheless, despite these probable uses, the gradually changing conception of the initial inherent in the Cîteaux *Moralia* suggests that its illuminations were not primarily conceived with an overtly public artistic function in mind. For the internal monastic audience, it seems to have been the personal element, not institutional control, that accounts for the polemical aspect of the Cîteaux *Moralia*. The artist of this manuscript needed no instructions along these lines from an aggressive abbot (assuming, for the sake of argument, that the artist of the Cîteaux *Moralia* was not Abbot Stephen Harding). Rather, he was living these spiritual polemics as had his institution since its foundation after the bitter flight of the first generation Cistercians from Molesme where some of them had been beaten and imprisoned for reformist views only eleven to thirteen years earlier. Indeed, it was apparently these very polemics that attracted the very polemical Bernard to Cîteaux just two years later.

For the external secular audience, the manuscript certainly presented a specific claim on the part of Cîteaux. It is instructive, however, to place it in the broader context of Romanesque manuscript illumination, especially that of the eleventh century, out of which it came. Following the general logic of George Duby's thesis that the royal inclination was to provide for luxuriously decorated liturgical books in order to adorn the liturgy properly speaking, through which its position at the top of the social hierarchy was made manifest,[37] it might be said that the luxurious decoration of the Cîteaux *Moralia* represents the breakdown of the feudal system in that the aristocratic monks luxuriously decorated non-liturgical, monastically oriented books for themselves, not for royal liturgies or royal donations—or ducal ones. It seems to be no coincidence that the imagery of power here is consistently knightly, not royal, the knightly class being precisely the one most responsible for the disintegration of royal power.

The emphasis in the Cîteaux *Moralia* is on personal and corporate spirituality, not the redemption of society as a whole. Thus, it is neither public art (for example, a luxurious Gospel book for public ceremonies) nor private art (for example, a Book of Hours intended for a specific individual) per se. Rather, it is something that is distinctly intermediate in both its conception and expression: personal art, more specifically, monastic personal art. It corresponds to the social level described by the contemporary Hugh of Saint Victor as somewhere between the private (*solitaria*) and the public (*publica*) spheres: that which relates to the affairs of a household (*rei familiaris officium*), whether familial or monastic, as an institution.[38] It is a personal expression for the, at times, personal use of the internal public of a community that disavowed private possessions. Although it is fundamentally an expression of the Cistercian ideological self-conception and may have served to unite the community, it is idiosyncratic, not part of a major intellectual or ideological program per se, nor the recipient or partial recipient of such a program handed down through so many iconographical generations—and this, in part, is its attraction.

Finally, a distinction has to be made as to exactly what kind of meditation is at play here. While the argument could be expanded greatly, for the sake of brevity let me limit it to one contemporary writer on art, the Cistercian author and friend of Bernard's, William of Saint-Thierry. According to William, every religious state or order has three types of persons: the lowest type or "animal man," the intermediate type or "rational man," and the highest type or "spiritual man."[39] The spiritual level known as animal man is not at all as negative as it might seem to the modern reader. The animal man is that religious person who is dependent on the senses. He or she can conceive of the spiritual only in terms of the physical, only by "forming a mental picture of bodies." Yet the adept animal man is truly virtuous, spurns the world, and manifests holy simplicity, "just like Job." And while "artworks and buildings" may be misused by the bad in regard to curiosity, pleasure, and pride, they are used by the good wisely.[40] But the "spiritual man" has no need of the physical—and so no need of artworks and luxurious buildings.[41] Thus while William may not have chosen to publicly characterize the first generation Cistercians as animal men, the initials of the Cîteaux *Moralia* do correspond to his conception of that spiritual level. At the same time, however, they are not the same type of art described by Gregory in his famous letters to Serenus, Bishop of Marseille, which were the theoretical basis for much of the justification of religious art in the Middle Ages. Here, Gregory describes a type of art whose primary function was simply to educate the illiterate in the narrative of the Bible.[42] The initials of the Cîteaux *Moralia* go far beyond this—in fact, they are virtually unconnected with it—in their intimate relation with an advanced spiritual text and in their exegetical spiritualization of the first generation Cistercian experience. Nevertheless, while they may not have been for "the people" by twelfth-century standards, they were representative of an increasingly outmoded, or at least less prestigious, form of monastic artistic spirituality, a form of spirituality that at Cîteaux was specific to the first generation.[43]

The Cîteaux *Moralia* is one of the most familiar but least understood illuminated manuscripts of the Romanesque period. It is so well known because of its striking illuminations of violence and daily life. It is poorly understood because these have largely been taken at face value. This lack of comprehension has come about because of an unawareness on the art theoretical level of exactly how spirituality and politics operate in the artistic process in this particular manuscript, and how this specific form of spirituality legitimized a very intimate and at first glance undisciplined attitude on the part of the artist toward his subject.

The key to understanding the illuminations of the Cîteaux *Moralia* consists primarily of three things, without even one of which it could never have taken its present form: the implicit and explicit methodology of the text of the *Moralia in Job* itself; the general vocabulary of violent spiritual struggle and the polemics of contemporary monastic culture;

and the idiosyncratic element of the individual who responded to the first in the visual vocabulary of the second. Thus these scenes of seemingly gratuitous violence and seemingly straightforward daily life are in fact the product of Gregory's demand that one become what one reads, that one internalize what one reads: in this case, the monk-artist internalizing the exegetical method of Gregory himself. In the same way that Gregory found it acceptable to analyze a line or even a word of text out of context, according to modern sensibilities, so the monk-artist was quite willing to do the same. The end result was the exegetical spiritualization of the first generation experience, the visual expression of Gregory's exegetical method. And while the depictions of violent spiritual struggle were generally conceived in terms of artistically nontraditional expressions of a traditional spirituality, the images of daily life grew directly out of the polemical situation of early-twelfth-century monastic reform.

But in the end, the use of art to express either of these was about to lose its frontline status—although only to a degree and only within certain circles. Whether depictions of the *opus Dei* or of *opus manuum* or of something else, what all of these initials had in common was that they were produced for *lectio divina*, and in this function were inherently distractive according to second generation Cistercian standards.[44] Clairvaux, the monastery of the charismatic and artistically ascetic Bernard, was rapidly becoming the defining center of Cistercian spirituality and its expression, both verbal and visual. And at Clairvaux, the basic premise of the use of figural art in the spiritual process was rejected out of hand, the cutting edge of Cistercian monasticism now turning its communal back on the historiated initial, although not on the superb sense of design and high standards of aesthetic accomplishment that had been its basis at Cîteaux. A glance at the initial *I* of Book Twenty-one (Fig. 23) and the initial *I* to the Book of Genesis of the Great Bible of Clairvaux (Fig. 59),[45] made there during Bernard's abbacy, drives home the radical change that had taken place, largely imposed from above. Indeed, the illuminations of the Cîteaux *Moralia* were not the "unexpected departures" of Bernard's description of the contemplative monk, but rather the "gradually ascending stages" of traditional monastic spirituality. And as such they were antithetical to the new Cistercian spirituality, regardless of what they represented, and were soon to be proscribed by the written legislation of the second generation.

NOTES

Preface

1. The date of IIII for the Cîteaux *Moralia* is taken from the date in a colophon at the end of the original first volume (Dijon, Bib. Mun. MS 170:92v; published in Załuska 1989, 202). For discussion of this, see esp. Davidson (1987, 47–48, who supports the date as valid for all of the Cîteaux *Moralia*. See also Oursel 1926, 29; Samaran 1959, vol.6:189, 462; Auberger 1986, 192–93; and Załuska 1989, 202.

On the question of Stephen Harding's role in the scriptorium of Cîteaux, see Porcher 1959, 18; Oursel 1959, 40–43; Oursel 1960, 20; Porcher 1962, 321; and Gras 1976, 96–97. For the suggestion (in a review of an article of 1955 by Oursel) that the artist of the early Cistercian illuminated manuscripts was a layperson, see J. A. Lefèvre, *Scriptorium* 10 (1956): 174–75; and Masai 1956, pt.2:143n.1, who seems to think that the artist was a visiting sculptor. I personally believe that there is no evidence to say whether Harding was an artist or not. The illuminations, however, are so imbued with a commitment to the ideals of Cistercian monasticism that I would be very surprised, to say the least, if the artist were anything other than a Cistercian monk.

Introduction

1. For example, see the section on "Frequency, Effect, and the Distractive Quality of Art" in Rudolph 1990a, 138–57, which in large part deals with the divergence of the Cîteaux *Moralia* from contemporary artistic conventions.

2. Bernard of Clairvaux, *De Consideratione* 5:3, vol.3:468–69, "At omnium maximus, qui, spreto ipso usu rerum et sensuum . . . non ascensoriis gradibus, sed inopinatis excessibus, avolare interdum contemplando ad illa sublimia consuevit." On the broader art historical significance of this passage, see Rudolph 1990a, 116–17.

3. On Gregory and the *Moralia in Job* in general, see Dudden 1905, vol.1:194–96; Rochais 1953, 255–56 (for the great popularity of Gregory in general and the *Moralia in Job* in particular in the genre of florilegia, such as the highly influential compilations of Odo of Cluny and Paterius); Laistner 1957, 107–8 (on the great influence of the *Moralia in Job* and its florilegia); Wasselynck 1956 (esp. 3, where he notes that the *Moralia in Job* was the classic work par excellence of Christian morality for the High Middle Ages); Dagens 1977; Ker 1972, 77; Besserman 1979, 51–56 (who notes that the *Moralia in Job* was "one of most important compendia of Christian doctrine to be had"); Leclercq 1982, 25–36 (where Gregory is presented as one of the

great formative influences on Western monasticsm); Smalley 1983, x, 32–35; Evans 1986; and Straw 1988 (on the spirituality of Gregory).

As to the exegetical method of the *Moralia in Job*, Gregory generally employs a triple sense, heavily emphasizing the moral or tropological interpretation; *Moralia ad Leandrum* 3–4, p. 4–6. A fourth sense is on occasion given. On Gregory's method, see Dudden 1905, vol.2:296–310; Wasselynck 1956, 9–14; de Lubac 1959, vol.1:187–89; Smalley 1983, 32–35; and Evans 1986, 87–95.

4. Isidorus Pacensis, *Chronicon* 13, *PL* 96:1257–58. Seville was raised to metropolitan status in 599, after the dedication of the *Moralia in Job*.

5. *Moralia* ad Leandrum 1, p. 2; Gregory the Great, *Registrum* 12:6, p. 975–76; the latter is cited by Dudden 1905, vol.1:195.

6. On the unlikelihood of Cîteaux being impoverished at the time of the making of the Cîteaux *Moralia*, see Rudolph 1987,1n.2. The distinction is not often enough made between the corporate prosperity of the Order and the individual voluntary poverty of the monks.

7. See Lekai 1977 and Auberger 1986 for bibliography.

8. For the legal documents, see *Exordium Parvum* 2, 6–7, 11–14, p. 58, 63–65, 71–75.

9. On the artistic situation at early Cîteaux, see Rudolph 1987 and 1990a, 133–57. The Cîteaux *Moralia* was apparently finished in 1111; Bernard arrived in 1113 (not 1112 as is claimed in some early documents; Bredero 1961, 62, 70–71). On the first and second generations, see Auberger 1986, 279–315.

10. It is sometimes forgotten that the Cistercians were in fact, and considered themselves to be, Benedictines, and that a number of monastic reform movements (including the Cluniac) claimed the Benedictine Rule as their ideal. Admittedly, the way had been prepared for the twelfth-century change in spiritual expression for some time, and the first generation was undoubtedly attuned to it to one degree or another.

11. Bernard of Clairvaux, *Ep.* 78:1, vol.7:201–2 (to Suger); *Ep.* 1:13, vol.7:10–11 (to Robert); *Apologia* 22, vol.3:99–100; *De Laude Novae Militiae* 1 and *passim*, vol.3:214–15; *Ep.* 2:12, vol.7:22 (to the canon regular). Numerous other examples exist. While the use of violence does appear in a few of the parables attributed to Bernard (there has been a great deal of disagreement about their actual authorship), it is not at all clear whether they were originally intended for the monks of Clairvaux; cf. *Parabolae* 1–3, vol.6, pt.2:261–76.

12. Stephen Harding, *Sermo*, *PL* 166:1375–76.

13. There are too many such passages to cite for Paul, but a few of the most notable are: Eph. 6:12 (where he notes that the struggle is not against flesh and blood, but against principalities and powers); 2 Tim. 2:3 (*miles Christi*); 2 Tim. 4:7 (where he states that he has fought the good fight). On spiritual struggle in Paul, see Forsyth 1987, 258–84. I refer to Athanasius and Prudentius because they were so fundamental to monastic culture. The *Vita Antonii* by Athanasius was one of the most widely

read books in monasticism. It is filled with images of demonic, monstrous, and semihominal spiritual struggle, and was translated into Latin early on. Along with the Lives of Paul the Hermit by Jerome and of Martin of Tours by Sulpicius Severus, the *Vita Antonii* by Athanasius was of such influence as to prompt no less than Augustine to request from Paulinus that he write a Life of Ambrose, hoping that it would achieve similar recognition; Paulinus, *Vita Ambrosii* 1, *PL* 14:27. All of these Lives contain violent, military, and/or semihominal imagery except, not surprisingly, the work requested by Augustine. Although the *Psychomachia* of Prudentius is extremely violent and bloody, it was much more to the demonology of Athanasius than to the late classicism of Prudentius that the Cîteaux *Moralia* is attuned. Cf. the passage of the *Psychomachia* in which Job himself figures, lines 162–71, p. 177–78. On spiritual combat in Gregory the Great in general, see Dagens 1977, 187–91. Other basic monastic sources that present spiritual struggle in terms of monstrous violence are referred to below.

14. Rudolph 1990a, 125–57.

15. On the Cîteaux *Moralia* in general, see Oursel 1926, 29–33, 70–72, and *passim* for art historical analysis; and Załuska 1989, 77–79, 200–204 for codicological, paleographical, and art historical analysis. Of special interest are Heslop 1986, 5–7 and Davidson 1987. See also Nordenfalk 1957, 203–6; Porcher 1959, 18–20; Oursel 1959; Samaran 1959, vol.6:189, 462; Oursel 1960, 11–12; Gutbrod 1965, 107–8, 119–26, 142–44, 159–60, 175–76, 185; Dodwell 1971, 89–93; Gras 1976, 98; Romanini 1978, 221–45; Auberger 1986, 192–95; Załuska 1989, 200–204 (essentially reprinted in Załuska 1990, 56–61); and Rudolph 1990a, 133–57.

16. A. K. Porter, in the introduction to Oursel 1928, 8; Dodwell 1971, 90; Pächt 1963, 71. On the artistic significance of the Cîteaux *Moralia*, see also Oursel 1926, 5–6; Porcher 1962, 320; Nordenfalk 1957, 176, 203, 206; Schapiro 1977, 7; and Pächt 1986, 58–60.

On the illuminated initial in general, see Nordenfalk 1951; Pächt 1963; Nordenfalk 1970; Alexander 1978a; and Pächt 1986, 45–94.

17. Heslop 1986, 2–3 (as a statement of principle), 5–7 (regarding the Cîteaux *Moralia*).

18. Schapiro 1977, 7; Dodwell 1971, 92.

19. The quotes are from Schapiro 1977, 6–7; originally published 1947. See also Oursel 1926, 32; Gutbrod 1965, 108, 123; Gras 1976, 98; and Auberger 1986, 195. With the exceptions noted below, Heslop (1986, 5) and Davidson (1987, 48–49) share the same opinion. Cf. Dodwell 1971, 92.

20. Viollet-le-Duc 1867, vol.1:127–28, vol.2:300, 387. Bernard of Clairvaux, *Apologia* 29, vol.3:106: "Ceterum in claustris, coram legentibus fratribus, quid facit illa ridicula monstruositas, mira quaedam deformis formositas ac formosa deformitas?" On the role of monstrous imagery in this passage, see Rudolph 1990a, 120–22, 334–36.

21. Auber 1884. The quote is from Auber 1866, 133 as cited by Mâle 1984, 49.

22. Mâle 1984, 49–61 (originally published in 1898). Mâle is referring to the early and highly influential "archaeologists," or art historians, as we generally say in the English-speaking world, Arcisse de Caumont and Adolphe-Napoléon Didron. See also Mâle 1978, 341 (originally published in 1922).

23. Vacandard 1884, 233. I have been unable to obtain A. Joly, *Un passage de saint Bernard à propos d'un portail de la cathédrale de Rouen* (Caen, n.d.), 8.

24. Schapiro 1977, esp. 6–7.

25. On Gombrich, see, for example, his chapter entitled "The Edge of Chaos" in Gombrich 1979, 251–84. On the element of the fantastic in the context of artistic freedom, see Cahn 1969, 10–14.

26. *Moralia* 4:Preface 1, p. 158: "Qui textum considerat et sensum sacrae locutionis ignorat, non tam se eruditione instruit quam ambiguitate confundit quia nonnumquam sibi litterae verba contradicunt." This distinction, one that is more fundamental than the traditional three or four levels of exegetical interpretation, is also recognized by Hugh of Saint Victor, "in una Scriptura duo similiter, littera et sensus" (*De Sacramentis* 1:9:2, *PL* 176:317).

Chapter One

1. Załuska (1989, 77) has noticed a certain tentativeness in the illuminations of Dijon, Bib. Mun. MS 168–170.

2. For a fine discussion of methods of illumination, see Alexander 1992.

All the illuminations of the Cîteaux *Moralia* are discussed in this study with the exception of those to Bks. 17 and 25, which are missing, and Bk. 14, which has the format of a rubric. Given that the entire folio that carried the initial to Bk. 17—which had been the opening initial of Dijon, Bib. Mun. MS 173 (the original second volume, as discussed below)—is missing and that only the first few words of the first sentence of that book are missing with it, it seems that the initial to Bk. 17 was a full-page initial, like the frontispiece; this has already been noted by Davidson 1987, 48.

3. On the view that Dijon, Bib. Mun. MS 168–170 and Dijon, Bib. Mun. MS 173 were by different artists, see Oursel 1926, 24, 31–33; Oursel 1960, 12; Gras 1976, 96–98 (following Oursel); and Romanini 1978, *passim*, but esp. 228. For the belief that the Cîteaux *Moralia* was largely by a principal artist with some illuminations by another, see Auberger 1986, 193–95; and Załuska 1989, 77–79, 201, 203.

4. Davidson 1987, 56n.63; Załuska 1989, 79n.42.

5. Załuska 1989, *passim*, but esp. 56–61, 202, 204. See Alexander (1978b), who argues that, in different circumstances, the scribe and artist were often the same person.

6. The use of *varietas* and its derivatives in expressions of praise are found in reference to every artistic medium, including manuscript illumination; for example, in reference to a book sometimes wrongly thought to be the Book of Kells, Giraldus Cambrensis, *Topographia Hibernica* 2:38, vol.5:123–24. Although it is impossible to be certain, it may that Hugh of Saint Victor was referring in his famous description of participants of varying ages in a monastic or canonial "school" to the ability of artists in his time to draw in different "modes": "Some depict figures in different modes and with diverse colors, applying their pen to parchment with practiced hand" (Alli figuras variis modis et diversis coloribus in membranis docta manu calamum ducente designant) (Hugh of Saint Victor, *De Vanitate Mundi* 1, p. 34).

7. *Moralia* ad Leandrum 2, p. 3.

8. On the format of the *Moralia in Job* in general, see Ker 1972, 81. There were also one- and three-volume formats.

9. Samaran 1959, vol.6:189; Davidson 1987, 47–48, esp. 47n.12; Załuska 1989, 201–3.

10. The sizes of the four current volumes are as follows: Dijon, Bib. Mun. MS 168 (335 x 250 mm), MS 169 (340 x 245 mm), MS 170 (350 x 240 mm), MS 173 (460 x 320 mm); Załuska 1989, 200, 203. On the common practice of varying the size of volumes within a set of the *Moralia in Job*, see Ker 1972, 81. On the continuity of text and image, see esp. Davidson 1987, 48; see also Oursel 1926, 18, 31–33; Porcher 1954, 98; Auberger 1986, 193, 195; and Załuska 1989, 78–79.

Załuska (1989, 57) notices an upgrading of the already fine quality of the calligraphy in Dijon, Bib. Mun. MS 173 on the part of a scribe whom she describes as one of the leading copyists of the scriptorium compared with his earlier work in the Cîteaux *Moralia* and the Bible of Stephen Harding. This seems to be a scribal response to the change of attitude toward the initials.

11. Dijon, Bib. Mun. MS 168:4v. See Załuska 1989, 201–2 for a codicological description of this insertion, including a diagram (fig. 8) that goes a long way toward explaining a fairly complicated arrangement.

12. Davidson 1987, 50–51 and *passim*.

13. Nordenfalk 1957, 203.

14. London, Brit. Lib. MS Cotton Julius A.VI:7v (Davidson 1987, fig. 26).

15. Bern, Bürgerbib. MS 264:80; illustrating *Psychomachia* lines 162–68. For the iconography of the illuminated copies of the *Psychomachia* in general, see Woodruff 1929.

16. Cambrai, Bib. Mun. MS 470:2. See Ker 1972 for the tradition of illuminated copies of the *Moralia in Job* in Britain. (The three initials to Bk. 11 given in Ker 1972[figs. 4, 7, and 8] act as a revelatory counterpoint to the Cîteaux *Moralia*'s initial to the same book.) As pointed out by Davidson (1987, 49), the tradition for bib-

lical illustrations was normally to show Job either as a leper sitting on a dunghill or as an Old Testament prophet.

17. Dijon, Bib. Mun. MS 12–15. Its colophon (13:150v) gives 1109 as a completion date (published in Załuska 1989, 193, 274–75).

18. Dijon, Bib. Mun. MS 14:60 (Song of Sol.; Oursel 1926, pl. VIII), 15:56v (John), 14:128v (Wis). On the initial to John, see below. On the initial to Wisdom, see Rudolph 1990a, 146–47.

19. Dijon, Bib. Mun. MS 15:68.

20. Dijon, Bib. Mun. MS 15:99v (Oursel 1926, pl. XXI). The details of the clothing of the figure who is stood upon in the middle of the descender are found only in male clothing in the Bible of Stephen Harding, thus implying that the figure is male and that the initial does not refer to Paul's discussion of the married state in this epistle, even in an indirect way.

21. Dijon, Bib. Mun. MS 15:56v (Oursel 1926, pl. XIX).

22. Dijon, Bib. Mun. MS 13:2, MS 169:62v, and MS 135:135v. Ms 13:2 is the initial to Jerome's preface to Kings; MS 135:135v is the initial to Jerome's *Ep.* 55 (modern system) to the priest Amandus (a different numbering system in used in the Cistercian manuscript, where the letter is listed as *Ep.* 87). For the initials to the *Letters* of Jerome in general, see Oursel 1926, pls. XXXVIII–XLIV. As might be expected, there are exceptions to the rule, with the occasional initial conveying some type of symbolic content. I use Załuska's date for the *Letters* (Załuska 1989, 207).

Chapter Two

1. Dijon, Bib. Mun. MS 168:2.

2. Pächt 1986, 59–60, 81. On the inhabited scroll in general, see Pächt 1986, 80–89 with numerous examples of similar imagery; and Nordenfalk 1957, 174–76. On the same question of the convention of a man struggling in vegetation, see Alexander 1978a, 16–17 and Heslop 1986, 8–9. I believe that there is no connection between this initial and Gregory's request in *Moralia* ad Leandrum 5, p. 7, that the reader not seek "leaves of words" where no tree is allowed (i.e., in the temple of God); the same holds true for *Moralia* 35:49, p. 1810.

3. Dijon, Bib. Mun. MS 168:5. Davidson (1987, 48–49) sees this presentation as related to the text. This is not, however, what is commonly meant by the expression, since a presentation does not actually relate to the content of the text properly speaking.

4. Dijon, Bib. Mun. MS 168:7. Davidson 1987, 49.

5. *Moralia*: Preface 1–3, p. 8–10. This has already been noted by Davidson 1987, 49. The question of the authorship of the Book of Job was a standard part of contem-

porary education; cf. Hugh of Saint Victor, *Didascalicon* 4:3, p. 73, based on Isidore of Seville, *Etymologiae* 6:2:13 (unpaginated).

6. Dijon, Bib. Mun. MS 168:12.

7. Dijon, Bib. Mun. MS 168:21. Alexander (1978b, 91, following Nordenfalk 1957, 173) has proposed the term "arabesque" for this type of initial.

8. Dijon, Bib. Mun. MS 168:39v.

Chapter Three

1. *Moralia* 4:15–17, p. 173–75.

2. *Moralia* 4:42, p. 188–89: "Quisquis enim accingi in divino servitio properat, quid aliud quam se contra antiqui adversarii certamen parat ut liber in certamine ictus suscipiat, qui quietus sub tyrannide in captivitate serviebat? Sed in eo ipso quod mens contra hostem accingitur."

3. Dijon, Bib. Mun. MS 168:52v.

4. Dijon, Bib. Mun. MS 169:20v. The textual basis for this initial is too diffuse to cite, but see, for example, *Moralia* 7:36, p. 359–60: "Aliquando vero involutis gressuum semitis et nulla culpa devincitur et alia per aliam perpetratur. Nam saepe furto negationis fallacia jungitur et saepe culpa fallaciae perjurii reatu cumulatur. . . . Sed cum culpa culpae adjungitur, quid aliud quam involutis semitis atque innodatis vinculis pravorum gressus ligantur? Unde bene contra pervasam mentem sub Judaeae specie per Isaiam dicitur: 'Erit cubile draconum' [Isa. 34:13]. . . . Quid namque per dracones nisi malitia . . . designatur?"

5. Dijon, Bib. Mun. MS 168:71v.

6. *Moralia* 5:19–20, p. 231–32: "aliquando superna conscendere mentis saltibus sciunt, ne semper in profundis curarum lateant." While the theme of the equality of treatment of the good and the bad runs throughout the first part of the book, its most articulate statement is found at the opening; *Moralia* 5:1, p. 218–19.

7. Athanasius, *Vita Antonii* 85, p. 162; *Verba Seniorum* 2:1, PL 73:858. On the importance of the *Vita Antonii*, see Introduction, note 13; the *Verba Seniorum* is equally significant.

8. *Moralia* 5:20, p. 231–32: "Quid enim per venationem Esau nisi eorum vita figuratur, qui . . . carnem sequuntur?" *Glossa Ordinaria*, PL 113:146–47.

9. Dijon, Bib. Mun. MS 158:1. For the date of this manuscript, Załuska 1989, 210. On the weak visual force of paired symmetrical finial heads, see Rudolph 1990a, 139–43.

10. Dijon, Bib. Mun. MS 169:5.

11. Davidson 1987, 50–52.

12. Rouen, Bib. Mun. MS A:123:193v.

13. *Moralia* 6:42, p. 315: "Sed cum sauciata mens anhelare in Deum coeperit, cum

cuncta mundi huius blandimenta despiciens ad supernam se patriam per desiderium tendit, ad temptationem ei protinus vertitur, quicquid amicum prius in saeculo blandumque putabatur. . . . Voluptates priscae ad memoriam redeunt."

14. According to Leclercq (1973, 142), the figures in the initial refer to the idea of the jester of God; he makes no attempt to relate them to the text of the *Moralia in Job*. Leclercq's views are repeated by Załuska (1989, 79).

I believe that there is no relation between this initial and the tradition of Job as a patron of music; on this tradition, see Meyer 1954.

Chapter Four

1. Dijon, Bib. Mun. MS 170:32, MS 173:47, MS 173:80.

2. Dijon, Bib. Mun. MS 169:36v.

3. *Moralia* 8:41, p. 412–13: "Si exteriora fugiens, introrsus redeo, . . . vehementer me per ipsas meae providentiae imaginationes terres." This initial is based on the extended passage, *Moralia* 8:41–43, p. 411–15, which does not lend itself to succinct citation.

4. *Moralia* 8:66, p. 432–33. There seems to be a pattern of the use of green for purposes of content in the Cîteaux *Moralia*; see the discussion of the initials to Bks. 13, 27, 31, and 35. Green is the traditional color of regeneration and was characterized by Gregory in the *Moralia in Job* as referring to sanctity, to regeneration through spiritual desire, and to that which is eternal; *Moralia* 8:66, 18:52, 30:65, p. 432, 920, 1535.

5. Utrecht Psalter, Utrecht, Bibliotheek der Rijksuniversiteit MS 32:4.

6. *Moralia* 6:49, p. 320. On the liturgical and extra-liturgical uses of Ps. 7, see, for example, the Cistercian *Ecclesiastica Officia* 98, p. 213; the first and third nocturns in the thirteenth-century Cistercian *Officium Defunctorum* from Heilsbronn (Erlangen, Universitätsbibliothek MS 118 Irm. 401:222, 225), for a transcription of which I am grateful to Chysogonus Waddell; *Corpus Antiphonalium Officii*, vol.2:719, 759; and Smalley 1983, xxx.

7. Dijon, Bib. Mun. MS 169:62v.

8. *Moralia* 9:8, p. 460–61: "'Qui praecipit soli et non oritur; et stellas claudit quasi sub signaculo.' Aliquando namque in sacro eloquio solis nomine, praedicatorum claritas designatur. . . . Qui stellarum quoque claritate figurantur, quia dum recta peccatoribus praedicant, tenebras nostrae noctis illustrant. Unde et subtractis praedicatoribus, per prophetam dicitur: 'Prohibitae sunt stellae [sic] pluviarum'. . . . Et quasi stellae in nocte resplendent quia et cum terrena agunt offensurum jamjamque nostri operis pedem exemplo suae rectitudinis dirigunt. Sed quia expulsis praedicatoribus non fuit qui plebi Judaicae in perfidiae suae nocte remanenti vel claritatem contemplationis ostenderet, vel activae vitae lumen aperiret. Veritas quippe quae

hanc repulsa deservit, subtracto praedicationis lumine, merito suae pravitatis excae-
cavit. Recte dicitur: 'Qui praecipit soli et non oritur; et stellas claudit quasi sub
signaculo.' Oriri quippe ei solem noluit a qua praedicantium animum divertit. Et
quasi sub signaculo stellas clausit qui dum praedicatores suos per silentium intra
semetipsos retinuit, caecis iniquorum sensibus caeleste lumen abscondit." This is
part of the extended passage, *Moralia* 9:6–11, p. 459–64.

9. *Moralia* 9:8–9, p. 460–62. Elijah is clearly named and Enoch implied in a discussion of Apoc. 11:4 in this passage. See also the *Glossa Ordinaria* on Apoc. 11:4 (*PL*
114:730), where it is stated that both Elijah and Enoch were believed to have been
removed from the earth by God; *Moralia* 14:27, p. 714, which discusses the return of
these two prophets by name; and 4 Kings 2:1–13 and Heb. 11:5. The actual phrasing
in *Moralia* 9:9, p. 462, is "duo illi eximii praedicatores dilata morte subtracti sunt
(those two distinguished [or "exempt, "] i.e., from death] preachers were removed
with death deferred)." The demonstrative pronoun *illi* carries an implication of understood reputation not conveyable in its English equivalent. Thus the Latin passage would have been clearer to a medieval reader than its English translation is to
a modern one.

10. *Moralia* 9:6, p. 459.

11. *Verba Seniorum* 18:17, *PL* 73:983. Utrecht Psalter, Utrecht, Bibliotheek der Rijksuniversiteit MS 32:24v.

12. *Moralia* 30:36–37, p. 1515–18, esp. "Quid est ergo quod beatus Job de partu
ibicum cervarumque discutitur, nisi quia in cervis vel ibicibus magistrorum spirital-
ium persona signatur? . . . Ipsi [the Fathers] etiam cervae vocati sunt. . . . Possunt
vero cervarum significatione doctores . . . intellegi." *Moralia* 30:65, p. 1535, "Igitur
postquam praedicatorum dispensatio sub cervarum praetextu descripta est."

13. *Moralia* 9:86, p. 517–18. For an example of the use of hunting metaphors in
contemporary writing, see Bernard of Clairvaux, *In Psalmum "Qui Habitat"* 3,
vol.4:392–93; and the first antiphon of the first vespers of the *Officium de Sancto Victore*, vol.3:501. In both examples by Bernard the protagonist is portrayed as the
hunted, imagery that is unavoidable since it comes out of the biblical passages from
Psalms that he is required to comment upon or render into chant.

Although unlikely, it may be that the reference to the two constellations of Arcturus (Arcturus is both an alternative name for the constellation Boötes and the
brightest star in it) and Orion in *Moralia* (9:12–17, p. 464–69 suggested the general
theme of the hunt since their mythological origins incorporate hunting narratives.
Even so, this passage is not actually referred to in the initial. Either one or two dogs
appear in the myths of Boötes, Arcturus, and Orion, depending on the sources con-
sulted, not the three dogs shown here. Furthermore, Gregory's discussion of the
stars is strictly astronomical and meteorological, not mythological. I also think that
the comparison of the Oriones to those who preach in *Moralia* 9:14, p. 465–66 is un-

related to the initial of the Cîteaux *Moralia* since this would add the unnecessary confusion of turning the hunters into the hunted.

14. Dijon, Bib. Mun. MS 13:2, MS 135:135v.

15. *Moralia* 9:8–9, p. 461–62.

16. Seal of Louis VII, Paris, Arch. nat., K 25 n°73. Examples of double parchment pendants of the same general proportions are common; see Bedos 1980, figs. 148, 238, 260 *bis*, 364, and so on.

17. The artist of the Cîteaux *Moralia* seems to have begun to develop some of these artistic devices in the second half of the Bible of Stephen Harding (Dijon, Bib. Mun. MS 14-15).

18. For my reasons for saying this, see the section on "Frequency, Effect, and the Distractive Quality of Art" in Rudolph 1990a, 138–57, esp. the subsections "Quantity: Finial Heads and Full Bodies " and "Variety: Symmetrical Pairs and Hybridity."

19. Second Bible of Saint-Martial, Paris, Bib. Nat. MS lat. 8:1:198.

20. Theophilus, *De Diversis Artibus* 3:78, p. 141. My thanks to John Williams for this apt reference.

21. Paris, Bib. Nat. MS lat. 8:1:208v.

22. On the knightly predilection in the early Cistercian manuscripts, see Rudolph 1990a, 149–50.

23. *Exordium Parvum* 15, 16, p. 77, 80. *Moralia* 8:2 (*miles Dei*), 12:17 (the present life is a [spiritual] *militia*), 31:86 (*spiritalis miles*), 31:91 (*miles Dei, spiritalis certaminis miles*), p. 383, 639, 1609, 1612. The source for this is 2 Tim. 2:3 (*miles Christi Jesu*).

On the origin of the idea of *militia Christi*, see von Harnack 1905. On the ideas of the spiritual athelete and the *militia spiritualis*, see Malone 1950, 64–111. For recent bibliography on this subject, see Aho 1981, 84n.11. On the relation between the early Cistercians and the aristocracy, see Bouchard 1987, 131–33, 148–49. Because of the nature of both the images and the text, I see the initials of the Cîteaux *Moralia* as only indirectly related to the militant Christianity of the eleventh and twelfth centuries. For an overview on this subject, see Alexander 1993, esp. 18–24; my thanks to Jonathan Alexander for sending me an offprint of this article.

24. Harris 1987.

25. Dijon, Bib. Mun. MS 14:13v.

26. Dodwell 1971, 92–93; Heslop 1986, 7; and esp. Harris 1987, 8–9. For a considerably more profound manifestation of the dynamic of the monastic desire for contemporaneity as it relates to art than that found in the fashionable dress of the Cîteaux *Moralia*, see Rudolph 1990b.

27. Dijon, Bib. Mun. MS 173:20. *Moralia* 19:56, p. 1001: "fortes spiritalis pugnae describeret bellatores, ait: 'Omnes tenentes gladios et ad bella doctissimi'."

28. *Moralia* 19:56, p. 1001: "Habet quippe, sed non tenet gladium, qui divinum qui-

dem eloquium novit, sed secundum illud vivere neglegit. Et doctus esse ad bella jam non valet, qui spiritalem quem habet gladium minime exercet."

29. Heslop (1986, 7) sees this initial as representing "the fight against evil, " although unrelated to the text. Davidson (1987, 49) relates it to the same passage cited here but thinks that the image is "purely secular." Auberger (1986, 194–95) sees the images of violence in the Cîteaux *Moralia* in general as referring in an unspecific way to the struggle against the powers of evil.

30. Dijon, Bib. Mun. MS 173:29.

31. *Moralia* 20:8, p. 1007–8: "Sed electi quique quamdiu in hac vita sunt, securitatis sibi confidentiam non promittunt. Horis enim omnibus contra tentamenta suspecti, occulti hostis insidias metuunt. . . . Vigilandum quippe semper est. . . . [The saints] semper sint de temptatione suspecti. . . . Confidunt et timent."

32. Terence, *Phormio* 3:2:21–22 (unpaginated).

33. Dijon, Bib. Mun. MS 173:133v.

34. Heslop 1986, 6; referring to *Moralia* 31:1, p. 1549.

35. Gregory of Tours, *De Virtutibus Beati Martini* 4:26, p. 206. Prudentius, *Psychomachia* lines 21–27, p. 171. Michael is depicted without armor proper, though armed and with shield, in both the earliest and somewhat later work of the scriptorium of Cîteaux. Cf. the Bible of Stephen Harding, Dijon, Bib. Mun. MS 15:125; and the Legendary of Cîteaux, Dijon, Bib. Mun. MS 641:64 (Oursel 1926, pls.XX and XXXV).

36. *Moralia* 31:85–86, p. 1608–9: "bellum procul odorari, est . . . nequitias latentes indagare. De quo odoratu Dominus recte in Ecclesiae suae laudibus dicit: 'Nasus tuus sicut turris, quae est in Libano.' . . . Et quid per nasum, nisi provida sanctorum discretio designatur? Turris vero speculationis in altum ponitur, ut hostis veniens longe videatur. Recte ergo nasus Ecclesiae turri in Libano similis dicitur, quia sanctorum provida discretio dum sollicite circumquaque conspicit in altum posita, priusquam veniat culpa deprehendit. . . . Hinc uniuscuiusque electi animam Jeremias admonuit, dicens: 'Statue tibi speculam'. . . ventura vitiorum certamina ex alta consideratione praenoscere. . . . Quia ergo spiritalis militis cogitatione omne vitium prius quam subripere possit aspicitur." The imagery continues in *Moralia* 31:91, p. 1612–13, both passages being part of the extended metaphor of *Moralia* 31:55–91, p. 1590–1613. Gregory's exegesis on the tower is in part based on Basil of Caesarea, *Commentarius in Isaiam* 92, *PG* 30:270 (on Is. 2:15).

37. *Moralia* 31:91, p. 1612–13: "Sed miles Dei . . . bellum procul odoratur, quia mala praeeuntia, quid menti persuadere valeant, cogitatione sollicita. . . . Igitur quia . . . quemlibet spiritalis certaminis militem descriptum . . . narratione [of the watchtower] cognovimus, nunc eumdem iterum in avis significatione videamus, ut . . . discamus illius contemplationem. . . . Per avium speciem cognoscamus quantum per contemplationem volat."

38. *Moralia* 31:102, p. 1620: "Qui [Isaiah] cum activae vitae virtutes exprimeret, . . . ad quae contemplationis culmina ascendatur adjunxit, dicens: 'Iste in excelsis habitabit'." For Gregory's *locus classicus* on the active and contemplative lives, see Gregory the Great, *In Hiezechihelem* 2:2, p. 225–36. On the active and contemplative lives in general, and with extensive reference to artworks, see Constable 1995, 1–141.

39. On red, *Moralia* 30:24, p. 1507, "Quid per purpuram, nisi cruor ac tolerantia passionum, amore regni perpetui exhibita?" *Purpura* can refer to any color from our modern red to purple; Gregory specifies it here as the color of blood, the same color seen in the helmet. On green, *Moralia* 30:65, p. 1535: "Virentia autem vocata sunt, quae nulla temporalitate marcescunt. Huic ergo onagro virentia perquirere, est sancto unicuique viro, despectis rebus transitoriis, in aeternum mansura desiderare." On the symbolic use of green in the Cîteaux *Moralia* in general, see above, chapter 4, note 4.

It may be that the coloring of the tower was based on Apoc. 21:18 and more indirectly on Is. 54:12, both of which are discussed in the *Moralia in Job*. The body of the tower is green and the battlements yellow: cf. Apoc. 21:18, which states that the wall of the Heavenly Jerusalem was of jasper (an opaque green quartz when referred to in the Bible), the city proper of gold; cited in *Moralia* 34:26, p. 1752; the passage from Apoc. 21:18 is based on Is. 54:12, which is cited in *Moralia* 8:81, p. 445.

40. Interestingly, Chenu (1968, 225) gives a rather similar interpretation to an initial in a twelfth-century "monastic" copy of the *Moralia in Job* (given by Chenu as Troyes, Bib. Mun. MS 43) which, according to his description, is identical in all but the details identifying the individual figures. Unfortunately, I have been unable to actually locate this illumination, despite the kind help of the Conservator, Mme. A. Plassard. If it in fact exists, it may be that it was done by a monk of Clairvaux, much of whose former library Troyes holds, who had seen the Cîteaux *Moralia* and conceived his illumination accordingly.

Oursel (1926, 72) describes the initial to Bk. 31 as "possibly allegorical." Davidson (1987, 49) writes without further elaboration that the initial illustrates the tower of *Moralia* 31:85–86 mentioned above.

41. Dijon, Bib. Mun. MS 173:156.

42. *Moralia* 33:12, p. 1682: "Nullus Behemoth morsum ex sola confessione fidei plene evasisse se existimet. . . . Os quidem eius fide nos sublevante fugimus, sed magno studio curandum est, ne in hoc lubrica operatione dilabamur." For the use of the term "dragon" in conjunction with Behemoth, *Moralia* 33:30–31, p. 1699–1701.

43. On the iconography of the man between two beasts, see Mâle 1978, 353–54 and Baltrusaitis 1934, *passim*, but esp. 59–73.

44. *Moralia* 33:18–20, p. 1688–90.

45. Dijon, Bib. Mun. MS 169:88v. Heslop 1986, 5–6, referring to *Moralia* 10:1, p. 534.

46. The examples are legion. Cf. Suetonius, *De Vita Caesarum*, Domitian 4, p. 319–20; Augustine, *Confessiones* 6:13, p. 82–83; Benedict the Canon, *Mirabilia*

Urbis Romae 23, vol.3:334; Hugh of Saint Victor, *Didascalicon* 2:27, p. 44; Papias, *Vocabulista*, p. 34. On the practice of wrestling in the Middle Ages, see Carter 1992, 59, 85, 102, 128, and *passim*.

Second Bible of Saint-Martial, Paris, Bib. Nat. MS lat. 8:2:167. Sketchbook of Villard de Honnecourt, Paris, Bib. Nat. MS fr. 19093:28 (Villard de Honnecourt 1935:f. 28). Luttrell Psalter, London, Brit. Lib. MS Add. 42130:62 (Backhouse 1989, fig.72). On the tradition of the athlete in the art of the Renaissance, with reference to Early Christian and medieval literature, see Eisler 1961.

47. For example, Dijon, Bib. Mun. MS 14:14, 14:44v, 14:90v (Oursel 1926, pl.VII).

48. *Moralia* 10:3, p. 535–36: "Recti, de quibusdam quae ab eis non recte gesta sunt, correptionis vocem, ministerium caritatis aestimant. . . . Illi se protinus ad oboedientiam sternunt. . . . Illi correptionis adjutorium vitae suae patrocinium deputant . . . venturi judicis ira temperatur; isti cum se impeti redargutione conspiciunt, gladium percussionis credunt."

49. The inscriptions are the same color as the dark red of the clothing, suggesting that they are original.

50. *Lex Visigothorum* 5:3:1, p. 216: "Si quis ei, quem in patrocinio habuerit, arma dederit vel aliquid donaverit, aput ipsum que sunt donata permaneant."

51. Cf. *Moralia*, Preface 14–15, p. 19–20.

52. Davidson (1987, 51) tries to connect the iconography of Christ holding scales to an initial showing *Libra* holding scales in Bk. 7 of an Italian *Moralia in Job* of *c.*1100 (Bamberg, Staatsbibliothek, Msc. Bibl. MS 41:68; Davidson 1987, fig.8)—suggesting that the initial to Bk. 10 of the Cîteaux *Moralia* is related to the text of Bk. 7, not Bk. 10, and that the initial as presented here is "misplaced."

53. Dijon, Bib. Mun. MS 173:122.

54. *Moralia* 30:58, p. 1530: "Neque enim ad conflictum spiritalis agonis assurgitur, si non prius intra nosmetipsos hostis positus, gulae videlicet appetitus, edomatur. . . . Incassum namque contra exteriores inimicos in campo bellum geritur, si intra ipsa urbis moenia civis insidians habetur." This is part of an extended passage on gluttony, *Moralia* 30:58–62, p. 1530–33.

55. *Moralia* 30:59, p. 1530: "Nonnulli vero ordinem certaminis ignorantes, edomare gulam neglegunt et jam ad spiritalia bella consurgunt. Qui aliquando multa etiam quae magnae sunt fortitudinis faciunt, sed dominante gulae vitio, per carnis illecebram omne quod fortiter egerint perdunt."

56. Dijon, Bib. Mun. MS 173:111v.

57. Cf., for example, the Sacramentary of Mont-Saint-Michel, New York, Pierpont Morgan Library MS 641:66v. On the iconography of Ps. 90:13, see Verdier 1982. The replacement of the person of Christ with another figure is found elsewhere; for example, *Liber Ystoriarum Romanorum*, Hamburg, Staats- und Universitätsbibliothek, MS 151:123v, in Buddensieg 1965, pl.5a, with discussion of this type (p. 50).

58. *Moralia* 29:1, p. 1434: "Dominus . . . ait: *Estote perfecti, sicut et Pater vester cae-lestis perfectus est.* In illa itaque nativitate divina ab humano genere cognosci non poterat; proinde in humanitatem venit ut videretur, videri voluit ut imitaretur."

59. Augustine, *In Psalmos* 90:2:9, p. 1275–76. The quote is from Spicq 1944, 11; cited by Besserman 1979, 56.

60. Isidorus Pacensis, *Chronicon* 13, *PL* 96:1257–58.

61. *Moralia* 29:1, p. 1434: "Dominus Deus noster Jesus Christus in eo quod virtus et sapientia Dei est." Cf. 1 Cor. 1:24: "Christum Dei virtutem et Dei sapientiam."

62. Augustine, *In Psalmos* 90:9, p. 1275–76. This is stated with even greater clar-ity in Augustine, *Confessiones* 9:36, p. 153–54. It may also be that Augustine's further interpretation of the dragon as referring to heretical threats to the Church (not taken up in Bk. 29) was meant to be understood by the reader/viewer. This inter-pretation of Ps. 90:13 continued to be current; cf. Bernard of Clairvaux, *Ep.* 189:2, 330, vol.8:13, 8:267–68.

63. *Moralia* 29:41–44, p. 1462–64.

64. Dijon, Bib. Mun. MS 168:4v.

65. Bernard of Clairvaux, *Ep.* 1:13, vol.7:10–11: "Surge, miles Christi, surge, ex-cutere de pulvere, revertere ad proelium unde fugisti, fortius post fugam proeliatu-rus, gloriosius triumphaturus. Habet quidem Christus multos milites qui fortissime coeperunt, steterunt, vicerunt, paucos autem qui, de fuga conversi, rursus se periculo ingesserint quod declinaverant, rursus fugarint hostes quos fugiebant. . . . An quia fugisti ex acie, putas te manus hostium evasisse? Libentius te insequitur adversarius fugientem quam sustineat repugnantem, et audacius insistit a tergo quam resistat in faciem. Securus nunc, projectis armis, capis maturinos somnos, cum illa hora Chris-tus resurrexerit, et ignoras quod exarmatus, et tu timidior et hostibus minus timen-dus sis? Armatorum multitudo circumvallaverunt domum, et tu dormis? Jam as-cendunt aggerem, jam dissipant saepem, jam irruunt per postitium."

66. On the technical aspects of the later insertion of this folio, see Załuska 1989, 201–2.

67. Benedict of Nursia, *Regula* 42. While the passage is a well-known one, the reference to excitement comes from Smalley 1983, 24. The Benedictine Rule em-ploys overt military imagery in a number of important places; see Benedict of Nur-sia, *Regula* Prologue, 1, 58, 61.

68. My thanks to Karl Werckmeister for drawing my attention to the social rela-tion between the knight and squire.

Heslop 1986, 7 sees this initial as representing the fight against evil.

69. Dijon, Bib. Mun. MS 173:56v. Rudolph 1990a, 146–48.

70. *Moralia* 6:52, p. 321: "Possunt etiam per terrae bestias motus carnis intellegi, qui dum mentem nostram irrationabilia suadendo lacessunt, contra nos bestialiter insurgunt." *Moralia* 7:36, p. 360: "Onocentauri ergo sunt qui, subjecti luxuriae vitiis,

inde cervicem erigunt, unde humiliari debuerunt;" Gregory actually refers to ono-centaurs (a centaurlike creature formed from an ass rather than a horse), but given the radically unconventional mixing of species in the Cîteaux *Moralia*, such a dis-tinction is meaningless. *Moralia* 7:36, p. 360: "'Et pilosus clamabit alter ad alterum' [Isa. 34:14]. Qui namque alii pilosi appellatione figurantur nisi hi quos Graeci panas. . . . Pilosi ergo nomine cuiuslibet peccati asperitas designatur, quod et si quando quasi ab obtentu rationis incipit, semper tamen ad irrationabiles motus ten-dit. Et quasi homo in bestiam desinit, dum culpa per rationis imaginem incohans, usque ad irrationabilem effectum trahit.

71. *Moralia* 7:35, 6:52, p. 358–59, 321–22.

72. The surprising degree to which the medieval viewer could be aware of color symbolism as part of the overall content of an image is made abundantly clear in Hugh of Saint Victor's *The Mystic Ark*, a translation and study of which I am cur-rently preparing (*The Mystic Ark* 1, 2, 5, PL 176:681–82, 684, 688, 690–91).

73. *Moralia* 23:39, p. 1173–74: "Nox quippe est vita praesens, in qua quamdiu sumus, per hoc quod interna conspicimus, sub incerta imaginatione caligamus. . . . Mundi tumultuosa concupiscentia."

74. *Moralia* 23:40, p. 1174–75: "Consideranti menti, et sese per paenitentiam lac-eranti, quasi quaedam plagae percussionis sunt lamenta compunctionis. . . . Ista refi-ciunt dum affligunt."

75. *Moralia* 23:41–43, p. 1175–77, esp.: "Perfectam scilicet animam ista compunctio afficere familiarius solet, quia omnes imaginationes corporeas insolenter sibi ob-viantes discutit, et cordis oculum figere in ipso radio incircumscriptae lucis inten-dit. Has quippe figuram corporalium species ad se intus ex infirmitate corporis traxit. . . . Quia enim per illas infra se lapsa est, sine illis super se ire conatur. . . . Nosmetipsos inspicimus bene conditos . . . conditione nos integros, sed culpa vitiatos."

76. *Moralia* 23:47–49, 51, p. 1179–83, 1184–85.

77. *Moralia* 23:51–53, p. 1184–87; citing Rom. 7:23.

78. For Bernard of Clairvaux's opposing view of the hybrid in general as in con-flict of nature, see Rudolph 1990a, 120–22.

79. Dijon, Bib. Mun. MS 173:103v.

80. *Moralia* 28:43–46, p. 1429–33: "Quod mare quantum saeviat. . . . Latenter intus ea cum qua huc venimus vitae veteris procella fatigamur. . . . Temptationum pro-cellis mare saeviens. . . . Mare tumultuosum . . . inquietudinis suae confusione tene-bratur. . . . [Job] contra procellas cordis fortiter stat." This is part of an extended passage with which Bk. 28 culminates and in which such imagery is a constant (*Moralia* 35–46, p. 1422–33).

81. *Moralia* 28:46, p. 1432: "Si autem mens Dei ac proximi dilectione constringi-tur, cum temptationum motus quaelibet ei injusta suggesserint, obicem se illis ipsa

dilectio opponit, et pravae suasionis undam . . . frangit. . . . [God] insurgentis maris impetum per obserata claustra compescit. Ira fortasse in occulto exasperat, sed ne quies superna perdatur, perturbationi mentis officium linguae subtrahitur, ne usque ad vocem exeat, quod in sinu cordis tumultuosum sonat."

82. *Moralia* 7:58, 26:56, p. 378, 1309. Utrecht Psalter, Utrecht, Bibliotheek der Rijksuniversiteit MS 32:18 (Utrecht Psalter 1982:fol. 18). Stuttgart Psalter, Stuttgart, Württembergische Landesbibliothek, bibl. fol. 23:39v (Stuttgart Psalter 1965:fol. 39v).

Davidson 1987, 52n.44 sees sources for some of the details of this initial in the Préaux manuscript mentioned above (p. 22). While some of the Préaux initials may have acted as iconographic sources in a limited way, they are unrelated to the Cîteaux *Moralia* in content and sense.

83. Dijon, Bib. Mun. MS 173:7.

84. *Moralia* 18:1, p. 886: "Aliud in eis inquirere lectorem cogunt. . . . Cum interiecta aliqua obscurius invenimus, quasi quibusdam stimulis pungimur, ut ad aliqua altius intellegenda vigilemus."

85. *Moralia* 18:31 (nocturnal and storm imagery), 18:35–37 (humankind to be tried; sight of another), 18:46 (reprobate dragged to punishment), 18:59 (hidden darkness of allegories), 18:62 (reason), 18:68 (earthly life as a stormy sea), p. 905–6, 907–10, 915, 926, 928, 933. The extended passage, *Moralia* 18:46–92, p. 915–55, is rife with the imagery first of darkness, followed by its counterpart, light.

Despite the reference in *Moralia* 18:56, p. 923 to the Church as a lioness, I do not believe that the lion (which is sometimes a positive symbol and sometimes a negative one) refers to the Church in this initial. This is because of its negative function in the killing of a cervine creature which, in my experience, always has a positive interpretation. In this violence, it mirrors the action of the dragon, a constant symbol of evil, which one would instead expect the lion to destroy if the lion were in fact meant to refer to the Church. See also the discussion below on the significance of the crushing of necks in this initial.

86. Cf. *Moralia* 11:43, 12:49, 13:18, 34:1–2, 35:14, p. 610, 658–59, 678, 1733–34, 1783.

87. Davidson (1987, 52n.44) sees a connection between the figure of the boy and one of the initials of the Préaux manuscript. For a rather loose interpretation of this initial, one which attempts no relation to the text, see Gutbrod 1965, 142–44.

88. Cassian, *Conlationes* 7:32, p. 210–12.

89. Athanasius, *Vita Antonii, passim,* but esp. 23, 24, 25, 40, 42, p. 52–54, 55–56, 58, 84–86, 88–90.

90. 1 Cor. 2:14; esp. as taken up by William of Saint-Thierry, *Ad Fratres* 41–93, p. 176–216, and *passim*. Both the term and its meaning are taken up below.

91. Cahn 1982, 172.

92. Only *Moralia* 18:67, p. 932–33 makes reference to Apoc. 20:2–3, which refers

once to "the dragon," something that is not taken up in the text proper of the *Moralia in Job.*

93. Dijon, Bib. Mun. MS 170:6v.

94. *Moralia* 11:19, p. 597. Cf. Bernard of Clairvaux, *Apologia* 1–3, vol.3:81–83, where this issue actually heads his, and so to a large degree reform monasticism's, criticism of traditional monasticism. The early Cistercians rejected even the temptation of such gain by rejecting the basis of its source in the Cult of the Dead and the Cult of Relics; on this see Rudolph 1987. On the relation between art and the sacred economy in general, see Rudolph 1990a, 17–103, esp. 42–50.

95. *Vetus Latina*, Is. 9:6, vol.12:293. Jerome, *In Esaiam* 3:9, p. 127. "Magni consilii angelus" is found elsewhere from time to time, as in Eusebius' *Historia Ecclesiastica* 1:2 (*PG* 20:54), translated by Jerome; Haimo of Auxerre's *In Isaiam* 2:9 (*PL* 116:771), which was widely read from the tenth to the twelfth centuries (Smalley 1983, 39); and in contemporary writings, such as Hugh of Saint Victor, *De Tribus Diebus* 24, p. 138.

96. *Moralia* 11:26, p. 601: "Sed saepe contingit ut in occulto animus de ipsa sua sapientia in elationis fastum sublevetur et sub eis vitiis corruat, de quibus se victorem fuisse gaudebat. . . . Sed quia nonnumquam hi qui in vitiis jacere videntur ad paenitentiae lamenta currunt." In this passage, Gregory gives an alternative interpretation for the verse under discussion, stating that "Cum enim mysticos allegoriarum nudos . . . solvimus, in lumine dicimus quod in tenebris audivimus [with reference to Mt. 10:27]." I think that the logic of Gregory's discussion eliminates a relationship to the initial.

In *Moralia* 11:49, p. 613 14, Gregory writes how we stand with tears before our creator. *Moralia* 11:32–33, p. 605–6 deals with prayer and those who give up the present world. *Moralia* 11:28, p. 602 refers to the secret counsels of Christ, from darkness to light, possibly something that accounts for the dark blue ground here.

97. *Moralia* ad Leandrum 5, p. 7; cf. *Moralia* 4:15, 7:56, 18:55, 26:72, p. 172–73, 377, 922, 1319, where he refers to the Old Latin Version. On the efforts of the first generation to produce a critical edition of the Bible, see the colophon of the Bible of Stephen Harding (published in Załuska 1989, 274–75).

98. Jerome, *In Esaiam* 3:9, p. 127; Wilmart 1917, 154; *Moralia* 11:19, p. 597.

99. Suger, *Vie de Louis VI* 32, p. 262.

100. Benedict of Nursia, *Regula* 52; Cistercian statute 84, p.32. Bernard himself prayed in a standing position, undoubtedly not without some particular reason such as emulation of the Desert Fathers; William of Saint-Thierry, *Vita Prima* 1:39, *PL* 185:250. The examples of standing prayer in the Desert Fathers are many; see, for example, *Verba Seniorum* 7:1, 12:3, 12:8, 12:11, *PL* 73:893, 941, 942. The Desert Fathers also prayed in other postures.

According to Gutbrod (1965, 124–26), this initial may depict Stephen Harding and the book that the angel holds may be the Cîteaux *Moralia*. While admitting the difficult nature of the initials of the Cîteaux *Moralia*, Auberger (1986, 194–95 believes that as a group they may be understood as an attempt to integrate scenes of life into the meditation of the text without their having a direct relation to the text.

101. For example, *Exordium Parvum* 15, p. 77; Cistercian statute 5, 9, p. 14, 14–15; *Exordium Cistercii* 15, 23, p. 123, 124; Bernard of Clairvaux, *Apologia* 1, 12, 13, vol.3:82, 92–93, 93; William of Malmesbury, *Gesta Regum* 336, p. 383; Orderic Vitalis, *Historia Ecclesiastica* 8:26, vol.4:310–26. On the authority for monastic manual labor, see Benedict of Nursia, *Regula* 48, 7.

Recent interest in the depiction of lay labor has been strong; see Mane 1990 and 1992; Bartal 1992; and Williams 1993.

102. Benedict of Nursia, *Regula* 48: "quia tunc vere monachi sunt, si labore manuum suarum vivunt." Cf. Cistercian statute 5, p. 14.

103. Ulrich of Cluny, *Consuetudines Cluniacenses* 1:30, PL 149:675–77.

104. The sources offer no firm historical evidence for precisely when *conversi* were introduced into the Cistercian Order, although the latest research suggests it may have been as late as the second or even the third generation; cf. Auberger 1986, 442–43.

The usefulness of the Cîteaux *Moralia* as historical evidence does not extend to the color of the habits, which does not indicate the status of the figures one way or the other. Cf. Hélyot 1718, vol.5:348 on the tradition that the Cistercians began wearing white habits during the abbacy of Alberic, who died in 1109, the year that the Cîteaux *Moralia* was probably begun. On the earliest written evidence for their white habits, which postdates the illuminations (Rupert of Deutz, *Super Quaedam Capitula Regulae Benedicti* of 1125), see Van Engen 1983, 317. Given that at least four and possibly five different colors of robes may be distinguished in the Cîteaux *Moralia*, the least that one could say in this regard is that the artist is employing *varietas* (see above), and the most is that this particular manifestation of *varietas* may be a statement against what the Cistercians saw as an exaggerated contemporary concern with monastic clothing.

105. Dijon, Bib. Mun. MS 173:41.

106. *Moralia* 21:4–5, p. 1065–68; for example: "Per hos etenim corporis sensus quasi per fenestras quasdam exteriora quaeque anima respicit, respiciens concupiscit. . . . Quisquis vero per has corporis fenestras incaute exterius respicit, plerumque in delectatione peccati etiam nolens cadit; atque obligatus desideriis, incipit velle quod noluit. . . . Ne ergo quaedam lubrica in cogitatione versemus, providendum nobis est. . . . Alius itaque luxuriam iam perpetrat actione, huic serpens repit ex ventre. Alius autem perpetrandam versat in mente, huic serpens repit ex pectore."

107. *Moralia* 21:4, p. 1066: "Neque enim Eva lignum vetitum contigisset, nisi hoc prius incaute respiceret."

108. Luke 3:9 and Matt. 3:10. John the Baptist's metaphor is discussed in *Moralia* 17:3, p. 851–52, although without relation to this initial. Note that it is not the biblical Tree of the Knowledge of Good and Evil itself that is shown as being cut down here, but rather a metaphorical tree of temptation as it applies to an individual.

109. My thanks to Emero Stiegman for his kind permission to use his observation on the role of the layman in this initial. On the relief from Joigny, perhaps from the tomb of Adelaide of Champagne, see Skubiszewski 1992, 67.

110. Benedict of Nursia, *Regula* 55.

111. Cf. Bernard of Clairvaux, *Apologia* 1, 24–26, vol.3:81, 101–2, among other sources.

112. On the shift, or scapular, see Linderbauer 1922, 353–54. I distinguish the personal sheath knife seen here from the knife as an element of a complete set of writing instruments, such knives often being seen in depictions of authors, scribes, and artists.

113. Nowhere is this made clearer than in comparison with the first-century carving of the god Esus on the Pillar of the Nautes from Paris and now in the Musée de Cluny, a work that is extremely similar to the Cîteaux initial in all but scale; illustrated in *Lutèce* 1984, fig. 176. Although unusual, a relatively naturalistic scale can sometimes be found, as in the Beatus manuscripts; see for example, Paris, Bib. Nat. MS n.a. lat. 2290:89, illustrated in Grégoire 1985, fig. 132.

114. A general connection with the Cistercian emphasis on manual labor has been made for this initial by (Nordenfalk 1957, 205), who makes no connection between text and image; repeated by Gutbrod 1965, 159–60. Heslop (1986, 7) sees it as depicting obedience through monastic labor, without any relation to the text of the *Moralia in Job*.

115. Dijon, Bib. Mun. MS 170:75v.

116. *Moralia* 16:62, 16:66, p. 834, 837: "Potest agri nomine scripturae sacrae latitudo signari. . . . Sunt vero nonnulli qui, malum suae nequitiae cognoscentes, satiari pane justitiae festinant, percipere sacri eloquii dicta desiderant. . . . Spicas signare patrum sententias dicimus, quia dum saepe per figurata eloquia proferuntur, ab eis tegmen litterae quasi aristarum paleas subtrahimus, ut medulla spiritus reficiamur."

117. Utrecht Psalter, Utrecht, Bibliotheek der Rijksuniversiteit MS 32:49v. Luttrell Psalter, London, Brit. Lib. MS Add. 42130:172v (Backhouse 1989, fig. 25). *Moralia* 16:29, p. 815.

Heslop (1986, 7) sees this initial as depicting humble obedience through monastic labor and as unrelated to the text.

118. Dijon, Bib. Mun. MS 170:20.

119. *Moralia* 12:Preface, p. 628: "Mos justorum est tanto sollicitius praesentem vitam quam sit fugitiva cogitare, quanto studiosius noverint caelestis patriae bona aeterna perpendere."

120. *Moralia* 12:Preface 4, p. 628–30: "*Homo natus de muliere, brevi vivens tempore. . . . Breves dies hominis sunt. . . .* Statutum quoque est quantum in ipsa vita mortali temporaliter vivat. . . . Ita vir quisque sanctus in hac vita positus, dum longe se ab exitu vitae praesentis conspicit, longe se esse ab aeternis gaudiis gemit."

121. On the use of winding sheets in the Cistercian ritual of burial, *Ecclesiastica Officia* 94, p. 207. This was common monastic practice; cf. Ulrich of Cluny, *Consuetudines Cluniacenses* 29, *PL* 149:773; and Lanfranc, *Decreta Lanfranci*, p. 124. On the use of winding sheets for lowering the dead into the grave, see Rush 1941, 129.

122. Dijon, Bib. Mun. MS 14:191.

In the funeral portrait of Trebius Justus in Rome, his parents hold a sheet in a manner very similar to that of the initial to Bk. 12. Given that it holds wreaths, coins, and a vessel—all items associated with ancient Roman funeral ceremonies—one wonders if it might also be a winding sheet. (Despite the similarity of design between the sheet and the togas of Trebius Justus and his father, the former does not represent a toga since it is rectangular and togas were semicircular.) For an illustration, see Grabar 1966, fig. 244. On the wreath and coin as part of Roman funeral rites, see Toynbee 1971, 44. My thanks to Robin Jensen for her help in trying to definitively identify the sheet.

123. Lections five and six. Cf. the thirteenth-century Cistercian *Officium Defunctorum* from Heilsbronn (Erlangen, Universitätsbibliothek MS 118 Irm. 401:224–25). For the specific lessons, see Meyer 1954, 22; and for the liturgical context of their reading, Rowell 1977, 58–59, 64–67.

124. Dijon, Bib. Mun. MS 170:59.

125. *Moralia* 15:27–28, p. 765–66: "dolorem habuit in ipsa suae concupiscentiae fatigatione, qualiter concupita raperet, quomodo alia blandimentis, alia terroribus auferret; at postquam acquisitis rebus pervenit ad desiderium, alius hunc dolor fatigat, ut cum sollicito timore custodiat quod cum gravi labore meminit acquisitum. Hinc inde insidiatores metuit atque hoc se perpeti quod ipse fecit aliis pertimescit. Formidat potiorem alterum ne hunc sustineat violentum; pauperem vero cum conspicit, suspicatur furem. . . . In his itaque omnibus quia timor ipse poena est, tanta infelix patitur quanta pati timet. Post hoc quoque ad gehennam ducitur, aeternis cruciatibus mancipatur. . . . Mira autem est securitas cordis, aliena non quaerere sed uniuscuiusque diei contentum manere." This is probably the basis of Hugh of Saint Victor's wonderful description of the cares of the rich man (*De Vanitate Mundi* 1, p. 31–32).

126. *Moralia* 15:54, p. 782–83: "Vir igitur sanctus has inquorum cogitationes intuens aspernetur. . . . Quia nimirum esse bonum incomparabiliter videt, ad breve tempus eligit hic sub flagello gemere quam aeternae ultionis supplicia tolerare." Cf. *Moralia* 15:39, p. 774 for a similar statement.

127. Benedict of Nursia, *Regula* 48: "Omnia tamen mensurate fiant propter pusillanimes."

128. William of Saint-Thierry, *Vita Prima* 1:23–24, *PL* 185:240–41.

129. Heslop (1986, 7) sees the initial to Bk. 15 as a portrayal of humble obedience through monastic labor, though unrelated to the text. Caviness (1983, 106) suggests that it was meant to express the harmony of work under the reformed Cistercian rule.

The reference to laughing at the holy in *Moralia* 15:40–41, p. 774–75 does not fit the sense of this initial.

130. Dijon, Bib. Mun. MS 173:167.

131. I say that the figures are stocking-footed because, although their feet look much like those of the monks in the other initials, there is a clear depiction of an unlaced shoe drying in front of the fire. The monk on the right seems to be hold-ing his other shoe to the fire in order to dry it, while the one on the left seems to be doing the same with both of his.

For clarity's sake I treat the question of trials in a somewhat simplified manner. I recognize that material trials could also have acted as spiritual ones and do not wish to draw too strong a distinction between the material and the spiritual in these initials.

132. *Moralia* 34:5, p. 1736: "Sed quia electi quique incessanter conspiciunt quod in praesentis vitae penuriam ab illa potestatis ingenitae facultate ceciderunt, bene dic-itur: 'Ego vir videns paupertatem meam.' Quisquis enim haec adhuc visibilia ap-petit, peregrinationis suae malum non intellegit, et hoc ipsum videre quod patitur nescit." The opposition between pride and poverty of spirit is taken up in two ex-tended passages, *Moralia* 34:1–7 and 34:39–56, p.1733–38, 1761–73.

133. Załuska (1989, 18–19) notes the strange absence of interest in the Cîteaux *Moralia* by later generations as evinced by the almost complete lack of attention to it in the late-fifteenth-century inventory of the library of Cîteaux made under Abbot Jean de Cirey, an attitude that may be indirectly related to the defacement of this initial.

134. Cistercian statute 1, p. 13; cf. *Exordium Parvum* 15, p. 78. On the later alter-ation of Cistercian monastic seclusion, see Donkin 1959.

135. *Exordium Parvum* 17, p. 77.

136. For similar opinions on the subject, see Alexander 1990 and Camille 1987.

137. William of Saint-Thierry, *Vita Prima* 1:23–24, *PL* 185:240–41.

138. Dijon, Bib. Mun. MS 173:148.

139. *Moralia* 32:5, p. 1630–31: "Quisquis contra flagella semetipsum defendere ni-titur, flagellantis iudicium evacuare conatur. . . . Beatum itaque Job non idcirco fla-gella caelestia percusserunt, ut in eo culpas exstinguerent, sed potius ut merita augerent. . . . Qui quidem culpam suam inter flagella non inveniens, nec tamen fla-gella eadem causam sibi esse augendi meriti deprehendens . . . justum credat omne quod patitur. . . . Quisquis enim jam percussionem tolerat, sed adhuc causas per-

cussionis ignorat si justum credens hoc ipsum contra se judicium amplectitur, eo ipso ab injustitia sua jam correctus est, quo percussum se juste gratulatur." And to a lesser degree, see *Moralia* 32:1, 32:3, p. 1626, 1628. The theme of the flail is even more prominent in this passage than is practical to show here. On the importance of this theme in Gregory, see Dagens 1977, 188.

140. Harris (1987, 4) sees those initials of daily life involving laymen as "of a completely secular nature."

141. Dijon, Bib. Mun. MS 173:92v.

142. Oursel 1960, 28.

143. The four fingers of the left hand of the seated figure are a bit hard to make out, but they are depicted with the little finger out of parallel alignment with the others, identical to the arrangement of the right hand of the standing figure on the left. The act of carding is indicated in the Luttrell Psalter through the prominent appearance of a carding comb, which is a fairly large device; London, Brit. Lib. MS Add. 42130:193 (Backhouse 1989, fig. 57). Davidson (1987, 53n.51) suggests that the man is holding a bunch of grapes. The initial to Bk. 13 of the Cîteaux *Moralia*, however, shows what are unquestionably bunches of grapes, and the color and shape are distinctly different from the object in the initial to Bk. 27. In the former, the color is more or less natural and the individual grapes have a rather natural oval shape. In the latter, the color (overpainted according to Davidson, and if so, possibly without a sense for what the object originally was meant to portray) is not suggestive of grapes and the shapes of the individual elements are circular, not oval as in the earlier example. The possibility exists, although for iconographical reasons I in no way insist on it, that the figure is shown holding the clouds discussed in *Moralia* 27:19–22, p. 1344–47, the passage upon which this initial is based.

144. The passage is extended (*Moralia* 27:19–22, p. 1344–47) and the imagery changes a little; I refer to two related passages of *Moralia* 27:19, p. 1344: "Extendit nubes Dominus, dum ministris suis viam praedicationis aperiens, eos in mundi latitudine circumquaque diffundit. Bene autem dictum est: 'Quasi tentorium suum.' Tentorium quippe in itinere poni solet. Et cum praedicatores sancti in mundo mittuntur, iter Deo faciunt. Unde scriptum est: 'Ecce mitto angelum meum ante faciem tuam, qui praeparabit viam tuam' [Mal. 3:1; cf. Mt. 2:10, Lk. 7:27]. . . . Atque in hoc itinere tentorium Dei sunt haec eadem corda sanctorum, quibus quasi in via quiescendo tegitur, dum per haec ad mentes hominum veniens, agit quae disposuit et non videtur. Hinc est quod simul omnis synagoga tentorium vocatur, cum cessasse a praedicatione sacerdotes per Jeremiam Dominus queritur, dicens: 'Non est qui extendat ultra tentorium meum et erigat pelles meas.'" I follow the Douay-Rheims translation of *pelles* in the passage from Jeremiah.

145. Utrecht Psalter, Utrecht, Bibliotheek der Rijksuniversiteit MS 32:49v.

146. On the symbolic use of green, see above, chapter 4, note 4.

147. On Stephen Harding as the artist of the Cîteaux *Moralia*, see Peface, note 1.

148. On Bernard's criticism of long-haired servants, see Rudolph 1990a, 305–6. For his criticism of over-concern with dress among knights, *De Laude Novae Militiae* 3, 7, vol.3:216, 220.

Considering the question of a source for this initial, Davidson (1987, 53–54) attempts to tie it to an iconographically and compositionally unrelated form, believing that there is an indirect connection with the prototype of the initial to Bk. 27 in the Préaux *Moralia*. In the process, she states that the link with the text of Bk. 27 is "absent" in the Cîteaux *Moralia*.

149. Dijon, Bib. Mun. MS 170:32.

150. *Moralia* 13:25–27, p. 682–84; esp. 13:25, p. 682: "Unde factum est ut redemptoris nostri sanguinem quem persecutores saevientes fuderant, postmodum credentes biberent eumque esse Dei Filium praedicarent." These chapters are part of the extended passage, *Moralia* 13:1–28, p. 669–85.

151. On the symbolic use of green in the Cîteaux *Moralia*, see above, chapter 4, note 4.

152. Dijon, Bib. Mun. MS 141:75 (Auberger 1986, fig. II/III-19) is based on the initial from Bk. 13 of the Cîteaux *Moralia*, but it completely lacks the general exuberance of the *Moralia* initials.

153. *Exordium Parvum* 15, p. 77; Cistercian statute 9, 26, p. 14–15, 19.

154. *Exordium Parvum* 15, p. 78; Cistercian statute 8, 26, p. 14, 19.

155. Luttrell Psalter, London, Brit. Lib. MS Add. 42130:74v (Backhouse 1989, fig. 27).

156. Dijon, Bib. Mun. MS 173:47.

157. *Moralia* 22:2 (humility and pride); 22:10 (knowledge does not lead holy men to pride); 22:14 (some do good from love of praise, not love of God); 22:15–16 (some are brought down through pride in their own knowledge, etc.); 22:18 (the heart should be humble, pride makes one fall); 22:31–35 (on humility, the opposite of pride); p. 1092–93, 1099–1100, 1102–3, 1103–5, 1105–6, 1114–17; and so on.

Heslop (1986, 7) thinks that this probably shows the Fall of Pride but believes that it is not related to the text of Bk. 22. Auberger (1986, 194–95) includes this initial among those of seemingly gratuitous violence, which he believes generally refer to the struggle against evil. Załuska (1989, 79) notes that this initial represents the Fall of Pride but associates it with the text of a different book, *Moralia* 31:43, p. 1579–81.

158. Dijon, Bib. Mun. MS 173:80; Davidson 1987, 52n.44; Auberger 1986, 194.

159. *Moralia* 26:73, p. 1320–21: "Auctore autem Domino, quia in cunctis mundi partibus sancta Ecclesia culmine religionis excrevit, hanc ipsam temporalem potentiam, qua quidem bene utitur, obtrectando in vitium elationis inflectunt. . . . Quosdam quippe conspiciunt quia sub religionis obtentu vitio elationis intumescunt; et quod in quibusdam jure reprehendunt, hoc injuste ad crimen omnium pertrahunt;

nequaquam videlicet perpendentes quod sint in ea qui et despicientes noverint perfecte temporalia regere. . . . Etsi quidam fortasse intra ipsam sunt qui non Dei sed suae gloriae sub religionis praetextu deserviunt, studet tamen eos aut, si valet, districte corrigere, aut, si non valet, aequanimiter tolerare." This is part of the longer passage, *Moralia* 26:72–74, p. 1319–21. Along similar lines, see also *Moralia* 26:44–48, p. 1298–1303.

160. Lekai 1977, 28–29. Davidson (1987, 52n.44) suggests that the source for this initial may be found in the Préaux *Moralia* mentioned above (p. 22).

161. Dijon, Bib. Mun. MS 173:66.

162. *Moralia* 24:15, 24:21, p. 1198–99, 1202–3: "Nonnumquam tamen homines dicit eos quos a bestiis ratione distinguit, id est quos non atteri bestiali passionum motu demonstrat. . . . At contra hi qui carnali affectioni succumbunt, non jam homines, sed jumenta nominantur. . . . Cum ergo vocentur homines hi qui justitiae ratione suffulti sunt, et irrationabilia jumenta nominentur hi qui carnali delectationi deserviunt. . . . Justorum ergo debemus vitam conspicere, ut subtiliter deprehendamus nostram. Illorum videlicet species, quasi quaedam forma nobis imitanda proponitur. . . . Sed haec reprobi nesciunt, quia mentis oculos semper in infimis premunt, qui et si quando in via Domini veniunt, non ad meliorum vestigia, sed ad intuenda semper deteriorum exempla vertuntur." This is part of the extended passage, *Moralia* 24:15–23, p. 1197–1204. Cf. also *Moralia* 24:7–8 (humans take pleasure in sins of the flesh); 24:14 (every day the devil does to humankind what he did in the Garden of Eden); 24:48 (a discussion of the rejection of lust); p.1193–94, 1197, 1223. Bk. 24 opens with a consideration of the temptation of the elect and of all others as well; *Moralia* 24:1, p. 1189.

163. Gregory the Great, *Dialogorum Libri* 2:4:2, vol.2:152.

164. For the ape as a symbol of the sinner, see Janson 1952, 17–19, 29–56 (p. 45–56 for the Romanesque period).

165. Quarré (1938, 158) sees the two human figures as representing two jongleurs. This is taken up by Załuska (1989, 79), who suggests that there might be a moralistic meaning to the initial. Janson (1952, 49–50) thinks that the evil man in the Cîteaux initial may be an iconographical trace of the iconographical prototype of the trainer and ape. If Janson is correct and if the artist were consciously employing this level of meaning, then it would be meant in the sense of the devil as the master of temptation and of the ape as the tool of his trainer, the devil. Oursel (1960, 28) sees the figure of the short man as that of a juggler (*bateleur*). Gutbrod (1965, 123–24) gives a loose interpretation of this initial, without any connection to the text: the short man is a wildman or forest spirit, the tall man is an aristocrat who implores the ape, and so on. Auberger (1986, 194) sees them both as jugglers (*bateleurs*). Davidson (1987, 52–53) tries to connect this initial to one in the Préaux manuscript that is unrelated in structure, iconography, and content.

Conclusion

1. Dudden 1905, vol.1:194–95. For similar though sometimes less pointed reactions to the *Moralia in Job*, see Laistner 1957, 105 (to most modern tastes the *Moralia in Job* is exceedingly far-fetched and tiresome); Dagens 1977, 61 (the symbolism of Gregory may at times seem labored and even incoherent); and Leclercq 1982, 27 (Gregory is sometimes disconcerting in the character of his style and exegesis, giving the impression of being unsystematic, disorganized, or even overly diffuse).

2. *Moralia* ad Leandrum 3, p. 4: "ferculum ori offerimus, ut invitati lectoris quasi convivae nostri fastidium repellamus . . . ;" *Moralia* 1:33, p. 43: "In nobismetipsis namque debemus transformare quod legimus, ut cum per auditum se animus excitat, ad operandum quod audierit vita concurrat;" *Moralia* 2:1, p. 59: "Ibi etenim foeda ibi pulchra nostra cognoscimus." Cf. *Moralia* 4:Preface 1, p. 158, where Gregory states that one ought to unite or join oneself with Scripture.

3. Gregory the Great, *Dialogorum Libri* 4:49:2, vol.3:168: "Nam quidam mecum in monasterio frater Antonius nomine vivebat, qui multis cotidianis lacrimis ad gaudia patriae caelestis anhelabat. Cumque studiosissime et cum magno fervore desiderii sacra eloquia meditaretur, non in eis verba scientiae, sed fletum compunctionis inquirebat, quatenus per haec excitata mens eius inardesceret et ima deserens ad regionem caelestis patriae per contemplationem volaret."

Note also the relation between reading and meditation in Gregory the Great, *In Hiezechihelem* 1:7:8, p. 87. For the basis of the *lectio divina* in the Benedictine Rule, see Benedict of Nursia, *Regula* 4:55, 38, 42, 48, 49, 53, and 73. On monastic *lectio divina* itself, see Leclercq 1982, 13, 15–17. For the inseparabiltiy of reading and meditation in monastic culture, see Leclercq 1982, 15–17, 72–73, 99–100 and Werckmeister 1980, 168–169. Unfortunately, Mary Carruthers' fine study came to my attention too late to be integrated here; see Carruthers 1990, esp. p. 221–57.

4. Cassian, *Conlationes* 14:10, p. 410–11. Along these lines, see also *Conlationes* 14:1–2, p. 398–99: "There are stages so ordered and distinct that human humility may be able to climb to the sublime. If these stages succeed each other in turn with the method that we have mentioned, one is able to be brought to a height to which one would not be able to fly if the first stage had been eliminated." The diametrically opposed relation to the passage of Bernard's with which this study opened is striking, being distinctly concerned with "gradually ascending stages" rather than "unexpected departures." On the discussion of *theoretica* in this passage, see Leclercq 1982, 99–100, who points out that in monastic texts *theoria* is related to contemplation and prayer. Cassian's *Conlationes* was one of the staples of monastic culture. It is one of the few nonscriptural books specifically prescribed for reading in the Benedictine Rule and receives special attention as a model in the concluding chapter of the Rule (Benedict of Nursia, *Regula* 42, 73).

5. Jerome, *Ep.* 107:9, vol.5:154. The letters of Jerome had great currency within twelfth-century monasticism and at Cîteaux in particular, where they were copied in a luxuriously illustrated edition (Dijon, Bib. Mun. MS 135). Gregory of Tours, *In Gloriam Martyrum*, Preface, p. 37.

6. William of Saint-Thierry, *Ad Fratres* 172, p. 280.

7. This is nowhere brought home more pointedly and practically than in the translations, made from the Greek tradition, which favor these types of works over more overtly theological writings; see Leclercq 1982, 91–92.

8. Smalley 1983, 74. Osbert, *Epistola, PL* 175:CLXII.

9. *Moralia* 27:21, p. 1345–46.

10. Whitby *Vita Gregorii* 9, p. 90; and cf. Whitby *Vita Gregorii* 12–14, p. 94–95. On this passage, see Colgrave 1968, 91n.41 and his notes in general on this text. The anecdote is related by Bede and ascribed by him to "tradition" (*Historia Ecclesiastica* 2:1, p. 132–34). As an indication of how popular this story was, and how much this mentality was associated with Gregory, see also the shorter Life by Paul the Deacon, *Vita Gregorii* 15, p. 171–72; the longer Life by Paul the Deacon, *Vita Gregorii* 17–21, *PL* 75:50–52; and the Life by John the Deacon, *Vita Gregorii* 21, *PL* 75:71–72.

11. For Gregory's identification with his subject, see *Moralia ad Leandrum* 5, p. 6. Whitby *Vita Gregorii* 27, p. 122–24.

12. Morrison 1988, 205. The early-twelfth-century autobiographer and exegete, Guibert de Nogent, thought that the "best keys" to the art of exegesis were found in Gregory the Great (*De Vita Sua* 1:17, p. 138).

13. On finding the "truer" sense, *Moralia ad Leandrum* 4, p. 6, "Ut ergo uniuscuiusque loci opportunitas postulat, ita se per studium ordo expositionis immutat, quatenus tanto verius sensum divinae locutionis inveniat, quanto ut res quaeque exegerit, per causarum species alternat."

14. *Moralia* ad Leandrum 3–4, p. 4–6, esp.: "Quae modis alternantibus multipliciter disserendo ferculum ori offerimus, ut invitati lectoris quasi convivae nostri fastidium repellamus, qui, dum sibi multa apposita considerat, quod elegantius decernit, adsumat." See also *Moralia* 18:1, p. 886. Gregory's famous architectural metaphor of exegesis may have its impetus in Augustine, *De Civitate Dei* 20:1, p. 699.

15. Smalley 1983, vii–ix.

16. Dijon, Bib. Mun. MS 15:56v: "Arrius. Erat aliquando quando non erat." A more precise translation might read: "There once was [a point before time] when he [Christ] was not." This formula was identified by Cahn (1962, 59), who gives important literary sources for the passage and discusses the iconographical sources of the initial. Augustine attributes the formula to Arius himself; *De Trinitate* 6:1, p.228. The Arian formula and John 1:1 appear together in the Fathers too often to cite here, but the widely read Athanasius, *Vita Antonii* 69, p. 134 should be mentioned. On the importance of the *Vita Antonii*, see chapter 1, note 13.

17. Cahn 1962, 59–62. In Cahn 1982, 143 and 217, the figure is said to be Arius himself, a view taken up by Załuska 1989, 110 and Garnier 1982, vol.1:146. On the use of the term "Arian" to characterize non-Arian positions, see for example Russell 1965, 39, 213–14. Cahn fully discusses the broad misapplication of this term.

18. Cassiodorus, *Institutiones*, 1:7:1, p. 28. Chenu 1968, 315n.9. Augustine, *In Iohannis* 1:1–11, p. 1–6; esp. 1:7, p. 4: "Ecce oculos vestros et sensus istos corporis levatis ad nos, nec ad nos . . . sed ad ipsum evangelium, ad ipsum evangelistam."

19. Bernard of Clairvaux, *Ep.* 192, 330, 331, 332, 336, 338:2, vol.8:44, 268, 270, 272, 276, 278. The issue "there once was a time when he was not" was a contemporary one; cf. for example, Bernard of Clairvaux, *Sermones Super Cantica* 71:7, vol.2:19 and John of Salisbury, *Historia Pontificalis* 13, p. 33.

20. Cahn cites a convincing possible "inspiration" for the John initial in the Eadwi Gospels (Cahn 1987, 32 and fig. 3).

21. Cf. Benedict of Nursia, *Regula* 57. On the subject of the autonomy of the artist, see Berliner 1945; Gilbert 1985 (my thanks to Professor Gilbert for kindly sending me an offprint of his study); Skubiszewski 1990 (my thanks to M. Skubiszewski for also kindly sending me a copy of his study); the question of the independence of the artist runs throughout Alexander 1992, but see esp. 89–94; there is some further bibliography in a review by J. Hamburger in *Art Bulletin* 75 (1993) 323–24.

22. To cite only one example of the copying of religious books as a spiritual exercise, Orderic Vitalis repeats a story about a man who was a bad monk but a good scribe. After his death, his most notable effort at copying was weighed against his sins, letter by letter, sin by sin, with the bad monk winning by only one letter (*Historia Ecclesiastica* 3, vol.2:50). The story is part of an extended passage that deals with the copying of manuscripts, *Historia Ecclesiastica* 3, vol.2:48–52. There is a very interesting depiction of this general idea in Munich, Bayerische Staatsbibliothek, MS Clm. 13031:1 (reproduced in Legner 1985, vol.1:241). The production of artworks in particular could also be a spiritual exercise; among many others, see Theophilus, *De Diversis Artibus* 1:Preface, 2:Preface, 3:Preface, p. 1, 36, 63. This attitude is also the basis, in part, of countless presentation scenes of the type where the book is presented to a heavenly being.

For the exegetical process as potentially under the same divine inspiration as the original biblical text, see Smalley 1983, 12 for ample documentation.

23. On the *Moralia in Job* as written under the inspiration of the Holy Spirit, see Whitby *Vita Gregorii* 26–27, p. 120–22, where the well-known incident regarding the Holy Spirit dictating the Homilies on Ezekiel to Gregory is related to the *Moralia in Job*. Anselm of Laon also claimed that the *Moralia in Job* was dictated to Gregory by the Holy Spirit (Smalley 1983, 12).

Theophilus, *De Diversis Artibus* 3:Preface, p. 62–63. On Theophilus, see Van Engen 1980. See also Guibert de Nogent who, in writing about the various factors at play in composing a sermon, encourages the introduction of new interpretations and ascribes the knowledge necessary for this to God: in effect, he attributes the process of creating original exegesis to God, even at this level of discourse (*Quo Ordine*, PL 156:22, 25, 29). Gerhoch of Reichersberg thought that the method of interpretation for a text was the same as that for a painting (cited by Morrison 1988:196).

24. On florilegia in general, see Rouse 1982.

25. Benton 1982, 264.

26. *Moralia* 4:Preface 1 (as in Introduction, note 26). *Moralia* ad Leandrum 3–4, 1:33, 2:1 (as in Conclusion, notes 2 and 14).

27. Dijon, Bib. Mun. MS 173:174.

28. For Bernard's criticisms, see Chapter 4, note 148.

29. On the restoration of Job, see *Moralia* 35:21–49, p. 1787–1811; esp. 35:22, p. 1787–88. On the traditional iconography of Job, see Davidson 1987, 49.

The hawk is elsewhere described as exemplifying the character of the elect and as referring to the renewed and virtuous people of the Gentiles, although it is not necessary to read such a meaning here (*Moralia* 31:12, 31:93, p. 1558, 1614). The knight is both dressed in green and appears before a green ground; on the color green as referring to regeneration and sanctity in the *Moralia in Job*, see Chapter 4, note 4.

Dodwell (1971, 92–93) states that this figure (which he mistakes for a woman) refers to secular pride, feeling that there is no relation with the text. Heslop (1986, 7) also believes that there is no direct relation with the text, likewise thinking that the initial probably refers to pride. Harris (1987, 8–9) tries to associate it with contemporary criticisms of excessive lay dress, although she finds it "difficult to explain" (p. 4) why such criticism should appear in a writing like the *Moralia in Job* in the first place.

30. Davidson 1987, 47n.12.

31. I believe that it was the personal function that led to the later division of the manuscript, the smaller volumes making personal reading more practical, the brutal result of their dismemberment apparently averting similar mistreatment of the original second volume.

32. Hugh of Saint Victor, *De Meditatione* 2:2, p. 48.

33. On the use of art as a spiritual aid, see the chapter "Art as a Spiritual Distraction to the Monk" in Rudolph 1990, 104–124. On art as a spiritual aid and to educate the illiterate, see Camille 1985, and Kessler 1985a, 1985b, and 1989; my thanks to Herb Kessler for offprints of these fine studies.

34. My thanks to Chrysogonus Waddell for bringing the significance of this punctuation to my attention. On medieval punctuation in general, see Parkes 1993, esp. 35–40; see 38–39 for a discussion of the importance of Cistercian punctuation; my thanks to my father for making me aware of this book.

Father Waddell has confirmed that the *Moralia in Job* was read in the refectory and at the *collatio*. On this see Benedict of Nursia, *Regula* 38 (there should be reading in the refectory), 42 (Cassian's *Conlationes*, the Lives of the Fathers, or something else edifying should be read after dinner). It may be that it was also read at matins; *Regula* 9 (commentaries by renowned and orthodox Fathers on the Old and New Testaments should be read at matins).

35. *Exordium Parvum* 16, p. 80. On the *Exordium Parvum*, see Bredero 1961.

36. *Exordium Parvum* 17, p. 81. It is my belief that the holding of ducal courts at Cîteaux was legislated against only after the arrival of Bernard and the second generation. I say this because of the inclusion of the account of their prohibition in the *Exordium Parvum* with that of the early Cistercian legislation against art (as opposed to the earlier body of legislation of *Exordium Parvum* 15, p. 77–78), for whose enactment I have argued for a date of 1115 to 1119 (this is distinct from the date of the *Exordium Parvum* itself); see Rudolph 1987. On Cîteaux's general relations with the local aristocracy, see Bouchard 1987 and 1991.

37. Duby 1981, 41–46, which includes an evocative presentation of the knightly predilection of eleventh- and twelfth-century monasticism.

38. The term Hugh uses for this level is *privata*, which should not be confused with our modern word "private"; it is private only in the sense of not being public (*publica*) and is opposed to the sense of the private individual (*solitaria*), the latter being what we today would describe as "private"; *Didascalicon* 2:19, 6:14, p. 37–38, 131.

39. William of Saint-Thierry, *Ad Fratres* 41–42, p. 176–78; the extended passage is *Ad Fratres* 41–89, p. 176–214. I translate *animalis homo* (1 Cor. 2:14) as "animal man" because it is following this Vulgate form that it is commonly known in the scholarly literature. Most modern translations of the Bible render *animalis homo* as "unspiritual man" (RSV) or "unspiritual person" (*The Jerusalem Bible*), translations that fit William's usage very poorly.

40. William of Saint-Thierry, *Ad Fratres* 46–49, 59, p. 182–84, 190–92. I render *opificiis* as "artworks" because of its context: "Hinc enim in litteris, vel opificiis, vel aedificiis."

41. William of Saint-Thierry, *Ad Fratres* 146–158, p. 258–68. I will discuss the rational man and spiritual man further in future work planned on Suger's program at Saint-Denis. Bernard questions the use of art for "spiritual men" in *Apologia* 28, vol.3:282.

42. Gregory the Great, *Registrum* 9:209, 11:10, p. 768, 874 (*Ep.* 9:105 and 11:13 in *PL* 77). According to Gregory, art could have a secondary function of inducing compunction, something that can be closely tied to the presentation of biblical narrative; this is not the purpose of the illuminations in the Cîteaux *Moralia*. The passage on art in the letter to Secundinus is spurious; see *Registrum* appendix 10, p. 1110–11 (*Ep.* 9:52 in *PL* 77). On Gregory's letters, see Kessler 1985b, 85–86 and 1989,

298; Curschmann 1990; and Rudolph 1990a, 50–51, 107–8. I am in fundamental disagreement with the recent studies by Chazelle (1990) and Duggan (1989).

43. When I say outmoded or less prestigious, I am speaking in reference to new reform monasticism and its mainstream supporters, of which there were many. Also, I am not referring to the *Moralia in Job* itself. For another, different instance of the integration of art and the exegetical process—one in which an effort is very much made to stay contemporary through such an integration—see Rudolph 1990b.

44. On art as a distraction according to second generation standards, see Rudolph 1987 and 1990a, 104–24, 156–57, 180–91. See also Schapiro 1964, 3 and 58 on his alignment of the first and second generation Cistercians with the so-called first and second styles of manuscript painting at Cîteaux.

45. Troyes, Bib. Mun. MS 27:1:7.

BIBLIOGRAPHY

Primary Sources

Athanasius, *Vita Antonii*: *Vita di Antonio*. Ed. G. J. M. Bartelink. Milan, 1974.

Augustine, *Confessiones*: *Confessionum Libri XIII*. Ed. Lucas Verheijen. CC 27. Turnhout, 1981.

Augustine, *De Civitate Dei*: *Sancti Aurelii Augustini de Civitate Dei*. Ed. Bernhard Dombart and Alfons Kalb. CC 47–48. Turnhout, 1955.

Augustine, *De Trinitate*: *De Trinitate Libri XV*. Ed. W. J. Mountain. CC 50. Turnhout, 1968.

Augustine, *In Iohannis*: *In Iohannis Evangelium Tractatus CXXIV*. Ed. R. Willems. CC 36. Turnhout, 1954.

Augustine, *In Psalmos*: *Enarrationes in Psalmos*, Ed. E. Dekkers and J. Fraipont. CC 38–40. Turnhout, 1956.

Basil of Caesarea, *Commentarius in Isaiam*: *Commentarius in Isaiam Prophetam*. PG 30:117–668.

Bede, *Historia Ecclesiastica*: *Bede's Ecclesiastical History of the English People*. Ed. and tr. Bertram Colgrave and R.A.B. Mynors. Oxford, 1969.

Benedict the Canon, *Mirabilia Urbis Romae*: *Mirabilia Urbis Romae*. In *Kaiser, Könige und Päpste: III Beiträge zur allgemeinen Geschichte*, ed. Percy Ernst Schramm, 321–38. Stuttgart 1969.

Benedict of Nursia, *Regula*: *S. Benedicti Regula Monachorum*. Ed. Benno Linderbauer. Metten, 1922.

Bernard of Clairvaux: *Sancti Bernardi Opera*. Ed. Jean Leclercq and H.-M. Rochais. 8 vols. Rome, 1957–77.

Cassian, *Conlationes*: *Iohannis Cassiani Conlationes XXIIII*. Ed. Michael Petschenig. CSEL 13:2. Vienna 1886.

Cassiodorus, *Institutiones*: *Cassiodori Senatoris Institutiones*. Ed. R.A.B. Mynors. Oxford, 1961.

CC: Corpous Christianorum, Series Latina. Turnhout, 1953– .

Cistercian statute: In *Statuta Capitulorum Generalium Ordinis Cisterciensis*, ed. Joseph-Marie Canivez, vol.1:12–32. Louvain, 1933.

Corpus Antiphonalium Officii: *Corpus Antiphonalium Officii*. In *Manuscripti "Cursus Monasticus"*, ed. R.-J. Hesbert, vol.2. Rerum Ecclesiasticarum Documenta, Series Maior, Fontes 8. Rome, 1965.

CSEL: Corpus Scriptorum Ecclesiasticorum Latinorum. Vienna, 1866–   .

Ecclesiastica Officia: In "Les monuments primitifs de la règle cistercienne," ed. Philippe Guignard. *Analecta Divonensia* 10 (1878): 87–245.

Eusebius, *Historia Ecclesiastica*: *Historia Ecclesiastica. PG* 20:45–906.

Exordium Cistercii: In *Les plus anciens textes de Citeaux*, ed. Jean de la Croix Bouton and Jean Baptiste Van Damme, 110–16. Achel, 1974.

Exordium Parvum: In *Les plus anciens textes de Citeaux*, ed. Jean de la Croix Bouton and Jean Baptiste Van Damme, 51–86. Achel, 1974.

Giraldus Cambrensis, *Topographia Hibernica*: In *Giraldi Cambrensis Opera*, ed. James F. Dimock, vol.5:1–152. Rolls Series 21. London, 1868.

Glossa Ordinaria: *Glossa Ordinaria. PL* 113–114.

Gregory the Great, *Dialogorum Libri*: *Dialogues*. Ed. and tr. Adalbert de Vogüé and Paul Antin. Sources chrétiennes 251, 260, 265. 3 vols. Paris, 1978–80.

Gregory the Great, *In Hiezechihelem*: *Homélies sur Ezéchiel*. Ed. and tr. Charles Morel. Sources chrétiennes 327. Paris, 1986.

Gregory the Great, *Moralia in Iob*: *S. Gregorii Magni Moralia in Iob*. Ed. M. Adriaen. CC 143–143B. Turnhout, 1979–85.

Gregory the Great, *Registrum*: *Registrum Epistularum Libri*. Ed. Dag Norberg. CC 140–140A. Turnhout, 1982.

Gregory of Tours, *De Virtutibus Beati Martini*: *Gregorii Episcopi Turonensis Miracula et Opera Minora*. Ed. Bruno Krusch. Monumenta Germaniae Historica, Scriptores Rerum Merovingicarum 1:pt.2, 134–211.

Gregory of Tours, *In Gloria Martyrum*: *Gregorii Episcopi Turonensis Miracula et Opera Minora*. Ed. Bruno Krusch. Monumenta Germaniae Historica, Scriptores Rerum Merovingicarum 1:pt.2, 34–111.

Guibert de Nogent, *De Vita Sua*: *Autobiographie*. Ed. and tr. E.-R. Labande. Les classiques de l'histoire de France au moyen âge 34. Paris, 1981.

Guibert de Nogent, *Quo Ordine*: *Quo Ordine Sermo Fieri Debeat. PL* 156:21–32.

Haimo of Auxerre, *In Isaiam*: *Commentaria in Isaiam. PL* 116:715–1086.

Hugh of Saint Victor, *De Meditatione*: In *Six opuscules spirituels*, ed. and tr. Roger Baron, 44–59. Sources chrétiennes 155. Paris, 1969.

Hugh of Saint Victor, *De Sacramentis*: *De Sacramentis Christianae Fidei. PL* 176:183–618.

Hugh of Saint Victor, *De Tribus Diebus*: In *I tre giorni dell'invisibile luce, L'unione del corpo e dello spirito*, ed. Vincenzo Licarro, 48–157. Florence, 1974.

Hugh of Saint Victor, *De Vanitate Mundi*: In *Soliloquium de Arrha Animae und De Vanitate Mundi*, ed. Karl Müller, 26–48. Bonn, 1913.

Hugh of Saint Victor, *Didascalicon*: *Hugonis de Sancto Victore Didascalicon de Studio Legendi*. Ed. Charles H. Buttimer. Studies in Medieval and Renaissance Latin 10. Washington, D.C., 1939.

Hugh of Saint Victor, *The Mystic Ark*: *De Arca Noe Mystica*. PL 176:681–704.

Isidore of Seville, *Etymologiae*: *Etymologiarum sive Originum Libri XX*. Ed. Wallace M. Lindsay. Oxford, 1911.

Isidorus Pacensis, *Chronicon*: *Chronicon Pacense*. PL 96:1251–80.

Jerome, *Ep.*: *Saint Jérôme: Lettres*. Ed. Jérôme Labourt. Collection des Universités de France. 8 vols. Paris, 1949–63.

Jerome, *In Esaiam*: *Commentarii in Esaiam*. Rd. M. Adriaen and G. Morin. CC 73–73A. 2 vols. Turnhout, 1963.

John the Deacon, *Vita Gregorii*: *Vita Gregorii*. PL 75:59–242.

John of Salisbury, *Historia Pontificalis*: *John of Salisbury's Memoirs of the Papal Court*. Ed. and tr. Marjorie Chibnall. London, 1956.

Lanfranc, *Decreta Lanfranci*: *The Monastic Constitutions*. Ed. and tr. David Knowles. London, 1951.

Lex Visigothorum: *Liber Iudiciorum sive Lex Visigothorum*. Ed. Karl Zeumer. Monumenta Germaniae Historica, Leges, sect.1:vol.1.

Orderic Vitalis, *Historia Ecclesiastica*: *The Ecclesiastical History of Orderic Vitalis*. Ed. and tr. Marjorie Chibnall. 6 vols. Oxford, 1969–78).

Osbert, *Epistola*: *Epistola de Morte Hugonis*. PL 175:CLXI–CLXIV.

Papias, *Vocabulista*: *Papias Vocabulista*. Reprint, Turin, 1966.

Paul the Deacon, *Vita Gregorii* (shorter Life): "Paulus Diaconus, *Vita Gregorii* nach den Handschriften." Ed. Hartmann Grisar. *Zeitschrift für katholische Theologie* 11 (1887): 158–73.

Paul the Deacon, *Vita Gregorii* (longer Life): *Vita Gregorii*. PL 75:41–60.

Paulinus, *Vita Ambrosii*: *Vita Sancti Ambrosii*. PL 14:27–46.

PG: *Patrologia Graeco-Latina*. Ed. Jacques-Paul Migne. 162 vols. Paris, 1857–66.

PL: *Patrologia Latina*. Ed. Jacques-Paul Migne. 221 vols. Paris, 1844–64.

Prudentius, *Psychomachia*: In *Aurelii Prudentii Clementis Carmina*, ed. J. Bergman, 165–211. CSEL 61. Vienna, 1926.

Stephen Harding, *Sermo*: *Sermo Beatissimi Stephani*. PL 166:1375–76.

Stuttgart Psalter 1965: *Stuttgarter Bilderpsalter*. Ed. Bernhard Bischoff. Stuttgart, 1965.

Suetonius, *De Vita Caesarum*: In *C. Suetoni Tranquilli Opera*, ed. Maximilien Ihm, vol. 1. Stuttgart, 1961.

Suger, *Vie de Louis VI*: *Vie de Louis VI le Gros*. Ed. and tr. Henri Waquet. Les classiques de l'histoire de France au moyen âge 11. Paris, 1929.

Terence, *Phormio*: In *P. Terenti Afri Comoediae*, ed. Robert Kauer and Wallace M. Lindsay, unpaginated. Oxford, 1926.

Theophilus, *De Diversis Artibus*: *Theophilus: The Various Arts*. Ed. and tr. C. R. Dodwell. London, 1961.

Ulrich of Cluny, *Consuetudines Cluniacenses*: *Antiquiores Consuetudines Cluniacensis Monasterii*. PL 149:635–778.

Utrecht Psalter 1982: *Utrecht Psalter: Vollstandige Faksimile-Ausgabe im Originalformat der Handschrift 32, aus dem Besitz der Bibliotheek der Rijksuniversiteit te Utrecht*, Ed. Koert van der Horst, et al. Graz, 1982.

Verba Seniorum: *Verba Seniorum*. PL 73:851–1024.

Vetus Latina: *Vetus Latina: Die Reste der altlateinischen Bibel*. Vol. 12, *Esaias*. Ed. Roger Gryson. Freiburg, 1987–94.

Villard de Honnecourt 1935: *Villard de Honnecourt: Kritische Gesamtausgabe des Bauhüttenbuches ms. fr 19093 der Pariser Nationalbibliothek*. Ed. Hans Hahnloser. Vienna, 1935.

Vulgate: *Biblia Sacra: Iuxta Vulgatam Versionem*. Ed. Robert Weber. 2 vols. Stuttgart, 1983.

Whitby, *Vita Gregorii*: *The Earliest Life of Gregory the Great*. Ed. and tr. Bertram Colgrave. Lawrence, Kansas, 1968.

William of Malmesbury, *Gesta Regum*: *De Gestis Regum Anglorum*. Ed. William Stubbs. 2 vols. Rolls Series 90. London, 1887.

William of Saint-Thierry, *Ad Fratres*: *Lettre aux frères du Mont-Dieu*. Ed. and tr. Jean Déchanet. Sources chrétiennes 223. Paris, 1975.

William of Saint-Thierry, *Vita Prima*: *Sancti Bernardi Vita Prima*. PL 185:225–466 [only the first part of the *Vita Prima* is by William].

Secondary Literature

Aho 1981: Aho, James. *Religious Mythology and the Art of War*. Westport, 1981.

Alexander 1978a: Alexander, J. J. G. *The Decorated Letter*. New York, 1978.

Alexander 1978b: Alexander, J. J. G. "Scribes as Artists: The Arabesque Initial in Twelfth-Century English Manuscripts." In *Medieval Scribes, Manuscripts & Libraries: Essays Presented to N. R. Ker*, ed. M. B. Parkes and Andrew G. Watson, 87–116. London, 1978.

Alexander 1990: Alexander, J. J. G. "*Labeur* and *Paresse*: Ideological Representations of Medieval Peasant Labor." Art Bulletin 72 (1990): 436–52.

Alexander 1992: Alexander, J. J. G. *Medieval Illuminators and Their Methods of Work*. New Haven, 1992.

Alexander 1993: Alexander, J. J.G. "Ideological Representation of Military Combat in Anglo-Norman Art." *Anglo-Norman Studies* 15 (1993): 1–24.

Auber 1866: Auber, Charles. "Histoire et théorie du symbolisme religieux, I. Du symbolisme chez les anciens." *Revue de l'art chrétien* 10 (1866): 121–35.

Auber 1884: Auber, Charles. *Histoire et théorie du symbolisme religieux.* 4 vols. Paris, 1884.

Auberger 1986: Auberger, Jean-Baptiste. *L'unanimité cistercienne primitive: Mythe ou réalité?*, Cîteaux: Studia et documenta 3. Achel, 1986.

Backhouse 1989: Backhouse, Janet. *The Luttrell Psalter.* London, 1989.

Baltrusaitis 1934: Baltrusaitis, Jurgis. *Art sumérien, art roman.* Paris, 1934.

Bartal 1992: Bartal, R. "The Early Representations of Urban Society in Romanesque Sculpture: The Foundations of a New Iconography." *Studi Medievali* ser.3,33 (1992): 109–32.

Bedos 1980: Bedos, Brigitte. *Corpus des sceaux français du moyen âge* 1. Paris, 1980.

Benton 1982: Benton, John F. "Consciousness of Self and Perceptions of Individuality." In *Renaissance and Renewal in the Twelfth Century*, ed. Robert L. Benson and Giles Constable. 263–95. Cambridge, Mass., 1982.

Berliner 1945: Berliner, Rudolf. "The Freedom of Medieval Art." *Gazette des beaux-arts* ser. 6,28 (1945): 263–88.

Besserman 1979: Besserman, Lawrence. *The Legend of Job in the Middle Ages.* Cambridge, Mass., 1979.

Bouchard 1987: Bouchard, Constance. *Sword, Miter, and Cloister: Nobility and the Church in Burgundy, 980–1198.* Ithaca, N.Y., 1987.

Bouchard 1991: Bouchard, Constance. *Holy Entrepreneurs: Cistercians, Knights, and Economic Exchange in Twelfth-Century Burgundy.* Ithaca, N.Y., 1991.

Buddensieg 1965: Buddensieg, Tilmann. "Gregory the Great, the Destroyer of Pagan Idols: The History of a Medieval Legend Concerning the Decline of Ancient Art and Literature." *Journal of the Warburg and Courtauld Institutes* 28 (1965): 44–65.

Bredero 1961: Bredero, Adriaan. "Etudes sur la 'Vita Prima' de Saint Bernard." *Analecta Sacri Ordinis Cisterciensis* 17 (1961): 3–59.

Cahn 1962: Cahn, Walter. "A Defense of the Trinity in the Cîteaux Bible." *Marsyas* 11 (1962–64): 58–62.

Cahn 1969: Cahn, Walter. "The Artist as Outlaw and *Apparatchick*: Freedom and Constraint in the Interpretation of Medieval Art." In *The Renaissance of the Twelfth Century*, ed. Stephen K. Scher, 10–14. Providence, 1969.

Cahn 1982: Cahn, Walter. *Romanesque Bible Illumination.* Ithaca, N.Y., 1982.

Cahn 1987: Cahn, Walter. "Heresy and the Interpretation of Romanesque Art." In *Romanesque and Gothic: Essays for George Zarnecki*, ed. Neil Stratford, 27–33. Woodbridge, 1987.

Camille 1985: Camille, Michael. "Seeing and Reading: Some Visual Implications of Medieval Literacy and Illiteracy." *Art History* 8 (1985): 26–49.

Camille 1987: Camille, Michael. "Labouring for the Lord: The Ploughman and the Social Order in the Luttrell Psalter." *Art History* 10 (1987): 423–54.

Carruthers 1990: Carruthers, Mary. *The Book of Memory: A Study of Memory in Medieval Culture*. Cambridge, 1990.

Carter 1992: Carter, John M. *Medieval Games: Sports and Recreations in Feudal Society*. New York, 1992.

Caviness 1983: Caviness, Madeline. "Images of Divine Order and the Third Mode of Seeing." *Gesta* 22 (1983): 99–120.

Chazelle 1990: Chazelle, Celia. "Pictures, Books, and the Illiterate: Pope Gregory I's Letters to Serenus of Marseilles." *Word and Image* 6 (1990): 138–50.

Chenu 1968: Chenu, Marie-Dominique. *Nature, Man, and Society in the Twelfth Century*. Chicago, 1968.

Colgrave 1968: Colgrave, Bertram. *The Earliest Life of Gregory the Great*. Lawrence, Kansas, 1968.

Constable 1995: Constable, Giles, *Three Studies in Medieval Religious and Social Thought: The Interpretation of Mary and Martha, The Ideal of the Imitation of Christ, The Orders of Society*. Cambridge, 1995.

Curschmann 1990: Curschmann, Michael. "*Pictura laicorum litteratura?* Uberlegungen zum Verhältnis von Bild und volkssprachlicher Schriftlichkeit im Hoch- und Spätmittelalter bis zum Codex Manesse." In *Pragmatische Schriftlichkeit im Mittelalter: Erscheinungsformen und Entwicklungsstufen*, ed. Hagen Keller, et al., 211–29. Münstersche Mittelalter-Schriften 65. Munich, 1992.

Dagens 1977: Dagens, Claude. *Saint Grégoire le Grand: Culture et expérience chrétienne*. Etudes augustiniennes. Paris, 1977.

Davidson 1987: Davidson, C. Treat. "Sources for the Initials of the Cîteaux *Moralia in Job*." In *Studies in Cistercian Art and Architecture* 3, 46–68. Cistercian Studies Series 89. Kalamazoo, 1987.

Dodwell 1971: Dodwell, C. R. *Painting in Europe 800–1200*. Pelican History of Art. Harmondsworth, 1971.

Donkin 1959: Donkin, R. A. "The Site Changes of Medieval Cistercian Monasteries." *Geography* 44 (1959): 251–58.

Duby 1981: Duby, Georges. *The Age of the Cathedrals*. Chicago, 1981.

Dudden 1905: Dudden, F. Homes. *Gregory the Great: His Place in History and Thought*. 2 vols. London, 1905.

Duggan 1989: Duggan, Lawrence. "Was Art Really the 'Book of the Illiterate'?" *Word and Image* 5 (1989): 227–51.

Eisler 1961: Eisler, Colin. "The Athlete of Virtue: The Iconography of Asceticism." In *De Artibus Opuscula XL: Essays in Honor of Erwin Panofsky*, ed. Millard Meiss, vol. 1, 82–97. New York, 1961.

Evans 1986: Evans, G. R. *The Thought of Gregory the Great*. Cambridge, 1986.

Forsyth 1987: Forsyth, Neil. *The Old Enemy: Satan and the Combat Myth*. Princeton, 1987.

Garnier 1982: Garnier, François. *Le langue de l'image au moyen âge*. Paris, 1982.

Gilbert 1985: Gilbert, Creighton. "A Statement of the Aesthetic Attitude around 1230." *Hebrew University Studies in Literature and the Arts* 13 (1985): 125–52.

Gombrich 1979: Gombrich, Ernst. *The Sense of Order: A Study in the Psychology of Decorative Art*. Ithaca, N.Y., 1979.

Grabar 1966: Grabar, André. *Le premier art chrétien (200–395)*. Paris, 1966.

Gras 1976: Gras, Pierre. "Les manuscrits de Cîteaux." *Les dossiers de l'archéologie* 14 (1976): 94–99.

Grégoire 1985: Grégoire, Réginald, et al. *The Monastic Realm*. Milan, 1985.

Gutbrod 1965: Gutbrod, Jürgen. *Die Initiale in Handschriften des achten bis dreizehnten Jahrhunderts*. Stuttgart, 1965.

von Harnack 1905: Harnack, Adolf von. *Militia Christi: Die christliche Religion und der Soldatenstand in den ersten drei Jahrhunderten*. Tübingen, 1905.

Harris 1987: Harris, Jennifer. "'Thieves, Harlots and Stinking Goats': Fashionable Dress and Aesthetic Attitudes in Romanesque Art." *Costume* 21 (1987): 4–15.

Heslop 1986: Heslop, T. A. "'Brief in Words but Heavy in the Weight of its Mysteries.'" *Art History* 9 (1986): 1–11.

Hélyot 1718: Hélyot, Pierre. *Histoire des ordres monastiques*. Paris, 1718.

Janson 1952: Janson, H. W. *Apes and Ape Lore in the Middle Ages and the Renaissance*. London, 1952.

Ker 1972: Ker, Neil. "The English Manuscripts of the *Moralia* of Gregory the Great." In *Kunsthistorische Forschungen Otto Pächt*, ed. Artur Rosenauer and Gerold Weber, 77–89. Salzburg, 1972.

Kessler 1985a: Kessler, Herbert L. "Pictures as Scripture in Fifth-Century Churches." *Studia Artium Orientalis et Occidentalis* 2 (1985): 17–31.

Kessler 1985b: Kessler, Herbert L. "Pictorial Narrative and Church Mission in Sixth-Century Gaul." *Studies in the History of Art* 16 (1985): 75–91.

Kessler 1989: Kessler, Herbert L. "Diction in the 'Bibles of the Illiterate.'" *World Art: Themes of Unity in Diversity*, Acts of the XXVIth International Congress of the History of Art, ed. Irving Lavin, vol.2,297–304. University Park, 1989.

Laistner 1957: Laistner, M. L. W. *Thought and Letters in Western Europe*. Rev. ed. London, 1957.

Leclercq 1973: Leclercq, Jean. "*Ioculator et saltator*: S. Bernard et l'image du jongleur dans les manuscrits." In *Translatio Studii: Manuscript and Library Studies Honoring Oliver L. Kapsner*, ed. Julian G. Plante, 124–48. Collegeville, 1973.

Leclercq 1982: Leclercq, Jean. *The Love of Learning and the Desire for God: A Study of Monastic Culture*. 3rd. ed. New York, 1982.

Legner 1985: Legner, Anton, ed. *Ornamenta Ecclesiae: Kunst und Kunstler der Romanik*. Cologne, 1985.

Lekai 1977: Lekai, Louis. *The Cistercians: Ideals and Reality*. Kent, 1977.

Linderbauer 1922: Linderbauer, Benno. ed. *S. Benedicti Regula Monachorum*. Metten, 1922.

de Lubac 1959: Lubac, Henri de. *Exégèse médiévale: Les quatre sens de l'écriture*. Paris, 1959–64).

Lutèce 1984: *Lutèce: Paris de César à Clovis*. Paris, 1984.

Mâle 1978: Mâle, Emile. *Religious Art in France: The Twelfth Century*. Princeton, 1978.

Mâle 1984: Mâle, Emile. *Religious Art in France: The Thirteenth Century*. Princeton, 1984.

Malone 1950: Malone, Edward. *The Monk and the Martyr*. Washington, D.C., 1950.

Mane 1990: Mane, Perrine. "Iconographie et travail paysan." In *Le travail au moyen âge: Une approche interdisciplinaire*, ed. Jacqueline Hamesse and Colette Muraille-Samaran, 251–62. Publications de l'Institut d'Etudes Médiévales: Textes, études, congrès 10. Louvain-la-Neuve, 1990.

Mane 1992: Mane, Perrine. "Le travail au moyen âge: Comparison entre le text de l'Ancien Testament et les enluminures d'une Bible moralisée." In *L'image au moyen âge: Actes du colloque, Amiens, 19-23 mars 1986*, 193–206. Recherches en littérature médiévale 15. Göppingen, 1992.

Masai 1956: Masai, François. "De la condition des enlumineurs et de l'enluminure à l'époque romane." *Bulletino dell'Archivio paleografico italiano* n.s. 2–3 (1956–57): 135–44.

Meyer 1954: Meyer, Kathi. "St. Job as a Patron of Music." *Art Bulletin* 36 (1954): 21-31.

Morrison 1988: Morrison, Karl. *"I Am You": The Hermeneutics of Empathy in Western Literature, Theology, and Art.* Princeton, 1988.

Nordenfalk 1951: Nordenfalk, Carl. "The Beginning of Book Decoration." In *Essays in Honor of Georg Swarzenski*, ed. Oswald Goetz, 9–20. Chicago, 1951.

Nordenfalk 1957: Grabar, André, and Carl Nordenfalk. *Early Medieval Painting: From the Fourth to the Eleventh Century.* Lausanne, 1957.

Nordenfalk 1970: Nordenfalk, Carl. *Die spätantiken Zierbuchstaben.* Stockholm, 1970.

Oursel 1926: Oursel, Charles. *La miniature du XIIe siècle à l'abbaye de Cîteaux.* Dijon, 1926.

Oursel 1928: Oursel, Charles. *L'art roman de Bourgogne.* Dijon, 1928.

Oursel 1959: Oursel, Charles. "La bible de saint Etienne Harding et le scriptorium de Cîteaux (1109–vers 1134)." *Cîteaux* 10 (1959): 34–43.

Oursel 1960: Oursel, Charles. *Miniatures cisterciennes (1109–1134).* Mâcon, 1960.

Pächt 1963: Pächt, Otto. "The Pre-Carolingian Roots of Romanesque Art." *Romanesque and Gothic Art*, 67–75. Studies in Western Art 1: Acts of the Twentieth International Congress of the History of Art. Princeton, 1963.

Pächt 1986: Pächt, Otto. *Book Illumination in the Middle Ages: An Introduction.* Oxford, 1986.

Parkes 1993: Parkes, M. B. *Pause and Effect: An Introduction to the History of Punctuation in the West.* Berkeley, 1993.

Porcher 1954: Porcher, Jean. *Les manuscrits à peintures en France du VIIe au XIIe siècle.* Paris, 1954.

Porcher 1959: Porcher, Jean. *L'enluminure française.* Paris, 1959.

Porcher 1962: Porcher, Jean. *L'art cistercien.* La Pierre-qui-Vire, 1962.

Quarré 1938: Quarré, Pierre. In the *séance* for June 8 in the *Bulletin de la Société Nationale des Antiquaires de France* (1938): 155–60.

Rochais 1953: Rochais, H.-M. "Contribution à l'histoire des florilèges ascètiques du haut moyen âge latin." *Revue bénédictine* 63 (1953): 246–91.

Romanini 1978: Romanini, Angiola Maria. "Il 'Maestro dei Moralia' e le origini di Cîteaux." *Storia dell'arte* 33 (1978): 221–45.

Rouse 1982: Rouse, Mary A., and Richard H. Rouse. "Florilegia of Patristic Texts." In *Les genres littéraires dans les sources théologiques et philosophiques médiévales*, 165–80. Louvain-la-Neuve, 1982.

Rowell 1977: Rowell, Geoffrey. *The Liturgy of Christian Burial.* London, 1977.

Rudolph 1987: Rudolph, Conrad. "The 'Principal Founders' and the Early Artistic

Legislation of Cîteaux." In *Studies in Cistercian Art and Architecture* 3, ed. Meredith Parsons Lillich, 1–45. Cistercian Studies Series 89 Kalamazoo,1987.

Rudolph 1990a: Rudolph, Conrad. *The "Things of Greater Importance": Bernard of Clairvaux's* Apologia *and the Medieval Attitude Toward Art*. Philadelphia, 1990.

Rudolph 1990b: Rudolph, Conrad. *Artistic Change at St-Denis: Abbot Suger's Program and the Early Twelfth-Century Controversy over Art*. Princeton, 1990.

Rush 1941: Rush, Alfred C. *Death and Burial in Christian Antiquity*. Washington, D.C., 1941.

Russell 1965: Russell, Jeffrey B. *Dissent and Reform in the Early Middle Ages*. Berkeley, 1965.

Samaran 1959: Samaran, Charles and Robert Marichal. *Catalogue des manuscrits en écriture latine*. 7 vols. Paris, 1959–85.

Schapiro 1964: Schapiro, Meyer. *The Parma Ildefonsus: A Romanesque Illuminated Manuscript from Cluny and Related Works*. New York, 1964.

Schapiro 1977: Schapiro, Meyer. "On the Aesthetic Attitude in Romanesque Art." In *Romanesque Art*, 1–27. New York, 1977.

Skubiszewski 1990: Skubiszewski, Piotr. "L'intellectuel et l'artiste." In *Le travail au moyen âge: Une approche interdisciplinaire*, ed. Jacqueline Hamesse and Colette Muraille-Samaran, 263–321. Publications de l'Institut d'Etudes Médiévales: Textes, études, congrès 10. Louvain-la-Neuve, 1990.

Skubiszewski 1992: Skubiszewski, Piotr. "Le trumeau et le linteau de Moissac: Un cas du symbolisme médiéval." *Cahiers archéologiques* 40 (1992): 51–90.

Smalley 1983: Smalley, Beryl. *The Study of the Bible in the Middle Ages*. 3rd ed. Oxford, 1983.

Spicq 1944: Spicq, Ceslas. *Esquisse d'une histoire de l'exégèse latine*. Paris, 1944.

Straw 1988: Straw, Carole. *Gregory the Great: Perfection in Imperfection*. Berkeley, 1988.

Toynbee 1971: Toynbee, J. M. C. *Death and Burial in the Roman World*. London, 1971.

Vacandard 1884: Vacandard, Elphège. "Saint Bernard et l'art chrétien." *Précis analytique des travaux de l'Académie de Sciences, Belles-lettres et Arts de Rouen* 87 (1884): 215–44.

Van Engen 1980: Van Engen, John. "Theophilus Presbyter and Rupert of Deutz: The Manual Arts and Benedictine Theology." *Viator* 11 (1980): 147–63.

Van Engen 1983: Van Engen, John. *Rupert of Deutz*. Berkeley, 1983.

Verdier 1982: Verdier, Philippe. "*Dominus potens in praelio.*" *Walraf-Richartz-Jahrbuch* 43 (1982): 35–106.

Viollet-le-Duc 1867: Viollet-le-Duc, Eugène. *Dictionnaire raisonné de l'architecture.* 10 vols. Paris, 1867–70.

Wasselynck 1956: Wasselynck, René. *L'influence des Moralia in Iob de saint Grégoire le Grand sur la théologie morale entre le VIIe et le XIIe siècle.* Lille, 1956.

Werckmeister 1980: Werckmeister, O. K. "The First Romanesque Beatus Manuscripts and the Liturgy of Death." In *Actas del simposio para el estudio de los códices del "Commentario al Apocalipsis" de Beato de Liébana*, vol. 2,167–200. Madrid, 1980.

Williams 1993: Williams, Jane Welch. *Bread, Wine, and Money: The Windows of the Trades at Chartres Cathedral.* Chicago, 1993.

Wilmart 1917: Wilmart, André. "L'ancienne bibliothèque de Clairvaux." *Mémoires de la Société Académique d'Agriculture, des Sciences, Arts, et Belles-lettres du Département de l'Aube* 81 [ser.3:54] (1917): 127–90.

Woodruff 1929: Woodruff, Helen. "The Illustrated Manuscripts of Prudentius." *Art Studies: Medieval, Renaissance and Modern* 7 (1929): 33–79.

Załuska 1989: Załuska, Yolanta. *L'enluminure et le scriptorium de Cîteaux au XIIe siècle.* Cîteaux, 1989.

Załuska 1990: Załuska, Yolanta. *Manuscrits enluminés de Dijon.* Paris, 1991.

LIST OF ILLUSTRATIONS

Except where otherwise indicated, the illustrations are museum or library photographs, reproduced with permission.

INDEX

Abelard, 88
active and contemplative lives. *See* Gregory the Great: and the active and contemplative lives
Athanasius, 8, 30–31, 61, 122n.16
Augustine, 49, 54, 87–88, 122n.14

Benedict of Nursia, Regula, 5, 6, 56, 64–65, 66–67, 70–74, 79, 121n.4, 123n.21
Bern, *Bürgerbibliothek* MS 264 (Prudentius), 22–23, fig. 38
Bernard of Clairvaux, 6, 88, 90, 93, 96
—*Apologia*, 7, 8, 10, 113n.94
—and art as a spiritual distraction, 4, 7, 10, 96
—and the vocabulary of violent spiritual struggle, 6–7, 8

Cambrai, Bibliothèque Municipale MS 470 (Philippus Presbyter), 22–23 fig. 39
Cassian, 61, 84–85
Cassiodorus, 87
Cistercian Order
—artistic asceticism of, 5–6, 96. *See also* Troyes, Bibliothèque Municipale MS 27
—reform policy and/or polemics of, 5–6, 14, 63, 64, 67, 71–72, 92–93. *See also* Cîteaux Moralia: and Cistercian reform polemics
—spiritual expression of first and second generation Cistercians, 3–4, 5–8, 43, 81, 96. *See also* Cîteaux Moralia: and the first and second generation Cistercians
Cîteaux Moralia (Dijon, Bibliothèque Municipale MSS 168, 169, 170, 173), figs. 1–36
—and the "animal man" (*animalis homo*), 61, 94–95
—artistic authorship of, 97n.1
—and Cistercian reform polemics, 92–93, 95–96

—clothing, 66–67, 71, 73–74
—episcopal authority, recognition of, 81
—gluttony, 52–53
—manual labor, 64–68, 70–74, 96
—monastic seclusion, 65–67, 72–74, 78
—spirituality of avarice, 63–64, 96
—voluntary poverty, 68, 70–74
—and contemporaneity, 55, 77–78, 90–91, 95, 96
—*conversi*, supposed depiction of, 65, 75, 78
—date of, 97n.1
—and the direct observation of nature, 9, 34, 66–67, 69–70, esp. 73–74, 77–79
—and the exegetical process of Gregory the Great, 12–13, 51–52, 60, 67–68, 74–75, 84–91, 95–96, passim
—and the first and second generation Cistercians, 54, 62, 64, 77, 81, 90, 92, 95, 96
—format of, 20–22
—function of, 91–95
—and the gradual change of conception of the initial, 13, 15, 20, 21–22, 23, 27–28, 34–36, 41–42, 88, 89–91, 93, passim
—hands of, 15–20, 27, 35
—and humor, 59, 70–72, 75
—and the intrusion of the secular upon the sacred, 42–44, 77–79
—layout of, 20–22, 124n.31
—and *lectio divina*, 68, 84–91, 93, 94–95, 96
—and the literality and sense of the text, 12–13, 30, 32–33, 41, 60, 88, 89–90, passim
—and the meaning of monstrous imagery, 9, 10–13, 23–25. *See also* Cîteaux Moralia: and the semihomo; and Cîteaux Moralia: and the visual vocabulary of violence

ILLUSTRATIONS

e
RAT

N ERRA hVS NOMINE IOB;

t erat uir ille simplex & rectus timens
dm̃ & recedens a malo; Itaq; sunt ei
septẽ filii & tres filie, & fuit possessio
ei septẽ milia ouiũ, & tria milia camelo

1. Initial to the Book of Job, *Moralia in Job*. Dijon, Bib. Mun. MS 168:2.

2. Frontispiece and initial to the Letter to Leander, *Moralia in Job*. Dijon, Bib. Mun. MS 168:4v.

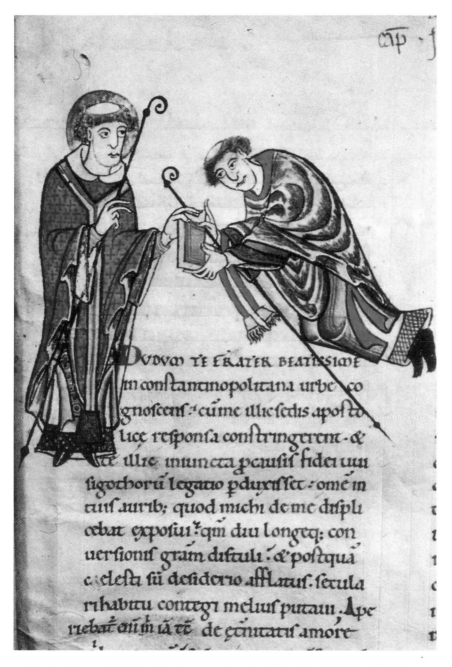

Dudum te frater beatissime in constantinopolitana urbe cognoscens : cum me illic sedis apostolice responsa constringerent · & te illic iniuncta perussis fidei uui sigothorum legatio pduxisset · omē in tuis auribus; quod michi de me displi cebat exposui : qm diu longeq: con uersionis gram distuli : & postquā celesti sū desiderio afflatus : secula ri habitu contegi melius putaui. Ape riebat enim iam tm de eternitatis amore

3. Illumination to the body of the Letter to Leander, *Moralia in Job*. Dijon, Bib. Mun. MS 168:5.

INCIPIWNT MORALIA BEATI GREGORII PAPAE.
PER CONTEMPLATIONEM SUMPTA INLI
BRVM IOB: LIBRI QVINQ: PARS PRIMA.
INTER MULTOS SEPE QVE
RITVR. QVIS LIBRI BEATI
IOB SCRIPTOR HABEATVR.
Et alii quidem moysen.
alii unu quelibet ppphe
tis. scriptore huius opis
fuisse suspicant; Quia
eni inlibro genescos iobab
de stirpe esau descendisse.
& bale filio beor inregnu
successisse describitur:
hunc beatu iob longe an
te moysi tempora extitis
se crediderunt. morem
pfecto sacri eloquii nesci
entes. quia insuperiorib;

4. Illumination to the Preface, *Moralia in Job*. Dijon, Bib. Mun. MS 168:7.

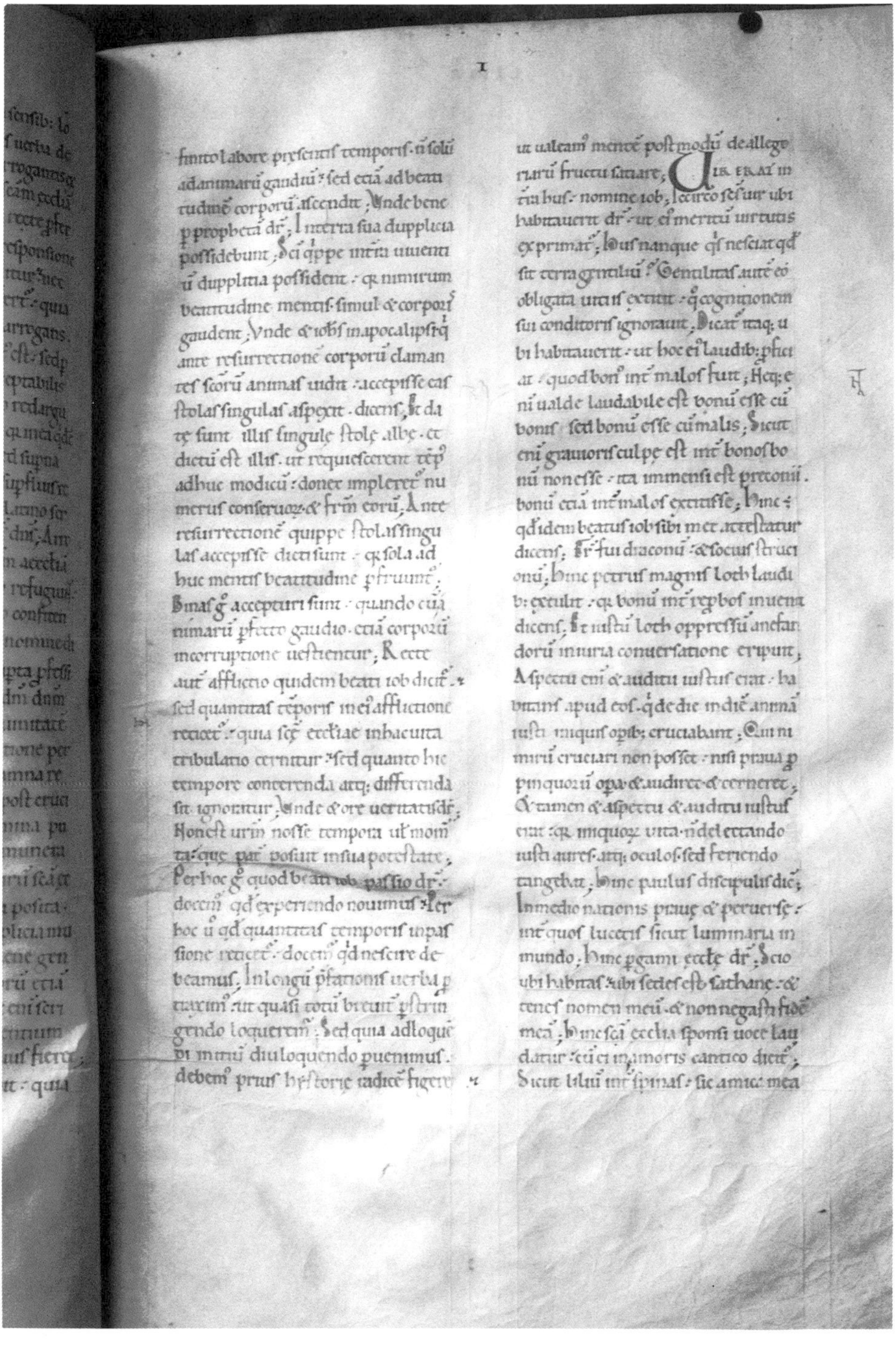

5. Initial to Book I, *Moralia in Job*. Dijon, Bib. Mun. MS 168:12.

6. Initial to Book 2, *Moralia in Job*. Dijon, Bib. Mun. MS 168:21.

é· sit nomen dñi benedictú; Nunc
eñi uere oftendim̄ quia accepta re
cte tenuim̄·· cũ pfecto equanimiter
ad momentú sublata toleramus;
EXPLICIT LIBER SECVND;
INCIP̃ LIBER ·III·
EAT VS ΦB
AD ꝏORTĒ PETITVS
inteptatione radui
tã creuit ex uulne
re·& antiquus ho
stis unde se bona ei
existimauit extin
guere·unde doluit
multiplicasse; Sed
quia primo certamine se succubu
isse considerat· ad alia se teptatio
num bella restaurat· & de sco uiro
mala adhuc impudent spat· quia

7. Initial to Book 3, *Moralia in Job*. Dijon, Bib. Mun. MS 168:39v.

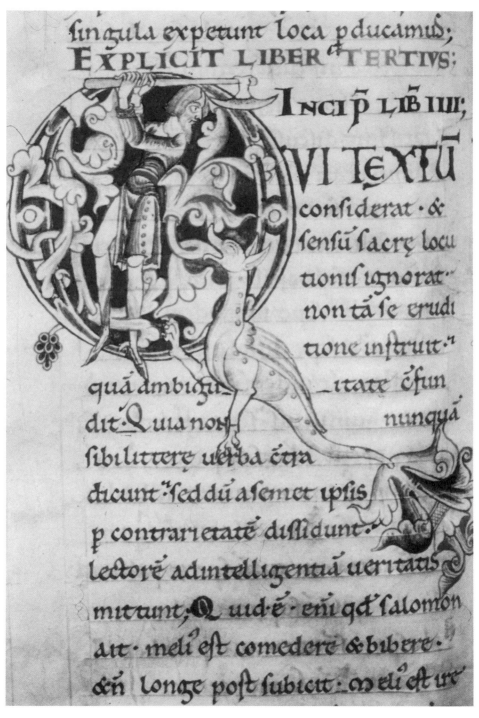

singula expetunt loca pducamus;
EXPLICIT LIBER TERTIVS;

INCIP LIB IIII;

VI TEXTV
considerat · &
sensu sacre locu
tionis ignorat·
non tā se erudi
tione instruit·ʳ

quā ambigui͞ _____ itate c̃fun
dit. Quia non _____ nunquā
sibi littere ueřba c̄tra
dicunt·ˢed dū asemet ipsis
p contrarietate͞ dissidunt·
lectore͞ adintelligentiā ueritatis
mittunt, Quid·ē· eñi qđ ſalomon
ait· meli͞ est comedere & bibere·
&ñ longe post subicit· c̃ eli͞ est uř

8. Initial to Book 4, *Moralia in Job*. Dijon, Bib. Mun. ms 168:52v.

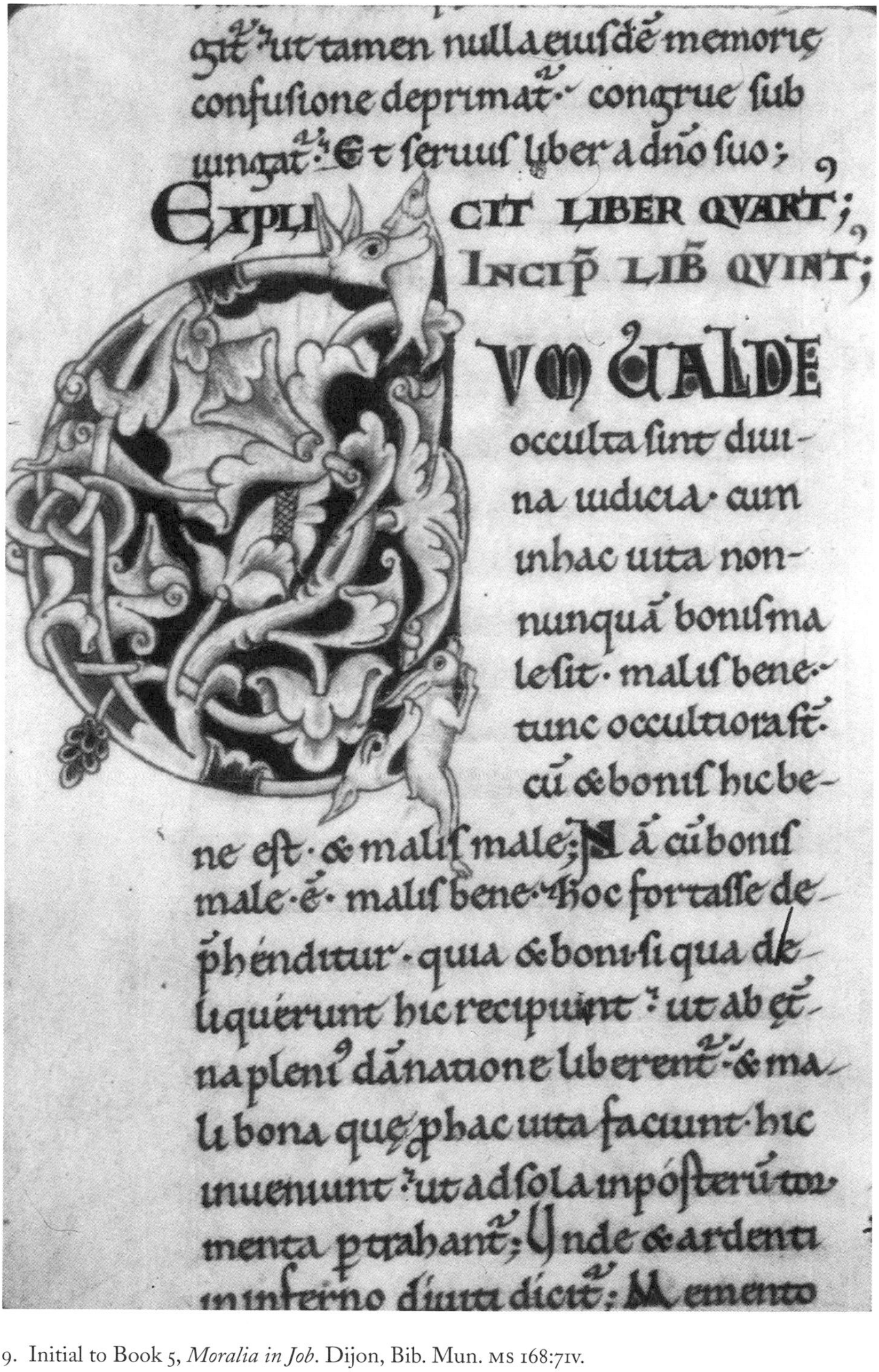

git ut tamen nulla eius dē memorię
confusione deprimat· congrue sub
iungat· Et seruus liber a dn̄o suo;
EXPLICIT LIBER QVART;
INCIP LIB QVINT;
CVM VALDE
occulta sint diui-
na iudicia· cum
in hac uita non-
nunquā bonis ma
le sit· malis bene·
tunc occultiora sẽt·
cū & bonis hic be-
ne est· & malis male; Nā cū bonis
male ē· malis bene· hoc fortasse de-
phenditur· quia & boni si qua de-
liquerunt hic recipiunt· ut ab ęt
na pleni dānatione liberent· & ma
li bona que p hac uita faciunt· hic
inueniunt· ut ad sola in posterū tor
menta ptrahant; Unde & ardenti
in inferno diuiti dicit· Memento

9. Initial to Book 5, *Moralia in Job*. Dijon, Bib. Mun. MS 168:71v.

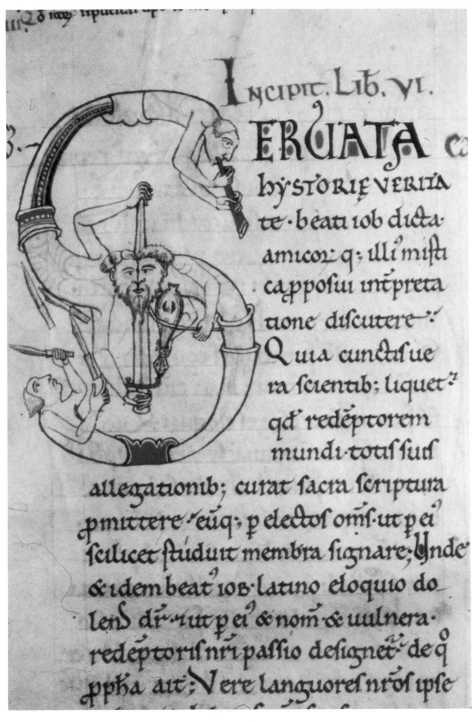

INCIPIT. LIB. VI.

ERUATA
hystorie veritate · beati iob dicta
amicor: q; illi misti cappofui interpretatione difcutere·:
Quia cunctif uera fcientib; liquet·
qd redeptorem mundi totif fuif
allegationib; curat facra fcriptura
pmittere·euq; p electof omf·ut p ei
fcilicet ftuduit membra fignare; Unde
& idem beat iob·latino eloquio dolenf dr·iut p ei & nom & uulnera·
redeptorif nri paffio defignet·de q
ppha ait; Vere languoref nrof ipfe

10. Initial to Book 6, *Moralia in Job*. Dijon, Bib. Mun. MS 169:5.

11. Initial to Book 7, *Moralia in Job.* Dijon, Bib. Mun. MS 169:20v.

etiā
p
ace
icū
cen
mu
tz;
idi:
uppe
mpo
de
ant
tip
psal
ula
dūe
tan
rīt
aq;
t.
am
cessi
tū

P RE
CE
DENT
IAM LIBELLO TRA
ctauimus; qd beatus iob uitā
nob suę humilitatis innotesc
dicens; Sup pupillū irruitis;
& subuertere nitimini amicū
urm; Quantę naq; infirmita
tis se ppendat insinuat; que
pupillū uocat; Quia u ab amo
re recedere; etiā lesa caritas
nescit; & subuerti se uelle que
ritur; & tamē se amicū ee te
statur; Cui uerba ut sepeiā
diximus; sic eidem specialiū con

12. Initial to Book 8, *Moralia in Job*. Dijon, Bib. Mun. MS 169:36v.

13. Initial to Book 9, *Moralia in Job*. Dijon, Bib. Mun. MS 169:62v.

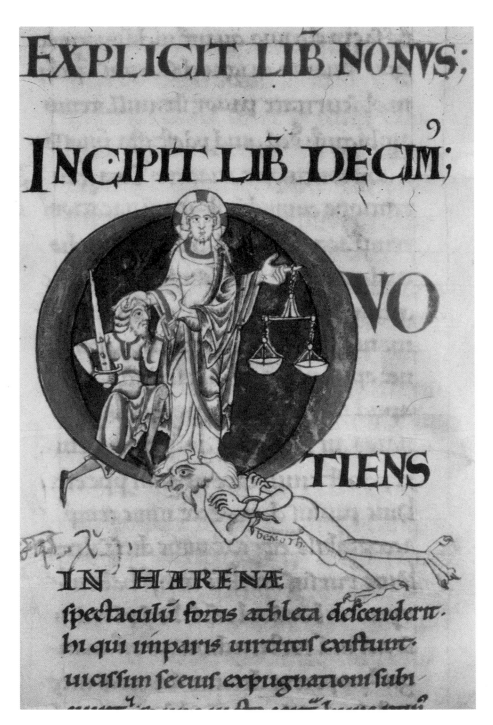

EXPLICIT LIB NONVS;

INCIPIT LIB DECIM;

VO

TIENS

IN HARENÆ
spectaculu fortis athleta descenderit.
hi qui imparis uirtutis existunt.
uicissum se eius expugnationi subi

14. Initial to Book 10, *Moralia in Job*. Dijon, Bib. Mun. MS 169:88v.

15. Initial to Book 11, *Moralia in Job.* Dijon, Bib. Mun. MS 170:6v.

16. Initial to Book 12, *Moralia in Job*. Dijon, Bib. Mun. MS 170:20.

uint · ab ipso solo aliena iuint · p quo
solo dicebant̃ : op̃ scs̃ uir nil in suis
actib; duplicitatis habuit̃ : que tes̃ti
uertas· de cordis simplicitate laudauit;

Explicit Liber Dvodecim;
Incip̃ Lib̃ XIII;

S

SE

ħoc
Pversorv̄ p̃priv̄
solet· qd̃ mala sua p conuictu̅ boni in
geruint· priusqua̅ de eis ipsi ueracit̃
accusentur; & du̅ metuint increpa
ri de his que faciunt· aduersantes
suis prauitatib; iustos hec facere
testantur; Scī aut̃ uiri patienter

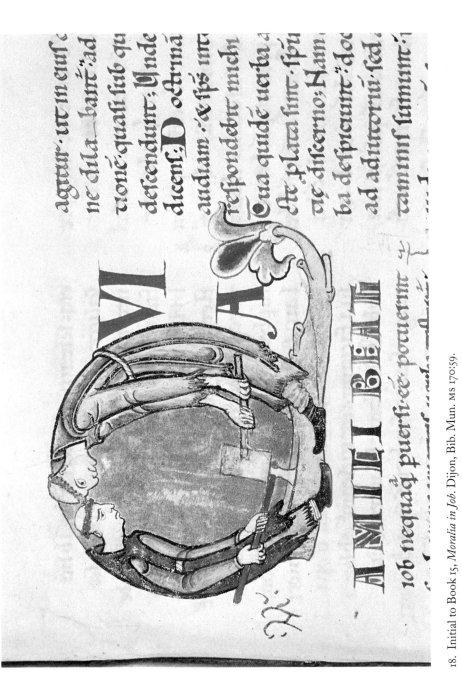

18. Initial to Book 15, *Moralia in Job*. Dijon, Bib. Mun. MS 170:59.

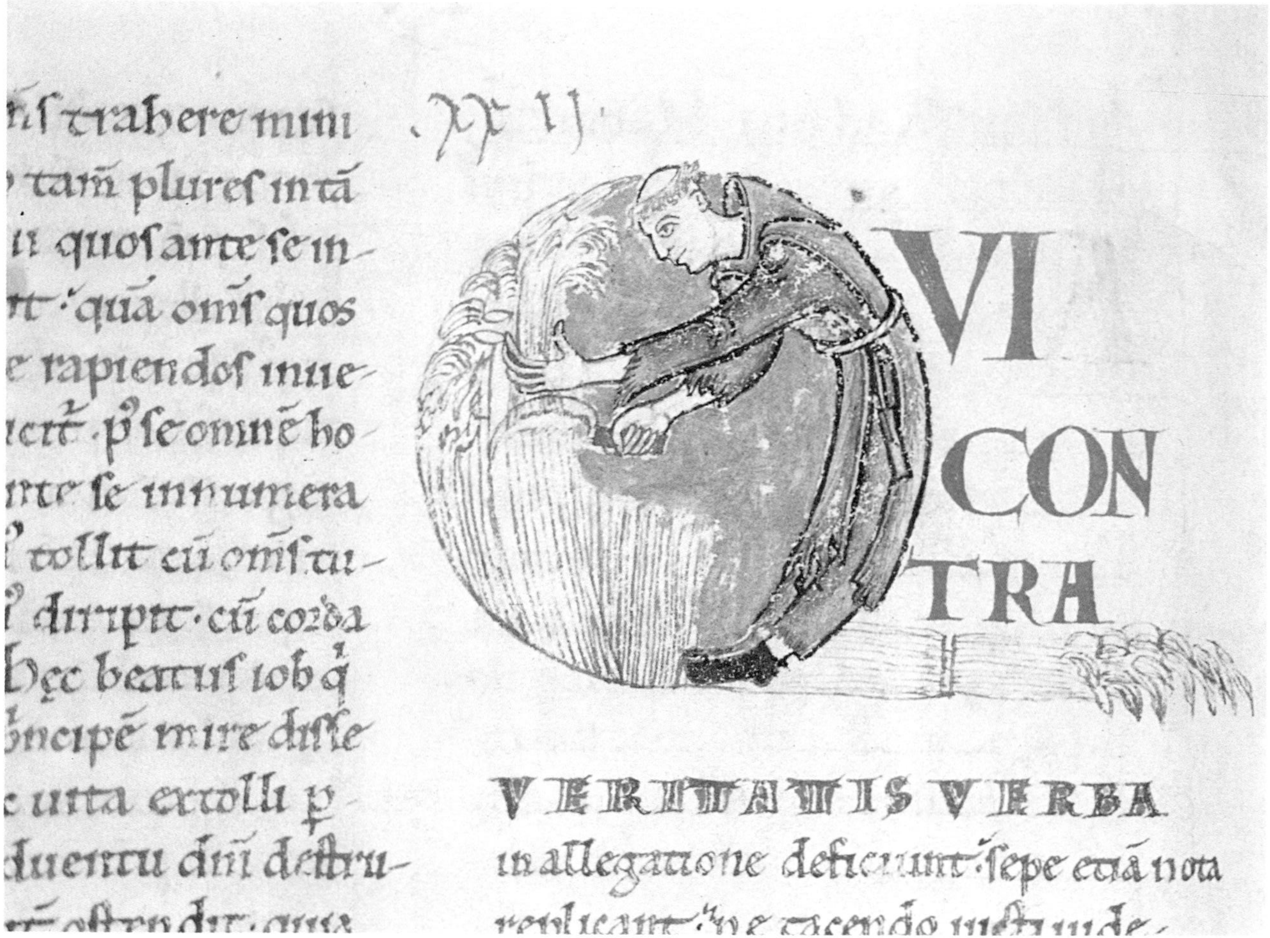

19. Initial to Book 16, *Moralia in Job*. Dijon, Bib. Mun. MS 170:75v.

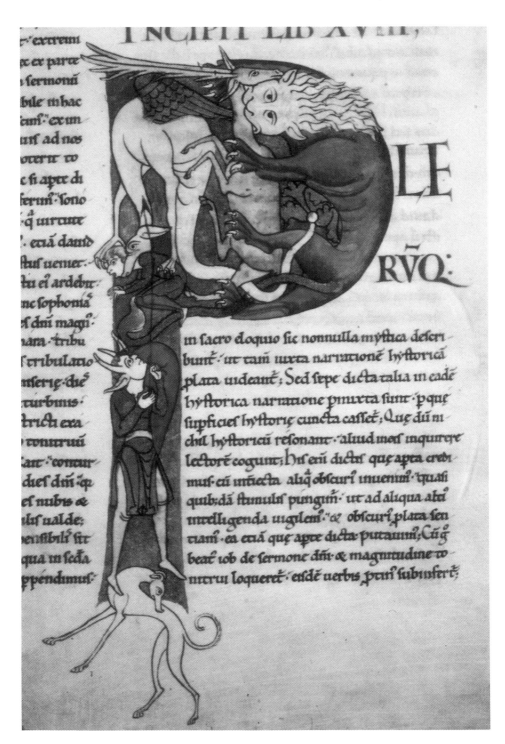

20. Initial to Book 18, *Moralia in Job*. Dijon, Bib. Mun. MS 173:7.

mus eī quē imitari possum̄ · q̄ & uidentes par-
ticipam̄ · & participantes imitam̄ ; Quę nimir̄z
uisio nc̄ fide inchoat̄ · sed tunc specie pficit̄ ·
quando coętn̄ā dō sapientiā quā m̄ p ora pre-
dicantiū · quasi p decurrentia flumina sumi-
mus̄ · in ipso suo fonte biberimus ;

EXPL LIB OCTAVDECIM͛ ;
INCIPIT NONDECIMVS ;

VID

MIR̄V

SI ETERNA DĪ SAPIENTIA conspici non ualet̄ ·
quando ipsa quoq; inuisibilia quę p eā sunt
condita · humanis oculis cōprehendi n̄ possunt ;

21. Initial to Book 19, *Moralia in Job*. Dijon, Bib. Mun. MS 173:20.

22. Initial to Book 20, *Moralia in Job*. Dijon, Bib. Mun. MS 173:29.

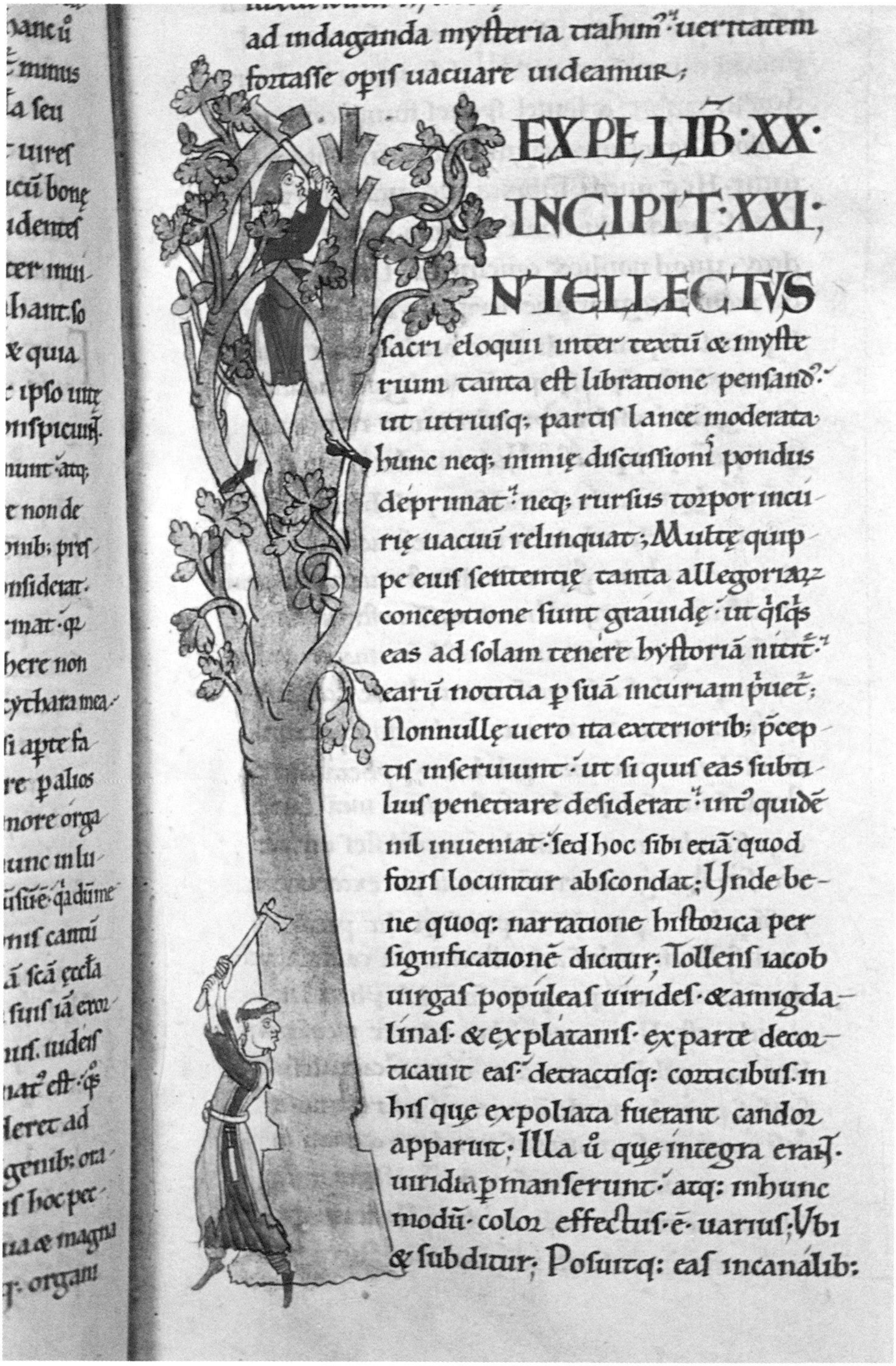

EXPL·LIB·XX·

INCIPIT·XXI;

NTELLECTVS
sacri eloquii inter textu̅ & myste
rium tanta est libratione pensand?
ut utriusq; partis lance moderata
hunc neq; nimie discussioni pondus
deprimat? neq; rursus torpor incu
rie uacuu̅ relinquat; Multe quip
pe eius sentente tanta allegoriaz
conceptione sunt grauide· ut qsqs
eas ad solam tenere hystoria̅ nititr
earu̅ notitia p sua̅ incuriam puet;
Nonnulle uero ita exterioribz pcep
tis inseruiunt· ut si quis eas subti
lius penetrare desiderat? intz quide̅
nil inueniat· sed hoc sibi etia̅ quod
foris locuntur abscondat; Unde be
ne quoq; narratione hystorica per
significatione̅ dicitur; Tollens iacob
uirgas populeas uirides· & amigda
linas· & ex platanis· ex parte decor
ticauit eas· detractisq; corticibus in
his que expoliata fuerant candor
apparuit· Illa u̅ que integra erat·
uiridia p manserunt· atq; inhunc
modu̅· color effectus·e̅· uarius; Ubi
& subditur; Posuitq; eas incanalib:

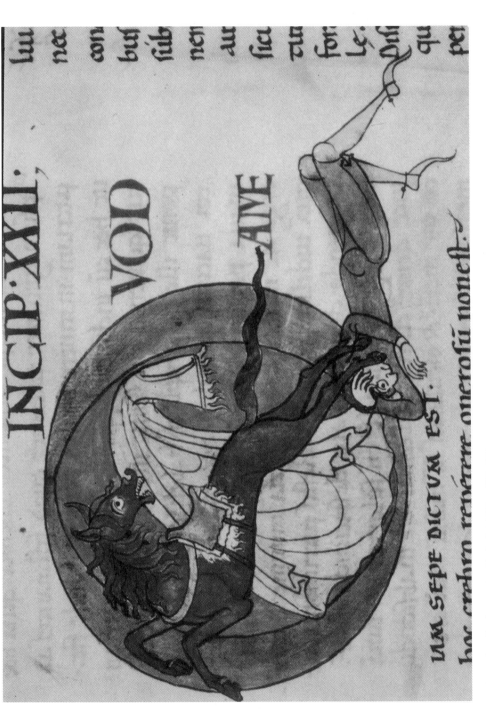

24. Initial to Book 22, *Moralia in Job*. Dijon, Bib. Mun. MS 173:47.

RE

FATI

ONEM

huiuf opif tocienf neceſſario repe
to. quocienf hoc indiftinctione uo-
luminu · locutionif mee pauſatione
ſuccido · ut cu legendi exordium
ſumte · priuſ ipſa memorie lectio
niſ cauſa renouet · & tanto robuſti'
ſurgat doctrine aedificiu · quanto
ex conſiderata cauſe origine ftudioſi'
ſponte unite fundamtu · Beat' iob
do ſoli ſibiq; cognit' intranquillitate' ad nam
noticia pducenduſ tactuſ e uerbere · ut odo-
re ſuaru uiru tanto lari' ſpangeret · quanto

E-
LIV
VIM

supne dispensationis insinuans. de electi
unius cuiusq; pcussione intulit dicens; Ap-
ppinquauit corruptioni anima ei. & uita illius mortiferis; Et du teptatu homine demonstrat unu. inqua teptatione sit postu huma-
nu genus ostendit uniuersu; Duq; narrat qd
specialit agat insingulis. liquido intimat

26. Initial to Book 24, *Moralia in Job*. Dijon, Bib. Mun. MS 173:66.

INCIP LIB XXVI·

ALOQVVTIONIBVS

suis hoc arrogantes uiri ha-
bere inter alia ꝓpriu so-
lent· qd ab auditorib; suis nequid fortasse inordina-
tu dixerint· tunc requirunt·̄
cu se laudabilr̄ aliquid
dixisse cognoscunt; hec
uidelicet faciunt· n̄ q̄ de
dictis suis ambigunt·̄ sed
quo audientiu iudicio fa-
uores quer; Nam inueniri
facile pocer·̄ q̄ animo puenc-
tanc·̄ si q̄squā cu eoꝝ bona laudat· etiā mala re-
ꝓhendat; Certu ꝗppe est
q̄ sicut inflanc laudibus·
ita correctionib; inflaman-
tur·̄ & aquolibet se ut iuste
reꝓhendi despiciunt· moxq;
in malis suis·fomitē defensionis exquir; quomodo & de bonis suis humilr̄ ambigunt·̄ q̄

27. Initial to Book 26, *Moralia in Job*. Dijon, Bib. Mun. MS 173:80.

28. Initial to Book 27, *Moralia in Job*. Dijon, Bib. Mun. MS 173:92v.

INCIP LIB · XXVIII;

PARS
VLTIMA;

OST

DĀPNA

REBVM. POST FVNERA PIGNORI.
poſt uulnera corporiſ. poſt uer
ba male ſuadentiſ uxoriſ. poſt
contumelioſa dicta conſolan
tium. poſt ſuſcepta forti ia
cula tot doloꝝ. de tanta uir
tute conſtantie laudanduſ
audice beat' iob fuerat. ſed
ſi iā deĩſentia ſcto eēt euocan
duſ. At poſt quā hic adhuc
duplicia recepturuſ ē. poſt.
quā ſaluti priſtine reſtituitur.

29. Initial to Book 28, *Moralia in Job*. Dijon, Bib. Mun. MS 173:103v.

30. Initial to Book 29, *Moralia in Job*. Dijon, Bib. Mun. ms 173:IIIv.

31. Initial to Book 30, *Moralia in Job*. Dijon, Bib. Mun. MS 173:122.

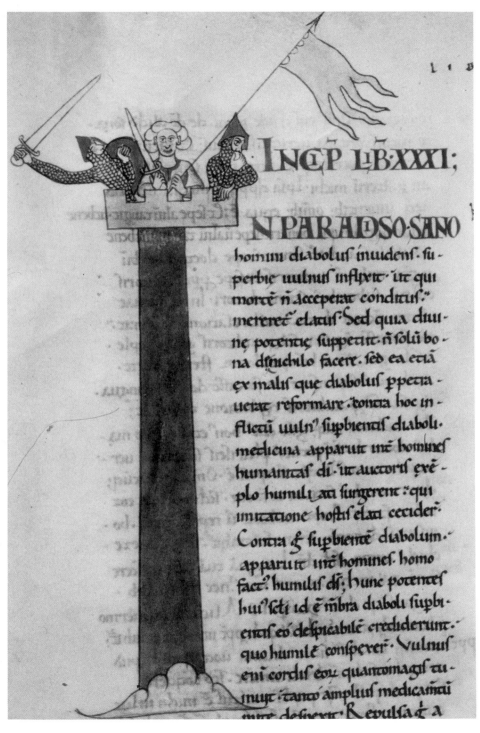

INCP̄ LIB·XXXI;

N PARAIDSO·SANO

homini diabolus inuidens. su-
perbie uulnus inflixit. ut qui
morte n̄ acceperat conditus:
meretur elatus. Sed quia diui-
ne potentie suppetit. n̄ solū bona d̄ nichilo facere. sed ea etiā
ex malis que diabolus ppetra-
uerat reformare: contra hoc in-
flictū uuln̄ superbientis diaboli.
medicina apparuit inr̄ homines
humanitas d̄i· ut auctoris exē-
plo humili ad surgerent: qui
imitatione hostis elati ceciderā.
Contra ꝗ superbientē diabolum.
apparuit inr̄ homines. homo
factus humilis d̄s; hunc potentes
hui͛ scli id ē vmbra diaboli supbi-
entis eo despicabilē crediderunt.
quo humilē conspexerā· Vulnus
eni cordis eoꝝ quantomagis tu-
muit: tanto amplius medicamen-
tū desiderat· Reuulsa ē a

INCIP LIB · XXXII;

CI
VIRI
QVO
APVD

Dñ altius̄ uirtutum dignitate pficunt:̄
eo ſubtil? indignos̄ ſe eē depēhendē:̄ qɛ dū p
rum lucis̄ fiunt:̄'dicẽd eos̄ uleroſiſ̄ lateōax

33. Initial to Book 32, *Moralia in Job*. Dijon, Bib. Mun. MS 173:148.

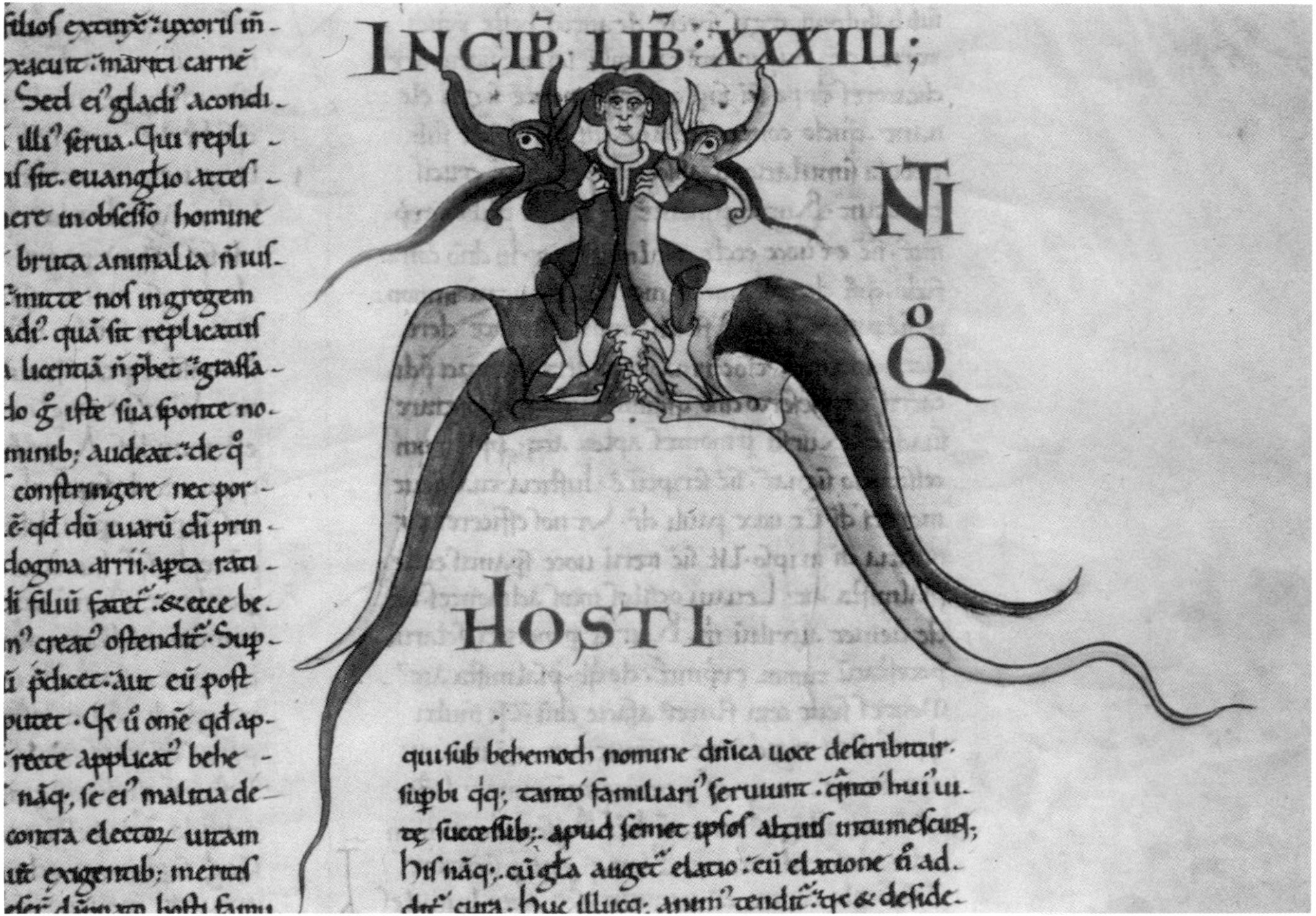

34. Initial to Book 33, *Moralia in Job*. Dijon, Bib. Mun. MS 173:156.

35. Initial to Book 34, *Moralia in Job.* Dijon, Bib. Mun. MS 173:167.

36. Initial to Book 35, *Moralia in Job*. Dijon, Bib. Mun. MS 173:174.

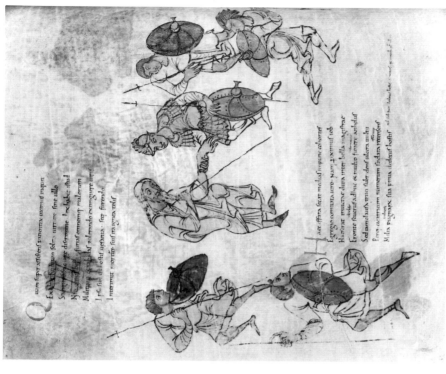

38. Illustration to Prudentius, *Psychomachia*, lines 162–68. Bern Bürgerbib. MS 264:80.

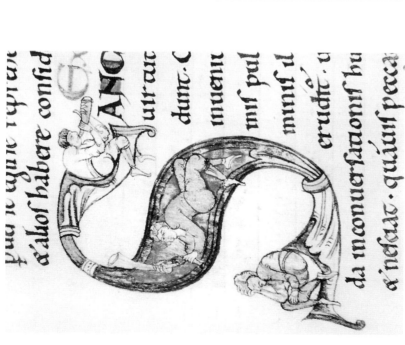

37. Initial to Book 32, *Moralia in Job*. Rouen, Bib. Mun. 498 MS A.123:193v.

40. Initial to John, Bible of Stephen Harding. Dijon, Bib. Mun. MS 15:56v.

39. Initial to Philippus Presbyter, *In Historiam Job Commentariorum Libri Tres.* Cambrai, Bib. Mun. MS 470:2.

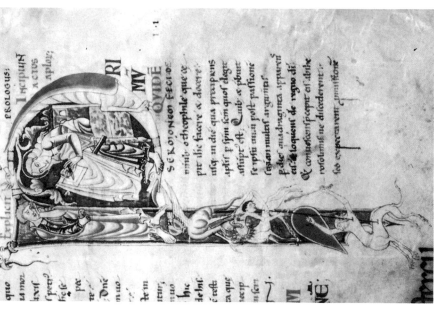

42. Initial to the Acts of the Apostles, Bible of Stephen Harding. Dijon, Bib. Mun. MS 15;68.

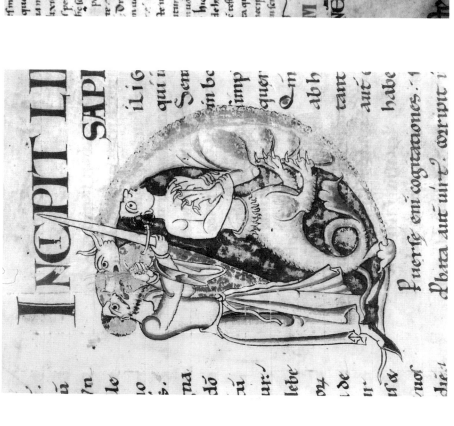

41. Initial to Wisdom, Bible of Stephen Harding. Dijon, Bib. Mun. MS 14:128v.

44. Initial to Epistle 55 (modern system), *Letters* of Jerome.
Dijon, Bib. Mun. MS 135:135v.

43. Initial to Jerome's preface to Kings, Bible of Stephen
Harding. Dijon, Bib. Mun. MS 13:2.

45. Frontispiece to *The City of God*.
Dijon, Bib. Mun. MS 158:1.

46. Illustration to Psalm 7, Utrecht Psalter. Utrecht, Bibliotheek der Rijksuniversiteit MS 32:4.

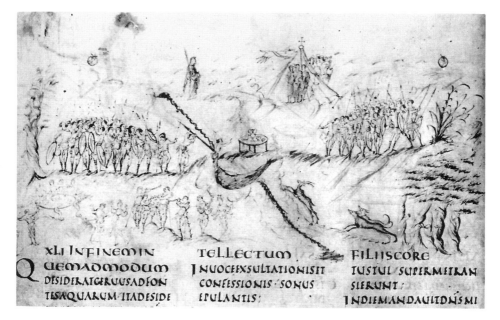

47. Illustration to Psalm 41, Utrecht Psalter.
Utrecht, Bibliotheek der Rijksuniversiteit
MS 32:24v.

48. Seal of Louis VII. Paris, Arch. Nat.,
K 25 n°73.

49. Initial to Job, Second Bible of Saint-Martial. Paris, Bib. Nat. MS lat. 8:1:198.

IREBAT INTERRABVS

50. Cloister capital 33, Saint-Pierre, Moissac.

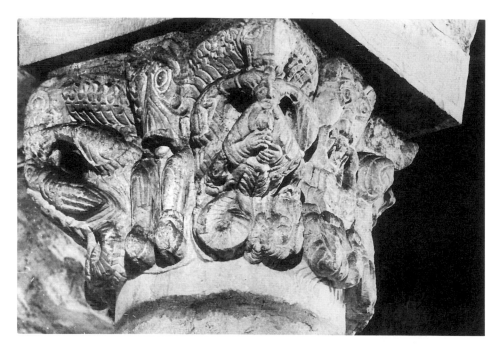

51. Rotunda capital 3,
Saint-Bénigne, Dijon.

52. Initial to Psalms, Second Bible of Saint-Martial.
Paris, Bib. Nat. MS lat. 8:1:208v.

54. Initial to the *oratio* for Easter Mass, Sacramentary of Mont-Saint-Michel. New York, Pierpont Morgan Library MS 641:66v.

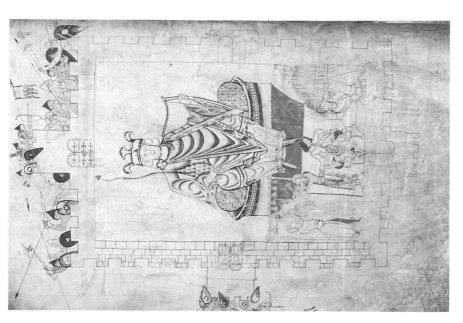

53. Illumination to Psalms, Bible of Stephen Harding. Dijon, Bib. Mun. MS 14:13v.

55. Tomb of Adelaide of Champagne (?), Saint-Jean, Joigny.

56. Illustration to Psalm 84, Utrecht Psalter. Utrecht, Bibliotheek der Rijksuniversiteit MS 32:49v.

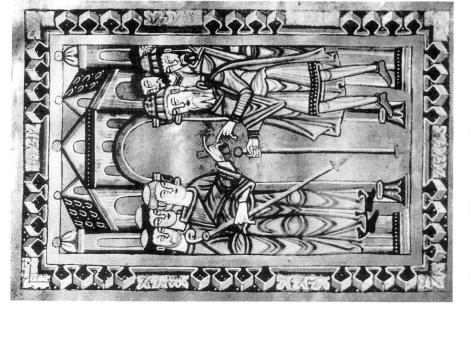

58. Illustration to Ildefonsus, *De Virginitate Beatae Mariae*, Parma Ildefonsus. Parma, Biblioteca Palatina MS lat. 1650:22.

57. Illustration to 2 Maccabees, Bible of Stephen Harding. Dijon, Bib. Mun. MS 14:191.

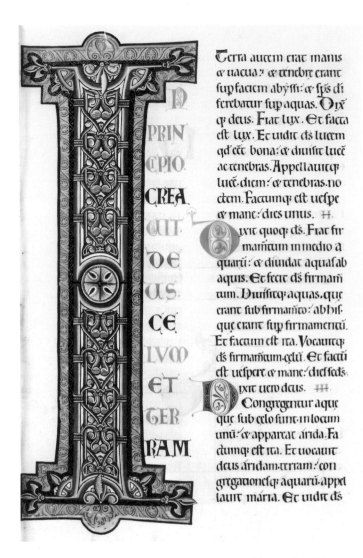

Terra autem erat inanis
& uacua; & tenebre erant
sup faciem abyssi: & sps di
ferebatur sup aquas. Dix
qp deus. Fiat lux . Et facta
est lux . Et uidit ds lucem
qd eet bona: & diuisit lucé
ac tenebras. Appellauitqp
lucé diem: & tenebras. no
ctem. Factumqp est uespe
& mane: dies unus. II.
Dixit quoqp ds. Fiat fir
mamtum in medio a
quarū: & diuidat aquas ab
aquis. Et fecit ds firmam
tum. Diuisitqp aquas. que
erant sub firmamto: ab his
que erant sup firmamentū.
Et factum est ita. Vocauitqp
ds firmamtum. celū. Et factū
est uespere & mane: dies secds.
Dixit uero deus. III.
Congregentur aque
que sub celo sunt · in locum
unū · & appareat arida. Fa
ctumqp est ita. Et uocauit
deus aridam · terram: con
gregationesqp aquarū · appel
lauit maria. Et uidit ds

59. Initial to Genesis, Great Bible of Clairvaux. Troyes, Bib. Mun.
MS 27:I:7.